table of contents

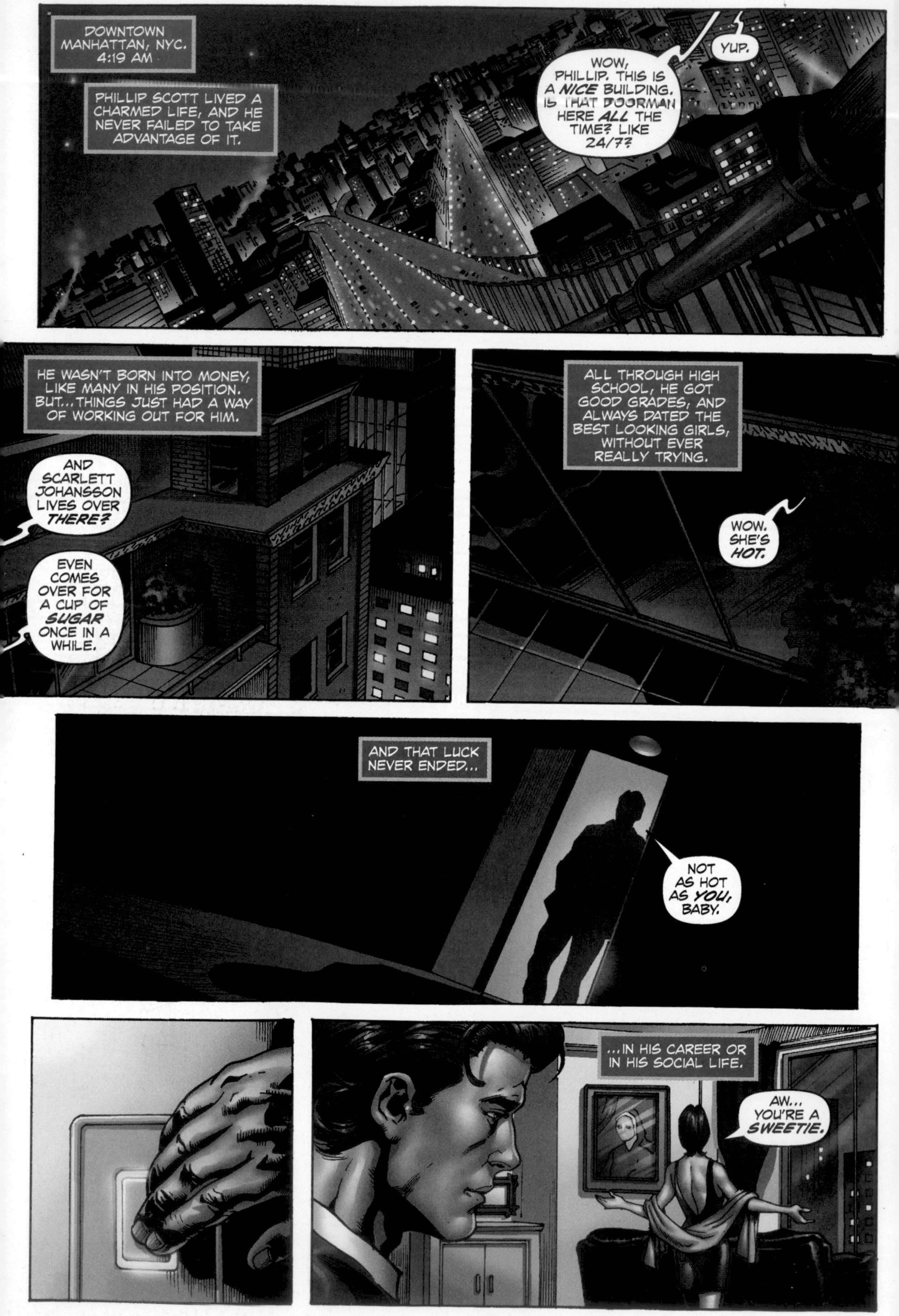
DOWNTOWN MANHATTAN, NYC. 4:19 AM
PHILLIP SCOTT LIVED A CHARMED LIFE, AND HE NEVER FAILED TO TAKE ADVANTAGE OF IT.
WOW, PHILLIP. THIS IS A NICE BUILDING. IS THAT DOORMAN HERE ALL THE TIME? LIKE 24/7?
YUP.
HE WASN'T BORN INTO MONEY, LIKE MANY IN HIS POSITION. BUT...THINGS JUST HAD A WAY OF WORKING OUT FOR HIM.
AND SCARLETT JOHANSSON LIVES OVER THERE?
EVEN COMES OVER FOR A CUP OF SUGAR ONCE IN A WHILE.
ALL THROUGH HIGH SCHOOL, HE GOT GOOD GRADES, AND ALWAYS DATED THE BEST LOOKING GIRLS, WITHOUT EVER REALLY TRYING.
WOW. SHE'S HOT.
AND THAT LUCK NEVER ENDED...
NOT AS HOT AS YOU, BABY.
...IN HIS CAREER OR IN HIS SOCIAL LIFE.
AW... YOU'RE A SWEETIE.

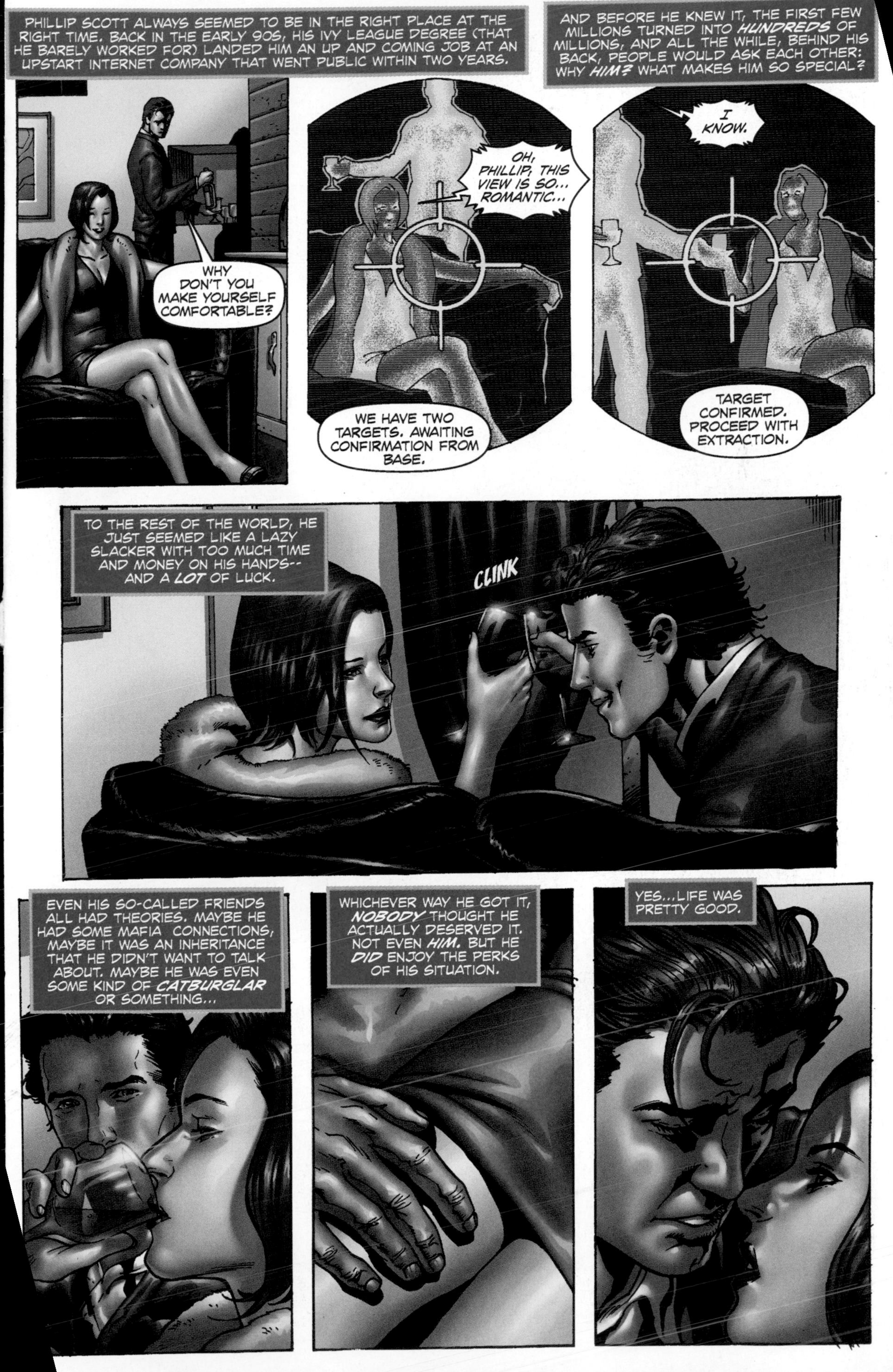
PHILLIP SCOTT ALWAYS SEEMED TO BE IN THE RIGHT PLACE AT THE RIGHT TIME. BACK IN THE EARLY 90S, HIS IVY LEAGUE DEGREE (THAT HE BARELY WORKED FOR) LANDED HIM AN UP AND COMING JOB AT AN UPSTART INTERNET COMPANY THAT WENT PUBLIC WITHIN TWO YEARS.
WHY DON'T YOU MAKE YOURSELF COMFORTABLE?
OH, PHILLIP, THIS VIEW IS SO... ROMANTIC...
WE HAVE TWO TARGETS. AWAITING CONFIRMATION FROM BASE.
AND BEFORE HE KNEW IT, THE FIRST FEW MILLIONS TURNED INTO HUNDREDS OF MILLIONS, AND ALL THE WHILE, BEHIND HIS BACK, PEOPLE WOULD ASK EACH OTHER: WHY HIM? WHAT MAKES HIM SO SPECIAL?
I KNOW.
TARGET CONFIRMED. PROCEED WITH EXTRACTION.
TO THE REST OF THE WORLD, HE JUST SEEMED LIKE A LAZY SLACKER WITH TOO MUCH TIME AND MONEY ON HIS HANDS-- AND A LOT OF LUCK.
CLINK
EVEN HIS SO-CALLED FRIENDS ALL HAD THEORIES. MAYBE HE HAD SOME MAFIA CONNECTIONS, MAYBE IT WAS AN INHERITANCE THAT HE DIDN'T WANT TO TALK ABOUT. MAYBE HE WAS EVEN SOME KIND OF CATBURGLAR OR SOMETHING...
WHICHEVER WAY HE GOT IT, NOBODY THOUGHT HE ACTUALLY DESERVED IT. NOT EVEN HIM. BUT HE DID ENJOY THE PERKS OF HIS SITUATION.
YES...LIFE WAS PRETTY GOOD.

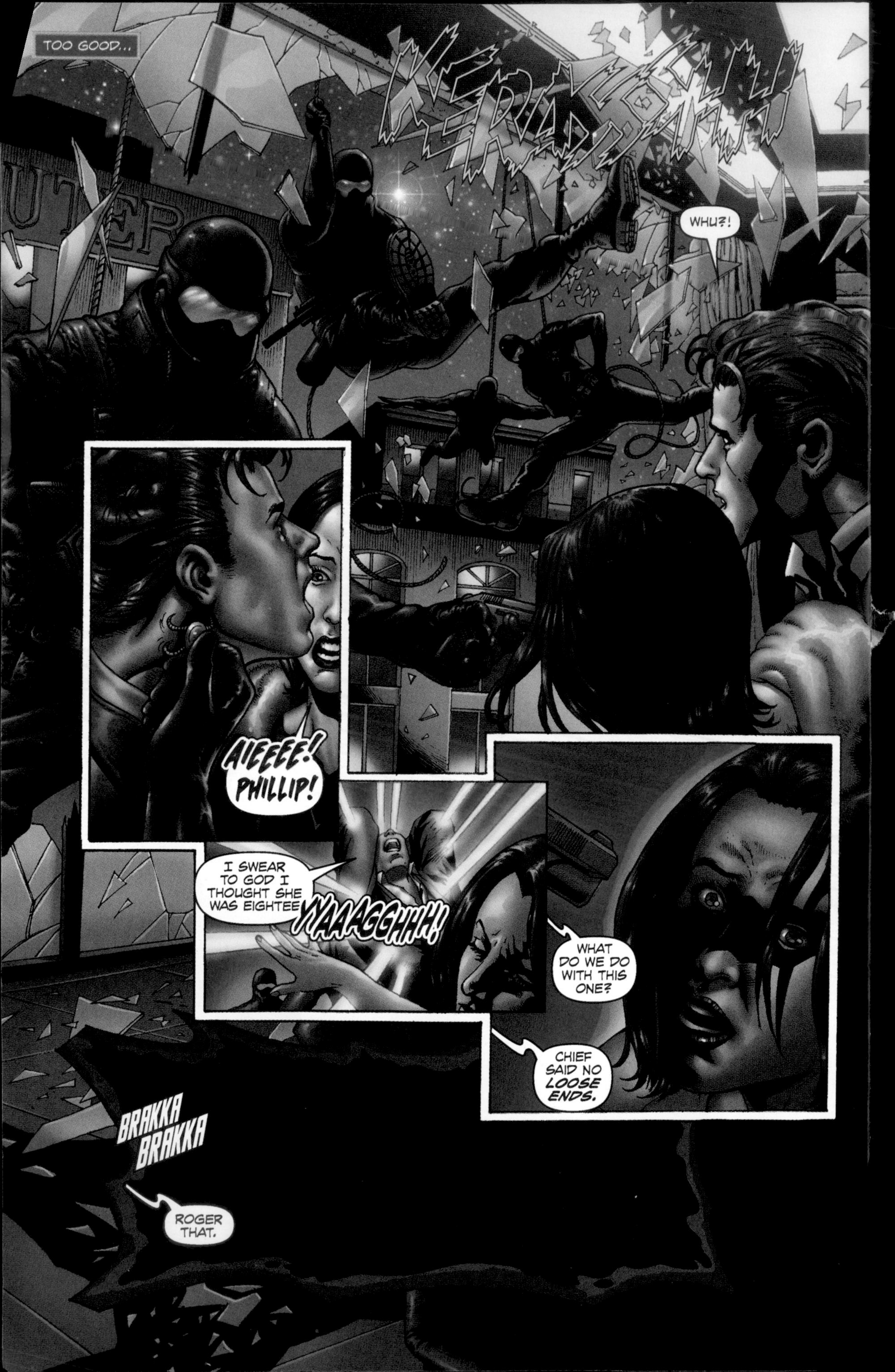

TOO GOOD...
KERRSSHH
WHU?!
AIEEEE! PHILLIP!
I SWEAR TO GOD I THOUGHT SHE WAS EIGHTEE
YYAAAGGHHH!
WHAT DO WE DO WITH THIS ONE?
CHIEF SAID NO LOOSE ENDS.
BRAKKA BRAKKA
ROGER THAT.

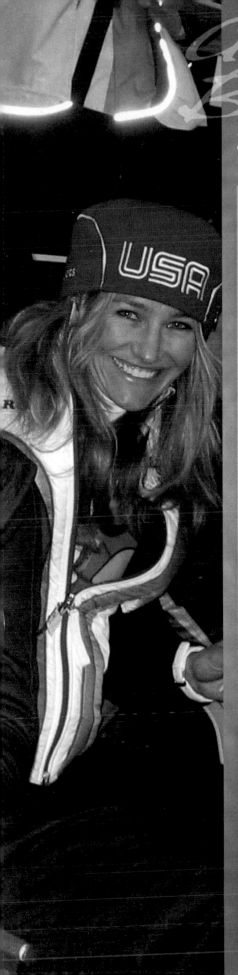

GRETCHEN BLEILER

2006 OLYMPIC SILVER MEDALIST, HALFPIPE
PROFESSIONAL SNOWBOARDER & PIONEER

BIRTHDATE 4/10/81
HOMETOWN TOLEDO, OH
RESIDES ASPEN, CO
HEIGHT 5FT 5IN

Gretchen Bleiler is one of the most accomplished female snowboarders in the world. To top off her incredible list of medals and contest wins, Gretchen most recently won the Silver medal at the 2006 Winter Olympic Games in Torino, Italy.

Gretchen aspired to compete in the Olympic Games from a very young age, and found her passion in snowboarding at age 11. She has been riding ever since and is now recognized as a role model and pioneer in the sport. Among her accomplishments, Gretchen jump-started the invert revolution for female riders as the first to land a Crippler 540 in competition, and won more halfpipe competitions in 2003, 2005 and 2006 than any other female snowboarder. This past season she won four of the five US Olympic halfpipe qualifiers and is also a two time X Games gold medalist.

In the 2006-2007 season, Gretchen will compete in halfpipe contests with the US snowboarding team, but also plans to ride in slopestyle contests and spend more time filming for snowboard videos.

When she's not competing, Gretchen enjoys surfing, mountain biking, interior design and fashion.

CAREER HIGHLIGHTS
- 2006 FIS World Cup 1st Place, Saas Fe, Switzerland
- 2006 Olympic silver medalist
- 2006 Overall Grand Prix Champion; won four of the five Grand Prix events determining Olympic team
- 2005 X Games and Gravity Games Gold Medalist
- 2005 US Open Halfpipe Champion
- FIS World Cup 1st Place, Bardonecchia, Italy
- Eight straight wins in 2003
- 2003 X Games Halfpipe Gold Medalist
- 2003 US Open Champion
- Won 2003 Overall Grand Prix Title
- One of only four females invited to coveted 2003 Arctic Challenge
- 2002 and 2003 Vans Triple Crown Overall Title Winner
- Won 2003 World SuperPipe Championships

AWARDS
- Voted 2006 Female Snowboarder of the Year at Fuel's inaugural Action Sports Awards
- Nominated for 2006 ESPY Award
- Won 2004 Colorado "Female Athlete of the Year" Award
- Earned Transworld Snowboarding's 2004 Reader's Choice Award
- Nominated for 2004 Laureus "Female Action Sports Athlete" Award
- Named Snowboarder and Transworld Snowboarding 2003 "Female Rider of the Year"
- Named 2006 "Female Snowboarder of the Year" in Fuel's inaugural Action Sports Awards

RM: One of the reasons we love Grace Stokes as an extreme athlete is that it gives us a way to travel the globe. Do you love the international element of your job, or does it become a grind?

GB: I love it. It's another amazing aspect of being a professional snowboarder. I not only get to go out and do what I love with my best friends, but I get to travel around the world doing it. I've been to New Zealand, Australia, all over Europe, Scandinavia, South America, Central America, Japan and of course all over the US. You learn so much from travel—seeing different cultures, and traditions, learning other languages, and getting new perspectives.

RM: Grace is a snowboarder by nature, but also excels at other sports. Do you feel it's realistic for an athlete to win at more than one sport?

GB: Yeah, definitely realistic. It's been done before. Both Shawn White and Cara Beth Burnside are both Summer and Winter X Games medalists in snowboarding and skateboarding. For me, I love surfing. And it is an X Games sport now, however I'm not holding my breath for that one!

RM: In our story, Grace is a little older and moving to a new career post X Games. Are you thinking of what you plan on doing after you finish being a competitor?

GB: At this point in my career, I have accomplished so many goals in snowboarding that I've always strived for—going to the Olympics and winning a medal has been a goal of mine since I was a little girl. I'm also a two-time X Games gold medalist. The XGames is the biggest event in snowboarding, so naturally when I first started in the sport, that was something I always dreamed of doing. But there are so many aspects to snowboarding that I haven't even touched on yet. I want to ride more slopestyle events, I want to try and get a great part in a snowboard movie. I want to go to the backcountry and learn how to land in powder consistently, I want to drop cliffs and find big mountain lines to ride. The opportunities are endless. So as you can see for me, I don't know what I want to do after snowboarding, because I have so much to do still within this sport.

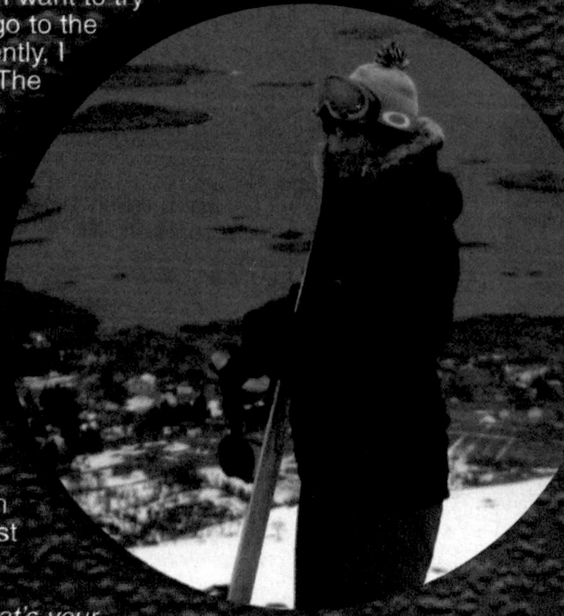

RM: Like you're designing snowboards.

GB: Yep. I have worked with K2, my board sponsor, for the past few years helping to come up with board graphic ideas as well as helping decide the way my snowboard, The Mix, actually rides. I also work closely with Oakley, my eyewear and outwear sponsor, to help develop their clothing lines and their women specific goggle, The Stockholm. Because being a snowboarder becomes a career and a business there are so many different avenues that you can explore. Snowboarding takes you more places than just down a mountain.

RM: In "The Innocents," Grace rides a motorcycle. What's your preferred mode of transportation?

GB: My preferred mode is my Lexus hybrid. But I used to ride a motorcycle, and I loved it! But at that time I was riding without a license (laughs). I didn't know you had to have a specific "motorcycle license" to be legal, I thought a driver's license would cut it. So needless to say I stopped riding until I got my license. However I still haven't found the time for it. This summer I was thinking about taking a course and getting it, because I have been thinking about it a lot lately. But now I live in Southern California with my boyfriend over the summer and fall. California is probably one of the more dangerous places to be on a bike. So one day when I have some time I'll get my license and a bike and ride it around Aspen, where it's a little bit safer.

RM: How do you feel about comic books? Do you have any favorites?

GB: Well, I love reading about strong, intelligent, independent women who go out and kick butt and make a positive effect on the world. I think it's a great message for girls of all ages, and it's fun to read. It's inspiring.

Inspiration

Real life muse and extreme sports champion Gretchen Bleiler talks with Spacedog's CEO Roger Mincheff about Karma, Comics, and Halfpipes in this exclusive behind-the-scenes.

Roger Mincheff: The heroine of "The Innocents," Grace Stokes, grew up with very strict enthusiast parents, and X Games were her ways of rebelling. Were your parents supportive of your career choice or did they view it as a rebellion?

Gretchen Bleiler: I've been very lucky to have always been encouraged and supported in everything I do, especially my snowboarding. But I grew up as a country club girl in Dayton, Ohio. I was on the swimming and diving team, I played golf, tennis and soccer. When we moved to Aspen, Colorado when I was ten, we sort of changed lifestyles. I went from the traditional sports to—hiking and camping, playing ice hockey and snowboarding. So snowboarding for me was just something totally new and different. I did face some adversity and questioning when I decided to defer a year from college to pursue snowboarding. And my grandmother always continued to talk to me about getting to college. But all of this was genuine concern for my best interest! But things have obviously turned out quite well; I make a great living by traveling around the world, learning valuable lessons daily, and by doing what I love, you can't beat that.

RM: So were you much of a Tomboy at all when you were young?

GB: Oh yeah. I have three brothers, two older. So whatever they were doing, I always wanted to do, and do just as well. When we moved to Aspen they had already been snowboarding for two years. And I just remember hearing about how good they were and seeing them do these cool tricks. So I decided I wanted to do it too. I would go out everyday on my snowboard, every day that I could, which was usually more than my friends wanted to go. So I ended up going out alone and I would push myself everyday to learn new tricks. Yes I definitely was a little tomboy.

RM: Grace is super talented, but as an Innocent, she's a bit of a slacker. Do you feel like you've ever slacked off at all? Do you ever have your "couch potato" moments?

GB: Yes, definitely. Being a professional snowboarder is tough because I have to be outside pushing myself and my level of snowboarding everyday no matter the weather, or in some instances the time of day, or the lighting, or the temperature, or the conditions. And sometimes I wake up and the last thing I want to do is go outside and snowboard! But I have to; it's what I do. And it's the best feeling in the entire world when you go out in these tough conditions and you do succeed. But in general as far as being a slacker, in the past I have only focused on snowboarding. And snowboarding is what I love. And in some ways anyone who is successful in what they do automatically becomes a role model in that category and this is the case for me. So now I want to go beyond what I have been doing and actually make a difference, not just in snowboarding, but in general. After the Olympics I heard something wonderful and it was this; you've proven yourself. You're an Olympian now. But this is just the first step. Now it's time to go out and make something of it. Use that celebrity, use this new title, and go and do something good for the world. So I'm sort of in that phase of my life right now. Kind of trying to figure out different charities and causes to get involved with, and not just be a snowboarder. Not just focusing on one thing, but using it to create a greater good.

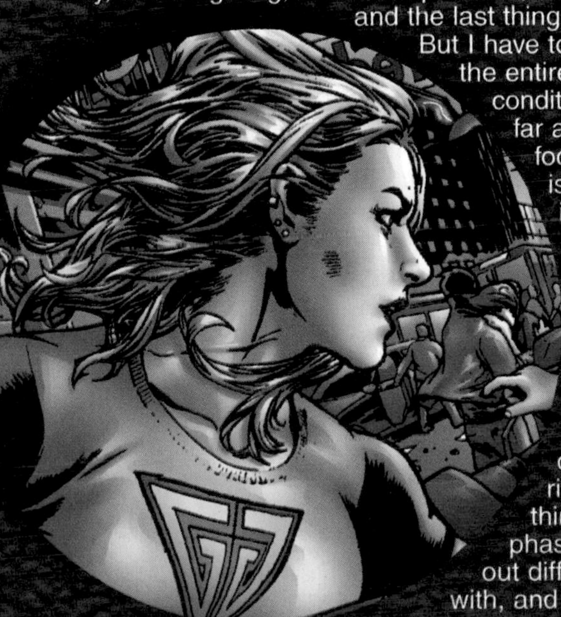

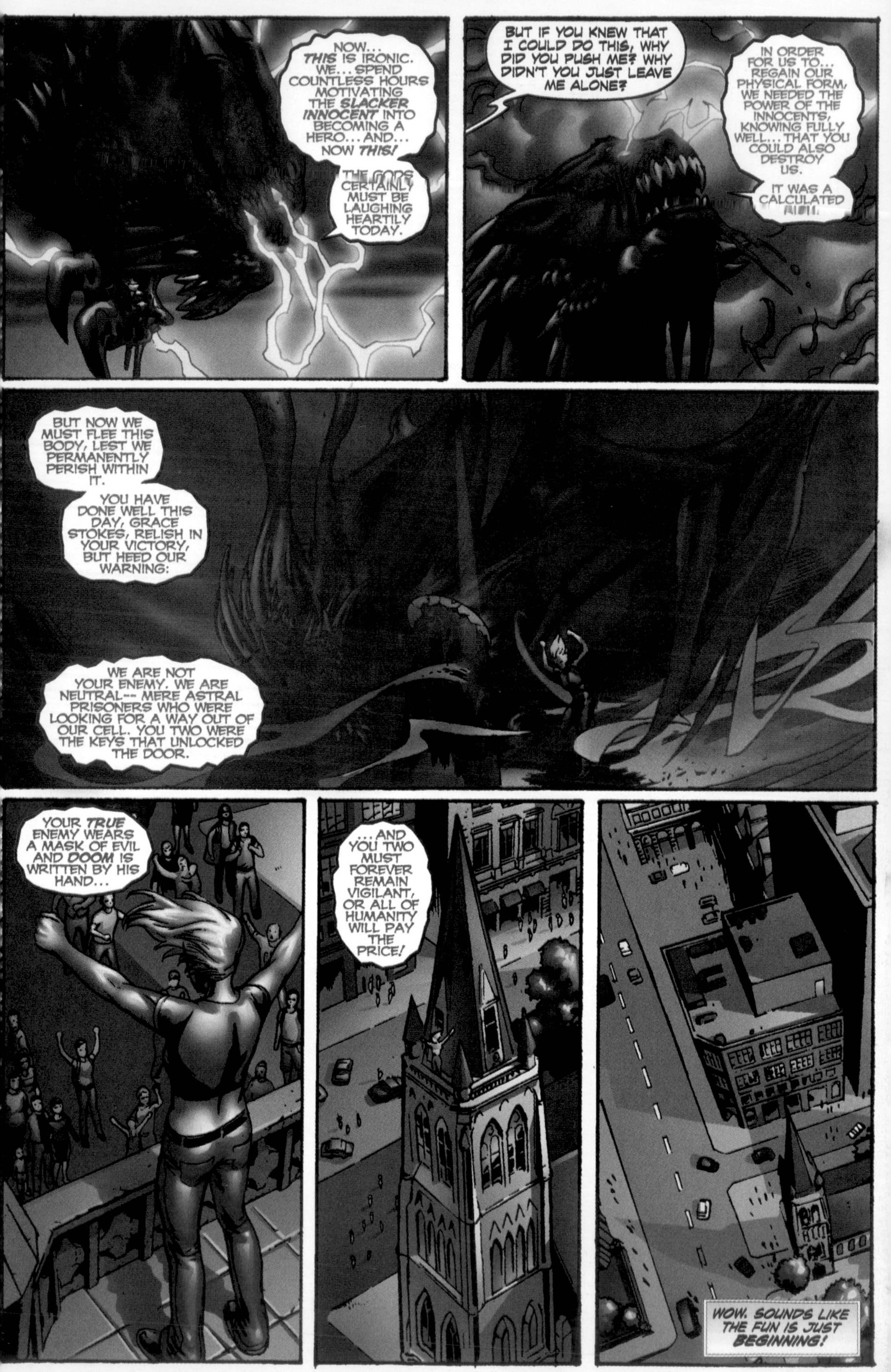
NOW... THIS IS IRONIC. WE... SPEND COUNTLESS HOURS MOTIVATING THE SLACKER INNOCENT INTO BECOMING A HERO... AND... NOW THIS!
THE GODS CERTAINLY MUST BE LAUGHING HEARTILY TODAY.
BUT IF YOU KNEW THAT I COULD DO THIS, WHY DID YOU PUSH ME? WHY DIDN'T YOU JUST LEAVE ME ALONE?
IN ORDER FOR US TO... REGAIN OUR PHYSICAL FORM, WE NEEDED THE POWER OF THE INNOCENTS, KNOWING FULLY WELL... THAT YOU COULD ALSO DESTROY US.
IT WAS A CALCULATED
BUT NOW WE MUST FLEE THIS BODY, LEST WE PERMANENTLY PERISH WITHIN IT.
YOU HAVE DONE WELL THIS DAY, GRACE STOKES, RELISH IN YOUR VICTORY, BUT HEED OUR WARNING:
WE ARE NOT YOUR ENEMY. WE ARE NEUTRAL-- MERE ASTRAL PRISONERS WHO WERE LOOKING FOR A WAY OUT OF OUR CELL. YOU TWO WERE THE KEYS THAT UNLOCKED THE DOOR.
YOUR TRUE ENEMY WEARS A MASK OF EVIL AND DOOM IS WRITTEN BY HIS HAND...
...AND YOU TWO MUST FOREVER REMAIN VIGILANT, OR ALL OF HUMANITY WILL PAY THE PRICE!
WOW. SOUNDS LIKE THE FUN IS JUST BEGINNING!

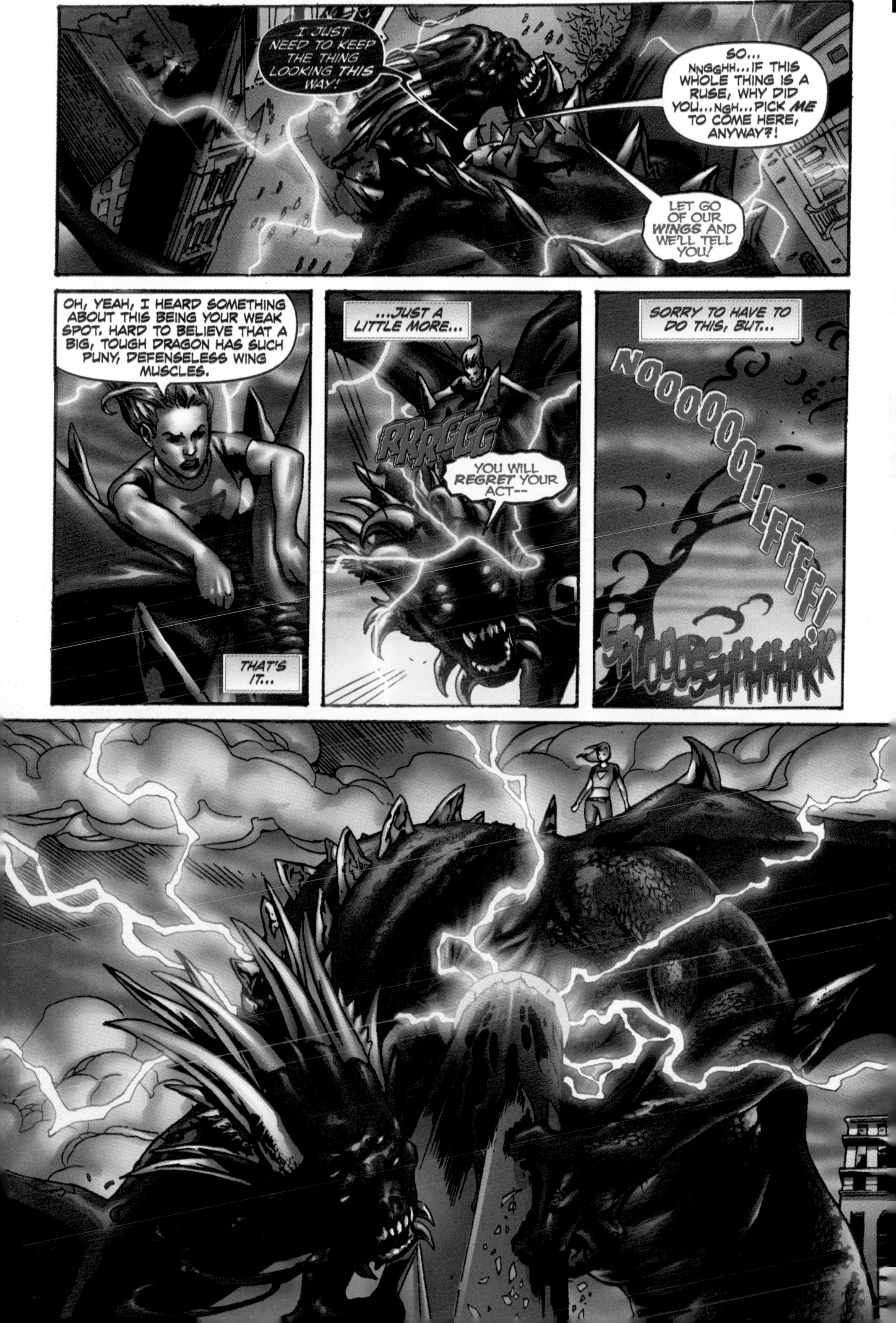
I JUST NEED TO KEEP THE THING LOOKING THIS WAY!
SO... NNGGHH...IF THIS WHOLE THING IS A RUSE, WHY DID YOU...NGH...PICK ME TO COME HERE, ANYWAY?!
LET GO OF OUR WINGS AND WE'LL TELL YOU!
OH, YEAH, I HEARD SOMETHING ABOUT THIS BEING YOUR WEAK SPOT. HARD TO BELIEVE THAT A BIG, TOUGH DRAGON HAS SUCH PUNY, DEFENSELESS WING MUSCLES.
THAT'S IT...
...JUST A LITTLE MORE...
RRRGGG
YOU WILL REGRET YOUR ACT--
SORRY TO HAVE TO DO THIS, BUT...
NOOOOOOOLLFFFFF!
SPLOOOSHHHHK

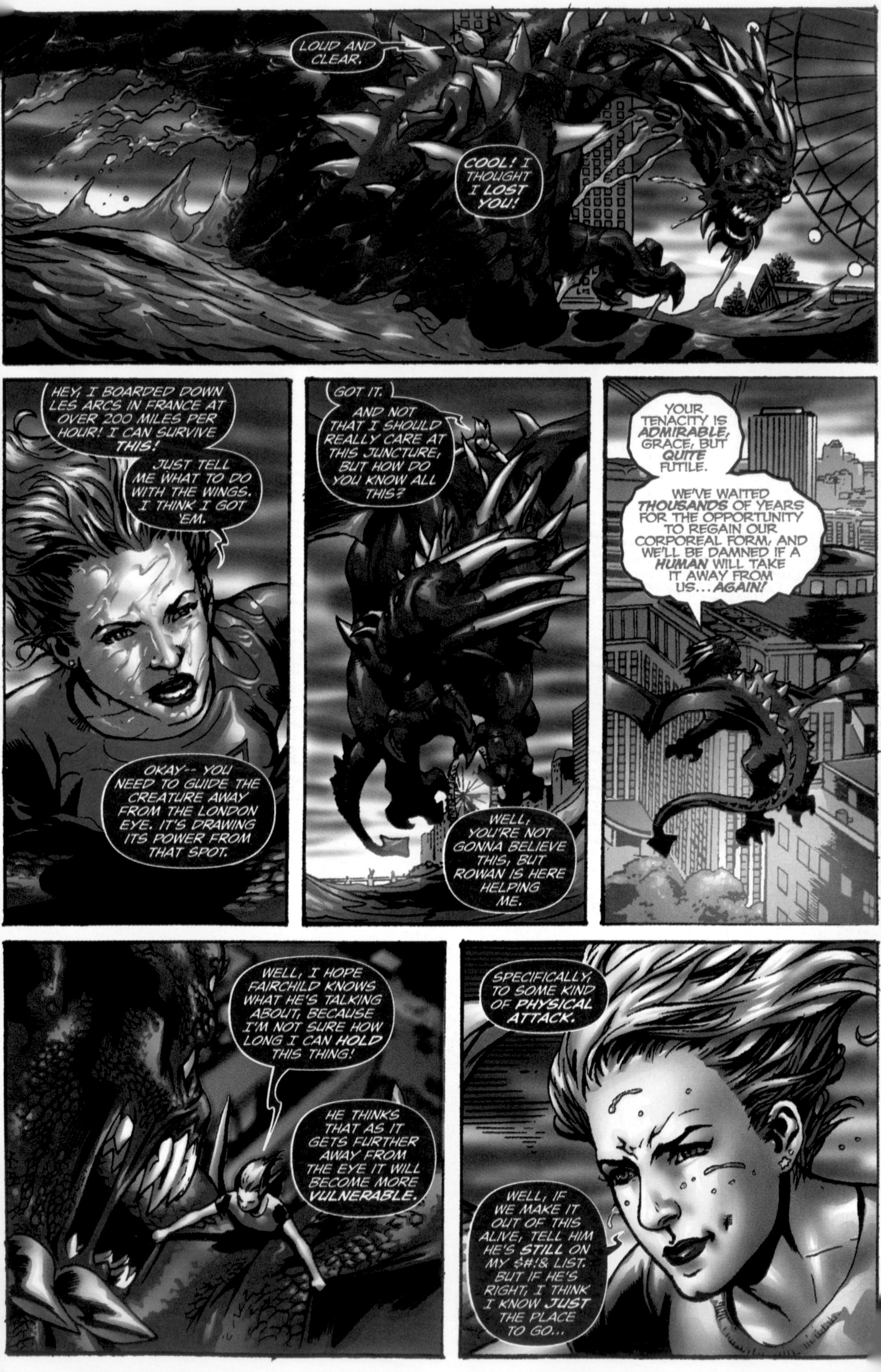
LOUD AND CLEAR.
COOL! I THOUGHT I LOST YOU!
HEY, I BOARDED DOWN LES ARCS IN FRANCE AT OVER 200 MILES PER HOUR! I CAN SURVIVE THIS!
JUST TELL ME WHAT TO DO WITH THE WINGS. I THINK I GOT 'EM.
OKAY-- YOU NEED TO GUIDE THE CREATURE AWAY FROM THE LONDON EYE. IT'S DRAWING ITS POWER FROM THAT SPOT.
GOT IT.
AND NOT THAT I SHOULD REALLY CARE AT THIS JUNCTURE, BUT HOW DO YOU KNOW ALL THIS?
WELL, YOU'RE NOT GONNA BELIEVE THIS, BUT ROWAN IS HERE HELPING ME.
YOUR TENACITY IS ADMIRABLE, GRACE, BUT QUITE FUTILE.
WE'VE WAITED THOUSANDS OF YEARS FOR THE OPPORTUNITY TO REGAIN OUR CORPOREAL FORM, AND WE'LL BE DAMNED IF A HUMAN WILL TAKE IT AWAY FROM US... AGAIN!
WELL, I HOPE FAIRCHILD KNOWS WHAT HE'S TALKING ABOUT, BECAUSE I'M NOT SURE HOW LONG I CAN HOLD THIS THING!
HE THINKS THAT AS IT GETS FURTHER AWAY FROM THE EYE IT WILL BECOME MORE VULNERABLE.
SPECIFICALLY, TO SOME KIND OF PHYSICAL ATTACK.
WELL, IF WE MAKE IT OUT OF THIS ALIVE, TELL HIM HE'S STILL ON MY $#!& LIST. BUT IF HE'S RIGHT, I THINK I KNOW JUST THE PLACE TO GO...

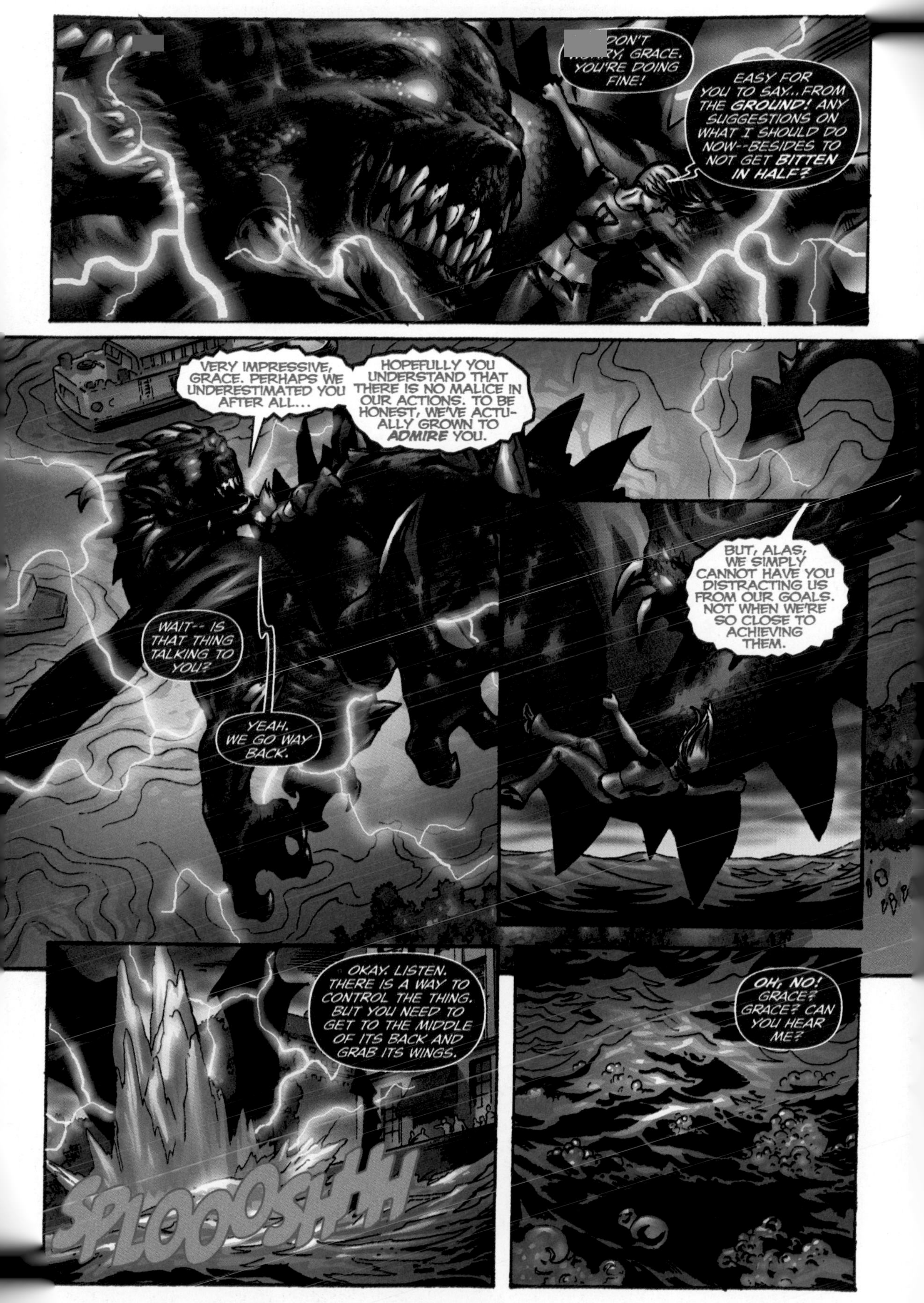

DON'T WORRY, GRACE. YOU'RE DOING FINE!
EASY FOR YOU TO SAY...FROM THE **GROUND!** ANY SUGGESTIONS ON WHAT I SHOULD DO NOW--BESIDES TO NOT GET **BITTEN IN HALF?**
VERY IMPRESSIVE, GRACE. PERHAPS WE UNDERESTIMATED YOU AFTER ALL...
HOPEFULLY YOU UNDERSTAND THAT THERE IS NO MALICE IN OUR ACTIONS. TO BE HONEST, WE'VE ACTUALLY GROWN TO **ADMIRE** YOU.
WAIT-- IS THAT THING TALKING TO YOU?
YEAH. WE GO WAY BACK.
BUT, ALAS, WE SIMPLY CANNOT HAVE YOU DISTRACTING US FROM OUR GOALS. NOT WHEN WE'RE SO CLOSE TO ACHIEVING THEM.
OKAY. LISTEN. THERE IS A WAY TO CONTROL THE THING. BUT YOU NEED TO GET TO THE MIDDLE OF ITS BACK AND GRAB ITS WINGS.
SPLOOOSHHH
OH, NO! GRACE? GRACE? CAN YOU HEAR ME?

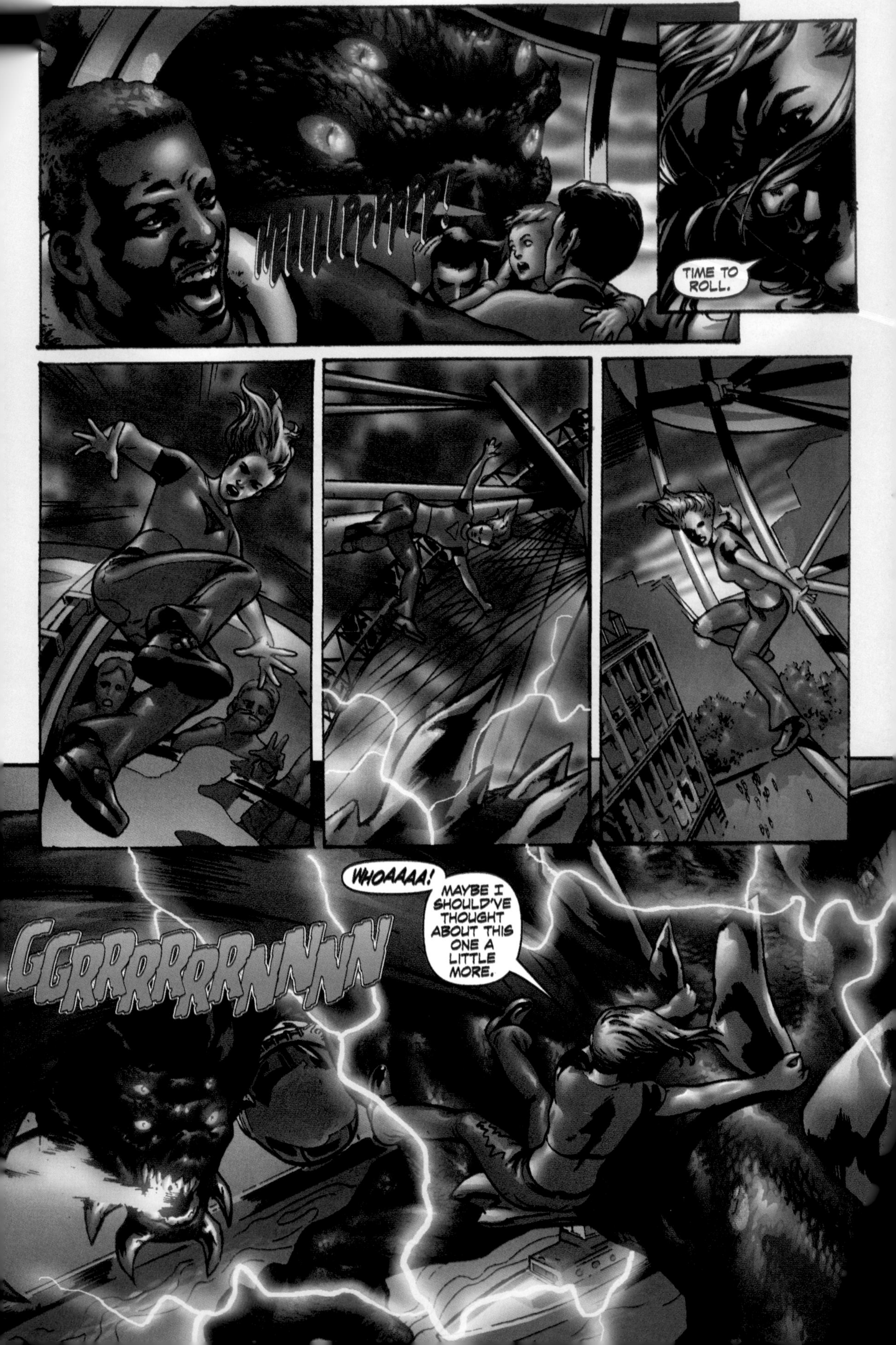
WHUUUUPPPPPP!
TIME TO ROLL.
GGRRRRRRNNNNN
WHOAAAA!
MAYBE I SHOULD'VE THOUGHT ABOUT THIS ONE A LITTLE MORE.

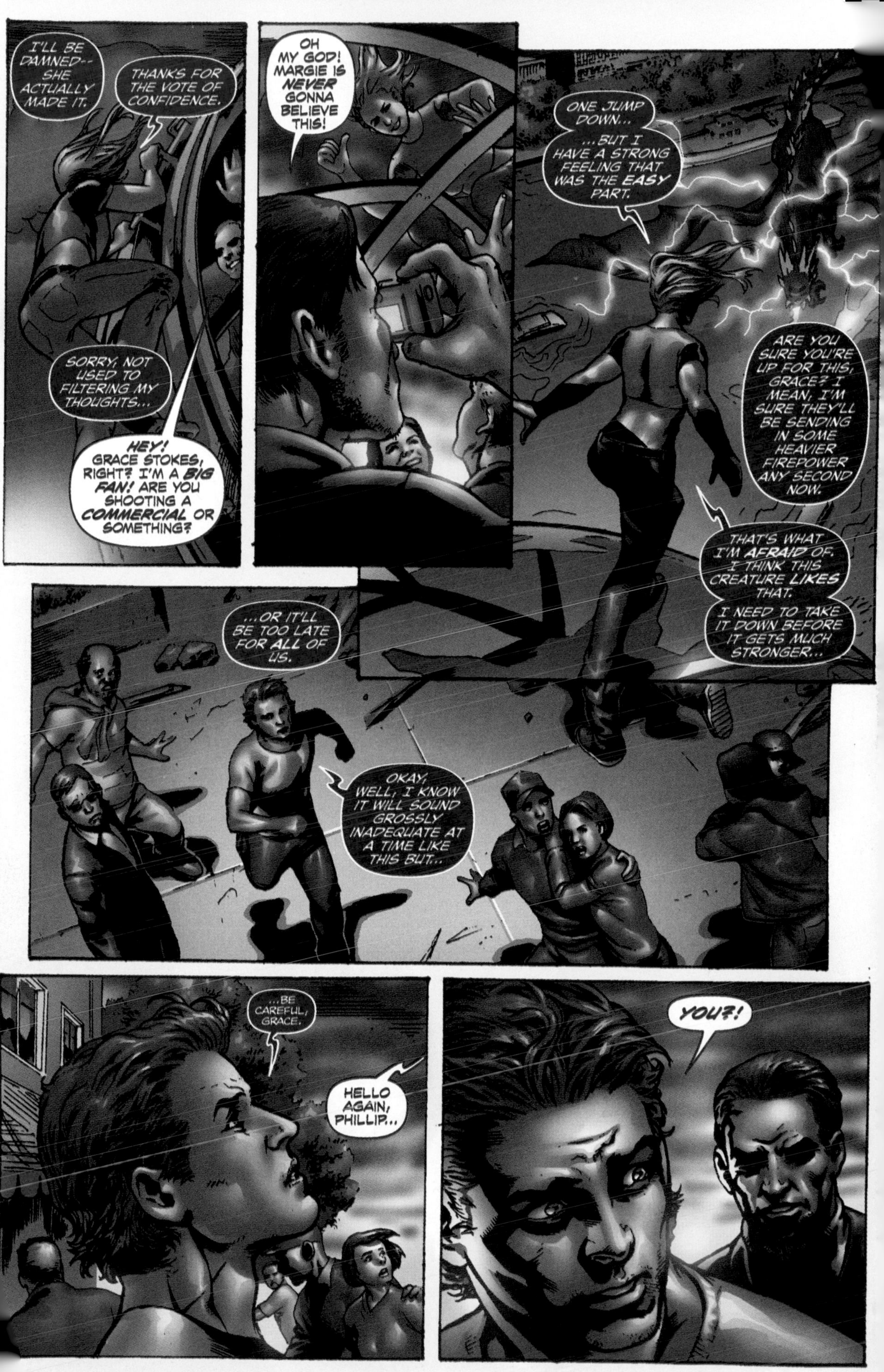
I'LL BE DAMNED-- SHE ACTUALLY MADE IT.
THANKS FOR THE VOTE OF CONFIDENCE.
SORRY, NOT USED TO FILTERING MY THOUGHTS...
HEY! GRACE STOKES, RIGHT? I'M A BIG FAN! ARE YOU SHOOTING A COMMERCIAL OR SOMETHING?
OH MY GOD! MARGIE IS NEVER GONNA BELIEVE THIS!
ONE JUMP DOWN...
...BUT I HAVE A STRONG FEELING THAT WAS THE EASY PART.
ARE YOU SURE YOU'RE UP FOR THIS, GRACE? I MEAN, I'M SURE THEY'LL BE SENDING IN SOME HEAVIER FIREPOWER ANY SECOND NOW.
THAT'S WHAT I'M AFRAID OF. I THINK THIS CREATURE LIKES THAT.
I NEED TO TAKE IT DOWN BEFORE IT GETS MUCH STRONGER...
...OR IT'LL BE TOO LATE FOR ALL OF US.
OKAY, WELL, I KNOW IT WILL SOUND GROSSLY INADEQUATE AT A TIME LIKE THIS BUT...
...BE CAREFUL, GRACE.
HELLO AGAIN, PHILLIP...
YOU?!

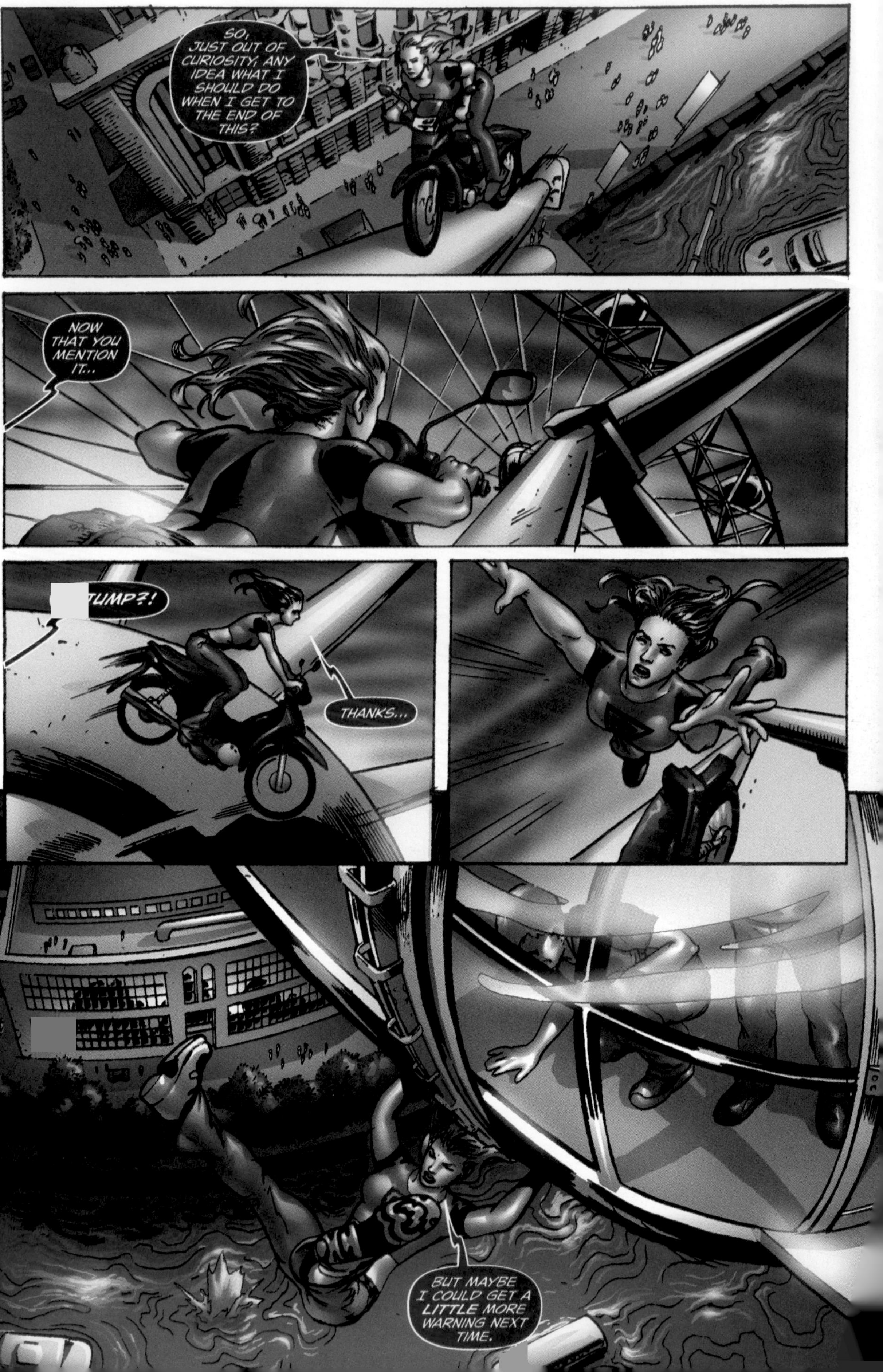
SO, JUST OUT OF CURIOSITY, ANY IDEA WHAT I SHOULD DO WHEN I GET TO THE END OF THIS?
NOW THAT YOU MENTION IT...
JUMP?!
THANKS...
BUT MAYBE I COULD GET A *LITTLE* MORE WARNING NEXT TIME.

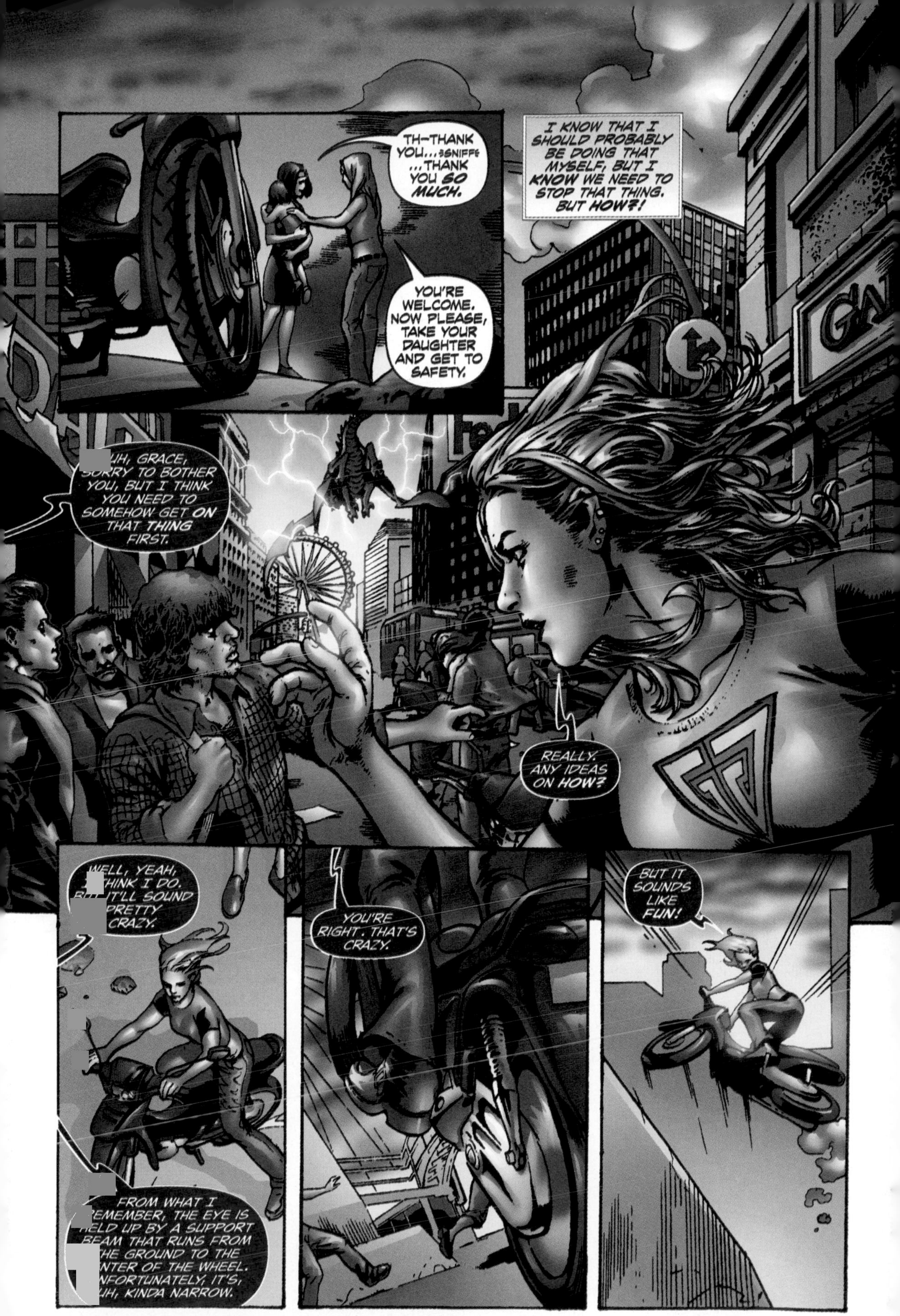
TH—THANK YOU... *SNIFF* ...THANK YOU SO MUCH.
YOU'RE WELCOME. NOW PLEASE, TAKE YOUR DAUGHTER AND GET TO SAFETY.
I KNOW THAT I SHOULD PROBABLY BE DOING THAT MYSELF, BUT I KNOW WE NEED TO STOP THAT THING. BUT HOW?!
UH, GRACE, SORRY TO BOTHER YOU, BUT I THINK YOU NEED TO SOMEHOW GET ON THAT THING FIRST.
REALLY. ANY IDEAS ON HOW?
WELL, YEAH, I THINK I DO. BUT IT'LL SOUND PRETTY CRAZY.
FROM WHAT I REMEMBER, THE EYE IS HELD UP BY A SUPPORT BEAM THAT RUNS FROM THE GROUND TO THE CENTER OF THE WHEEL. UNFORTUNATELY, IT'S, UH, KINDA NARROW.
YOU'RE RIGHT. THAT'S CRAZY.
BUT IT SOUNDS LIKE FUN!

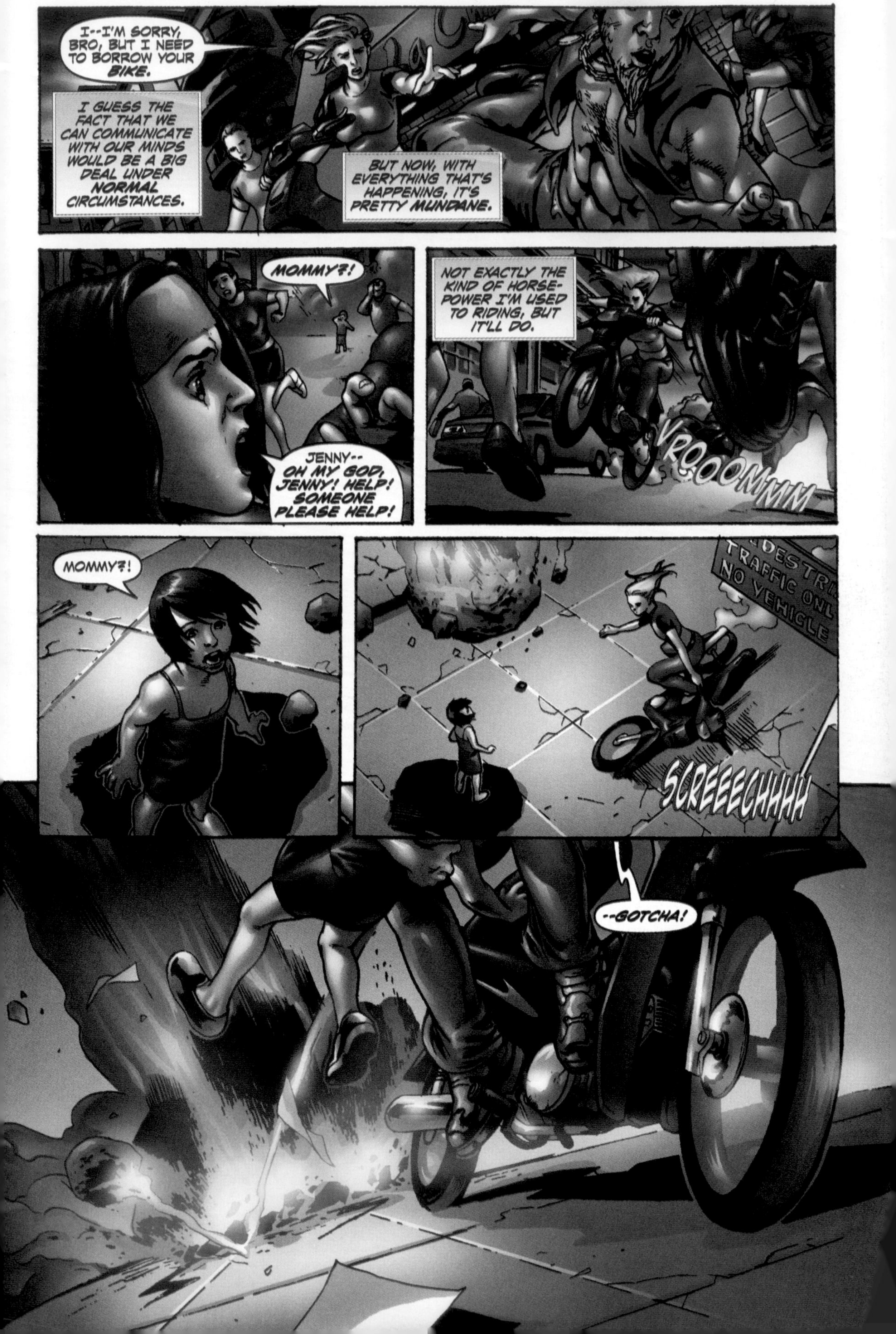
I--I'M SORRY, BRO, BUT I NEED TO BORROW YOUR BIKE.
I GUESS THE FACT THAT WE CAN COMMUNICATE WITH OUR MINDS WOULD BE A BIG DEAL UNDER NORMAL CIRCUMSTANCES.
BUT NOW, WITH EVERYTHING THAT'S HAPPENING, IT'S PRETTY MUNDANE.
MOMMY?!
JENNY-- OH MY GOD, JENNY! HELP! SOMEONE PLEASE HELP!
NOT EXACTLY THE KIND OF HORSE-POWER I'M USED TO RIDING, BUT IT'LL DO.
VROOOMMM
MOMMY?!
SCREEECHHHH
--GOTCHA!

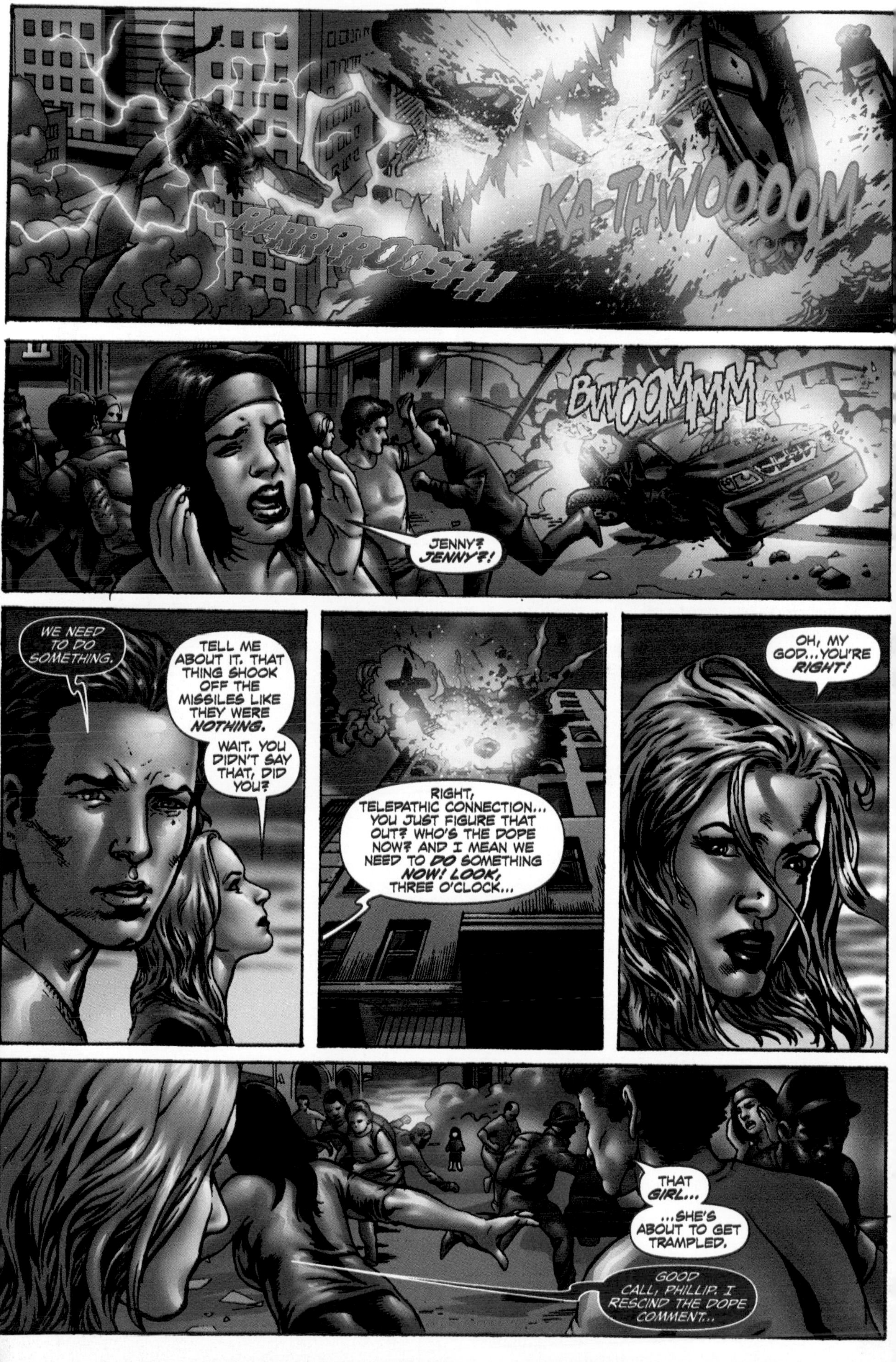
RARRRROOSHH
KA-THWOOOOM
BWOOMMM
JENNY? JENNY?!
WE NEED TO DO SOMETHING.
TELL ME ABOUT IT. THAT THING SHOOK OFF THE MISSILES LIKE THEY WERE NOTHING.
WAIT. YOU DIDN'T SAY THAT, DID YOU?
RIGHT, TELEPATHIC CONNECTION... YOU JUST FIGURE THAT OUT? WHO'S THE DOPE NOW? AND I MEAN WE NEED TO DO SOMETHING NOW! LOOK, THREE O'CLOCK...
OH, MY GOD...YOU'RE RIGHT!
THAT GIRL...
...SHE'S ABOUT TO GET TRAMPLED.
GOOD CALL, PHILLIP. I RESCIND THE DOPE COMMENT...

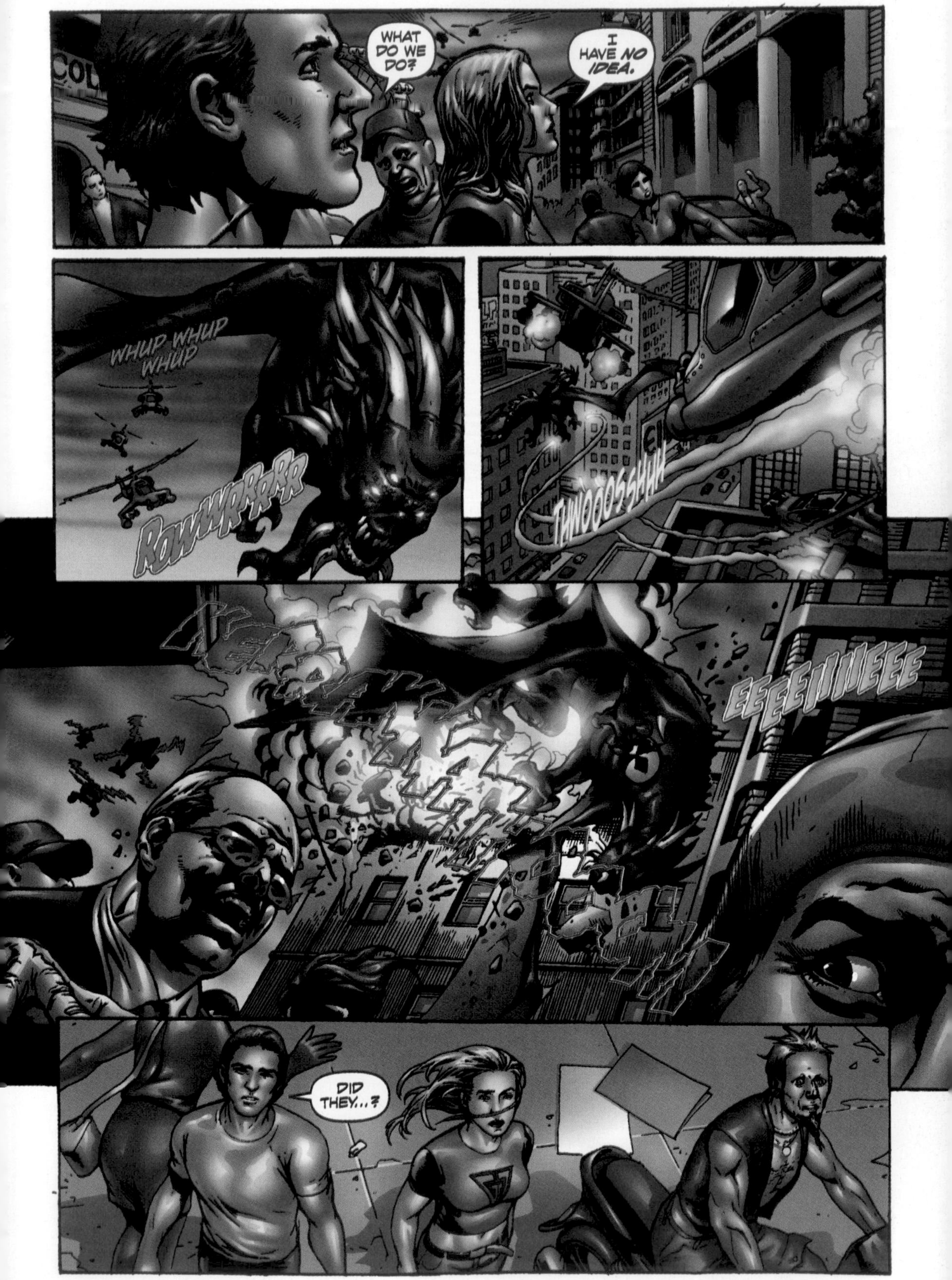
WHAT DO WE DO?
I HAVE NO IDEA.
WHUP WHUP WHUP
ROWWRRRRR
THWOOOSSHHH
EEEEIIIIEEE
DID THEY...?

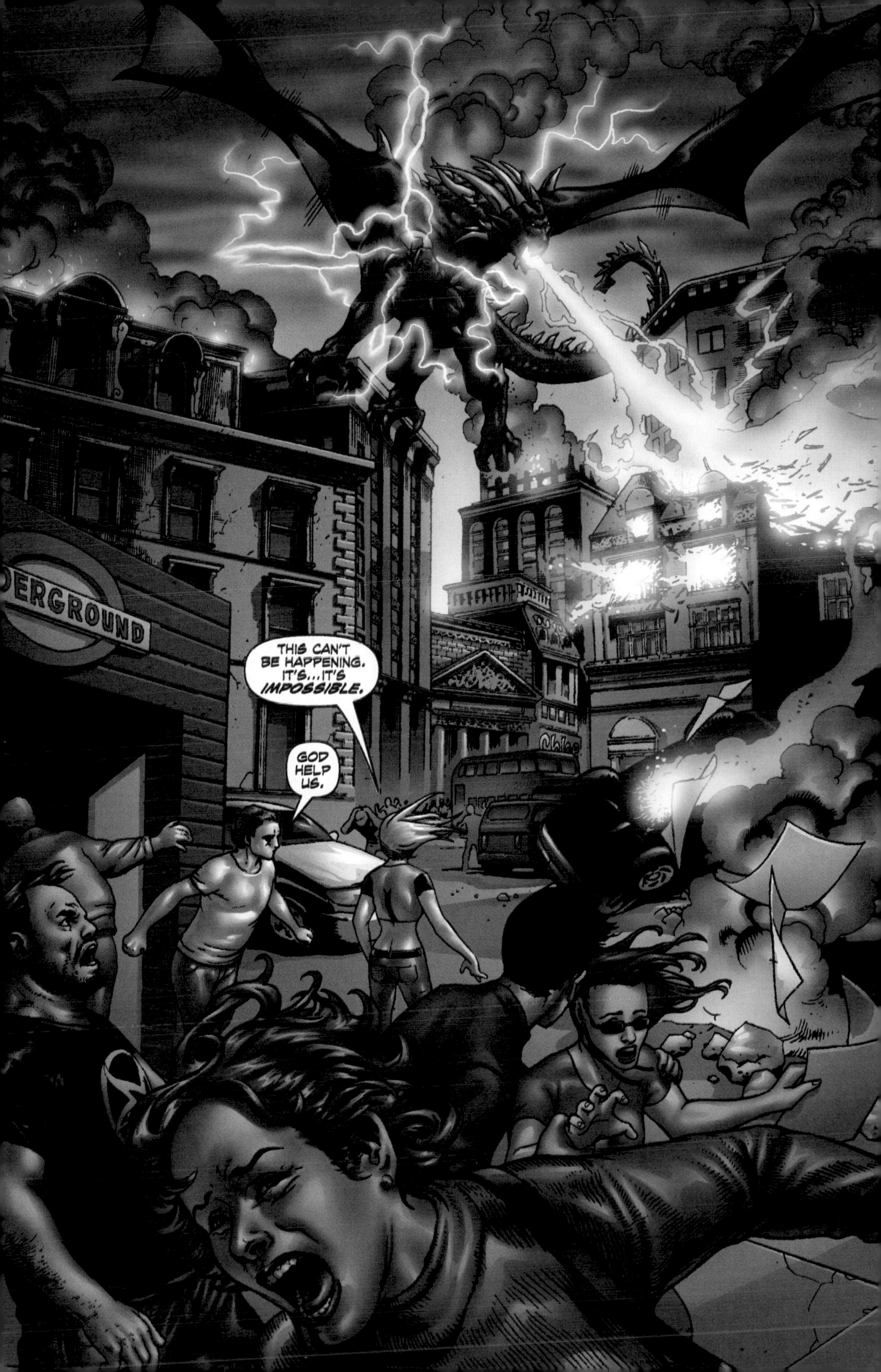
ERGROUND
THIS CAN'T BE HAPPENING. IT'S...IT'S IMPOSSIBLE.
GOD HELP US.

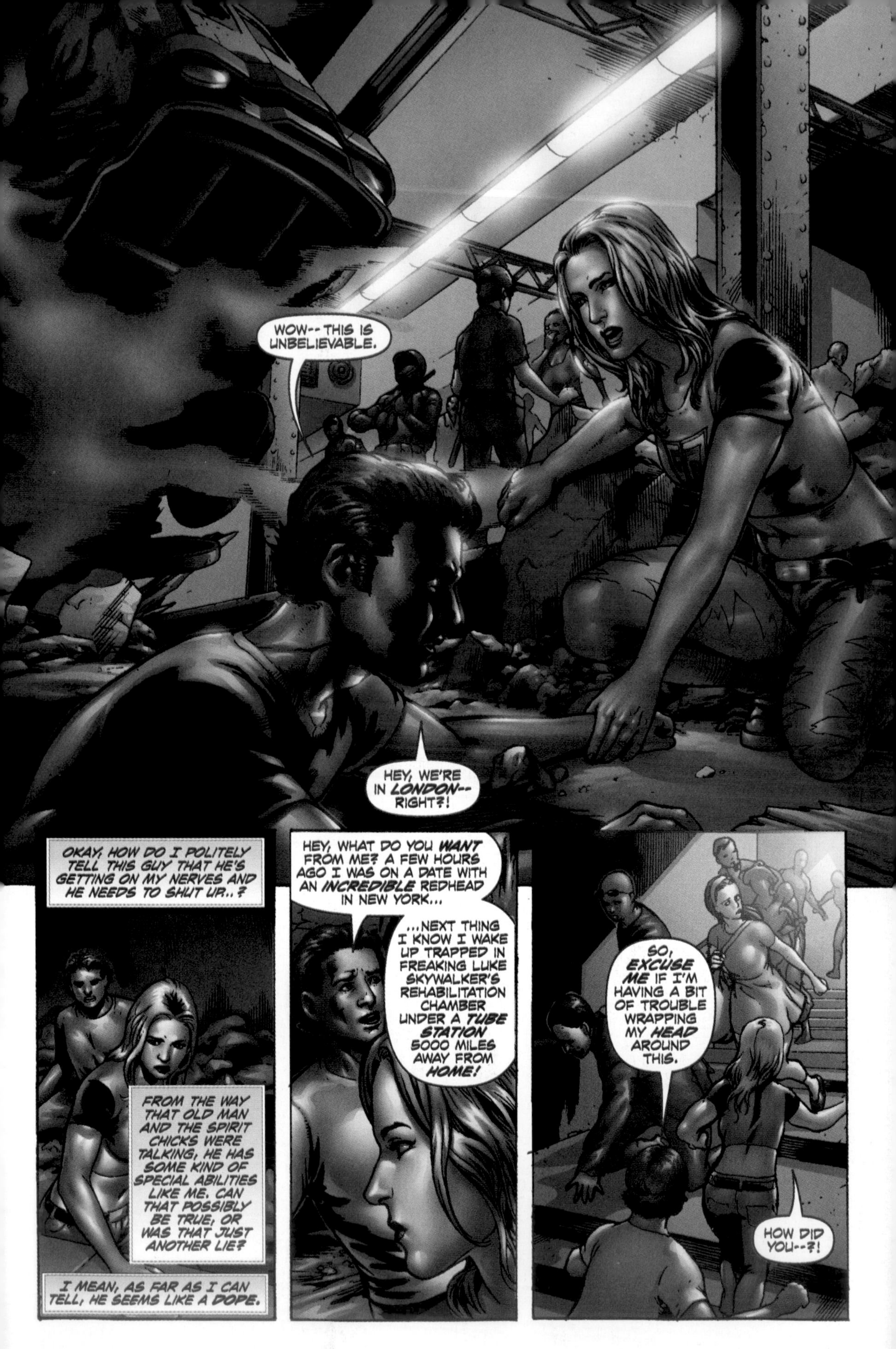
WOW-- THIS IS UNBELIEVABLE.
HEY, WE'RE IN LONDON-- RIGHT?!
OKAY, HOW DO I POLITELY TELL THIS GUY THAT HE'S GETTING ON MY NERVES AND HE NEEDS TO SHUT UP..?
FROM THE WAY THAT OLD MAN AND THE SPIRIT CHICKS WERE TALKING, HE HAS SOME KIND OF SPECIAL ABILITIES LIKE ME. CAN THAT POSSIBLY BE TRUE, OR WAS THAT JUST ANOTHER LIE?
I MEAN, AS FAR AS I CAN TELL, HE SEEMS LIKE A DOPE.
HEY, WHAT DO YOU WANT FROM ME? A FEW HOURS AGO I WAS ON A DATE WITH AN INCREDIBLE REDHEAD IN NEW YORK...
...NEXT THING I KNOW I WAKE UP TRAPPED IN FREAKING LUKE SKYWALKER'S REHABILITATION CHAMBER UNDER A TUBE STATION 5000 MILES AWAY FROM HOME!
SO, EXCUSE ME IF I'M HAVING A BIT OF TROUBLE WRAPPING MY HEAD AROUND THIS.
HOW DID YOU--?!

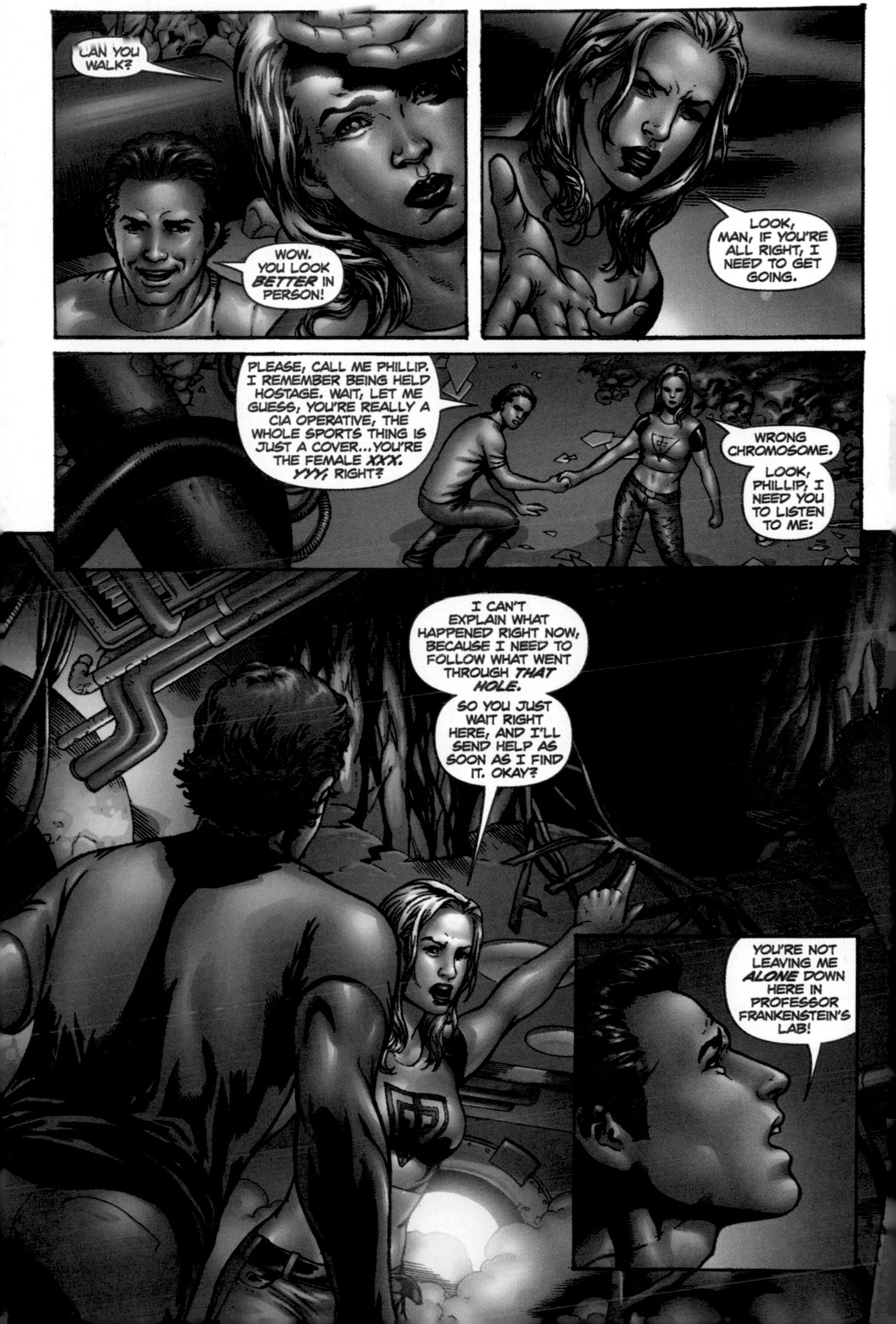
CAN YOU WALK?
WOW. YOU LOOK BETTER IN PERSON!
LOOK, MAN, IF YOU'RE ALL RIGHT, I NEED TO GET GOING.
PLEASE, CALL ME PHILLIP. I REMEMBER BEING HELD HOSTAGE. WAIT, LET ME GUESS, YOU'RE REALLY A CIA OPERATIVE, THE WHOLE SPORTS THING IS JUST A COVER...YOU'RE THE FEMALE XXX. YYY, RIGHT?
WRONG CHROMOSOME.
LOOK, PHILLIP, I NEED YOU TO LISTEN TO ME:
I CAN'T EXPLAIN WHAT HAPPENED RIGHT NOW, BECAUSE I NEED TO FOLLOW WHAT WENT THROUGH THAT HOLE.
SO YOU JUST WAIT RIGHT HERE, AND I'LL SEND HELP AS SOON AS I FIND IT. OKAY?
YOU'RE NOT LEAVING ME ALONE DOWN HERE IN PROFESSOR FRANKENSTEIN'S LAB!

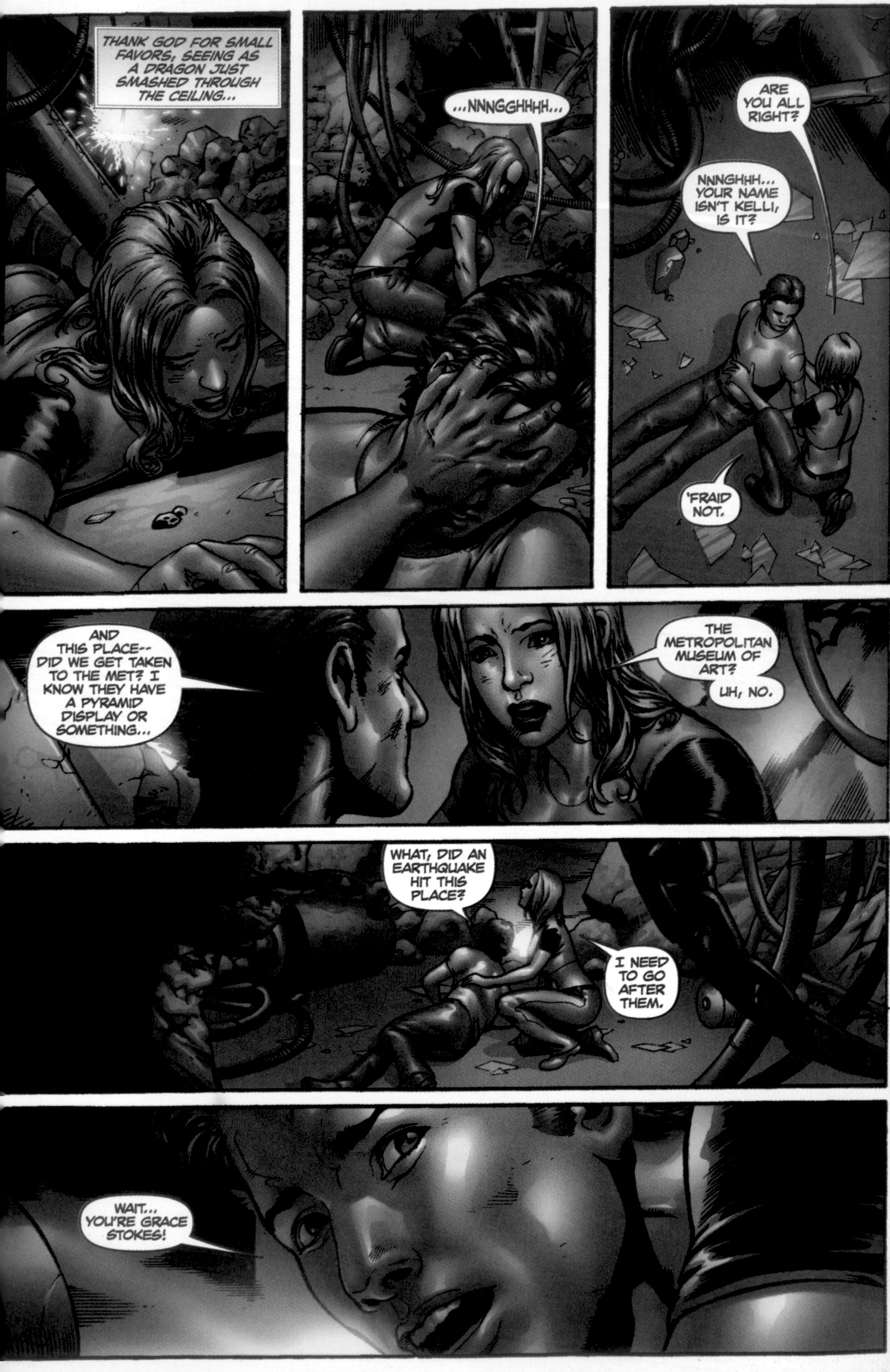
THANK GOD FOR SMALL FAVORS, SEEING AS A DRAGON JUST SMASHED THROUGH THE CEILING...
...NNNGHHHH...
ARE YOU ALL RIGHT?
NNNGHHH... YOUR NAME ISN'T KELLI, IS IT?
'FRAID NOT.
AND THIS PLACE-- DID WE GET TAKEN TO THE MET? I KNOW THEY HAVE A PYRAMID DISPLAY OR SOMETHING...
THE METROPOLITAN MUSEUM OF ART?
UH, NO.
WHAT, DID AN EARTHQUAKE HIT THIS PLACE?
I NEED TO GO AFTER THEM.
WAIT... YOU'RE GRACE STOKES!

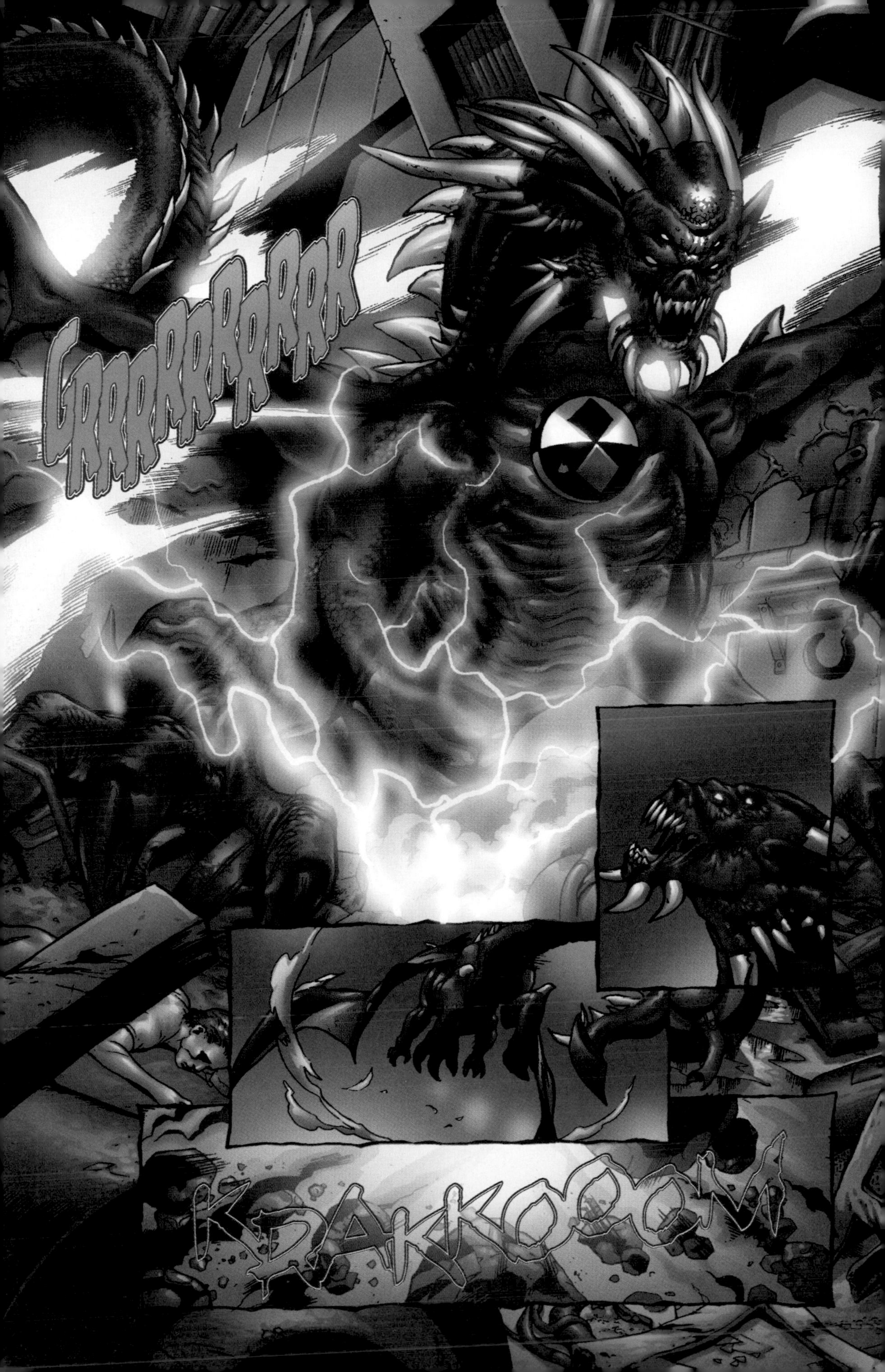
GRRRRRRRRRR
KRAKOOOM

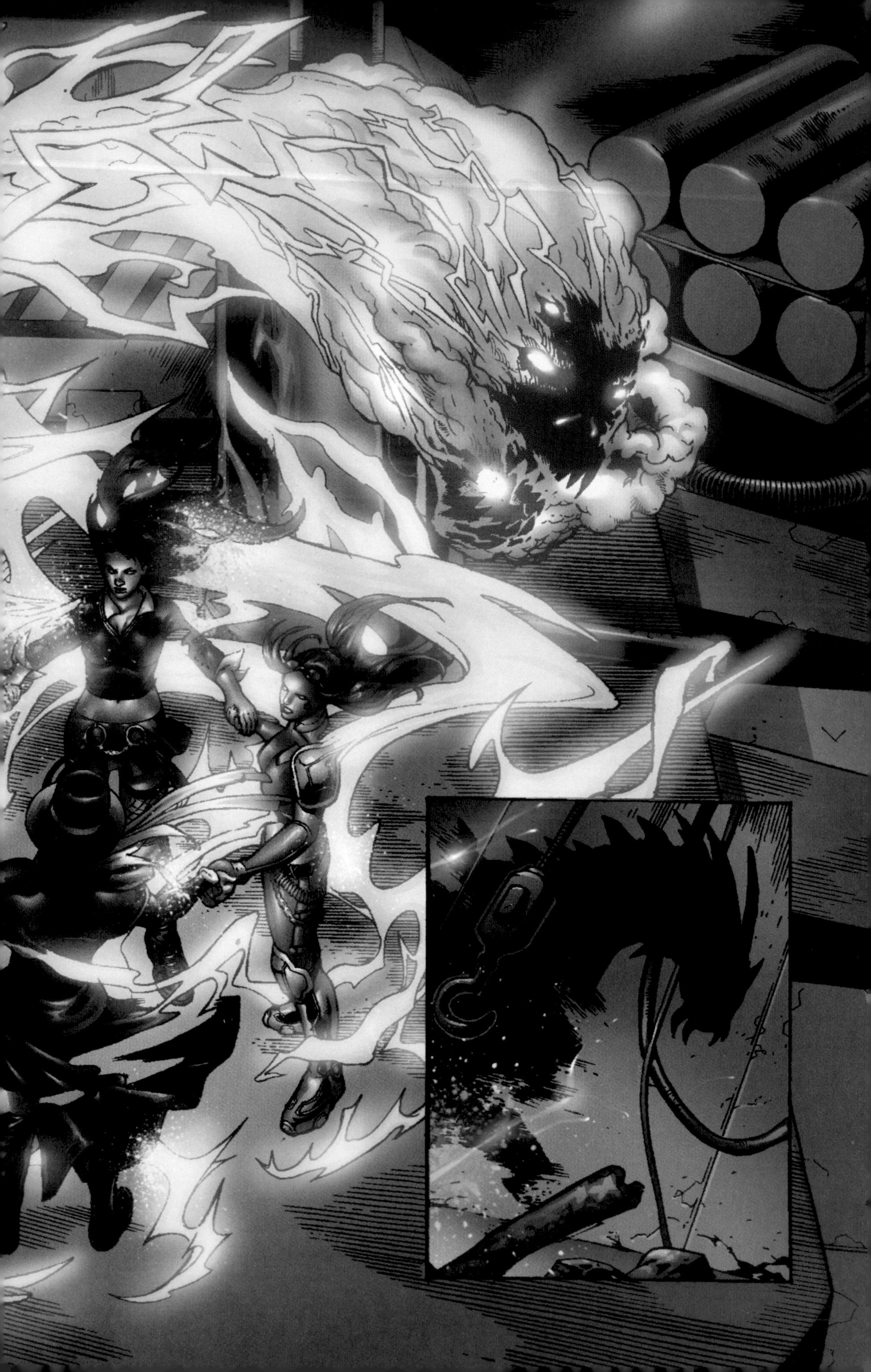

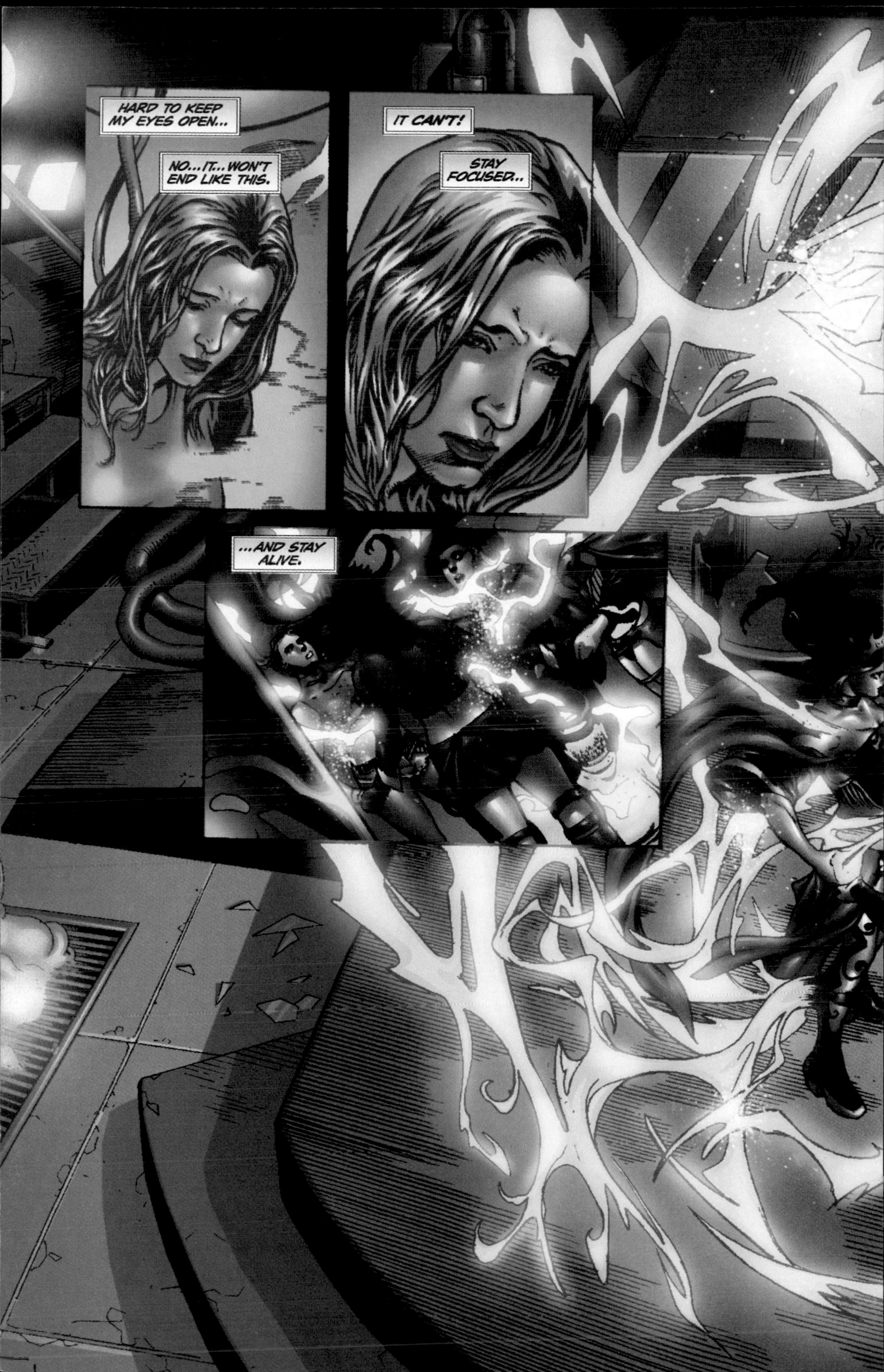
HARD TO KEEP MY EYES OPEN...
NO...IT...WON'T END LIKE THIS.
IT CAN'T!
STAY FOCUSED...
...AND STAY ALIVE.

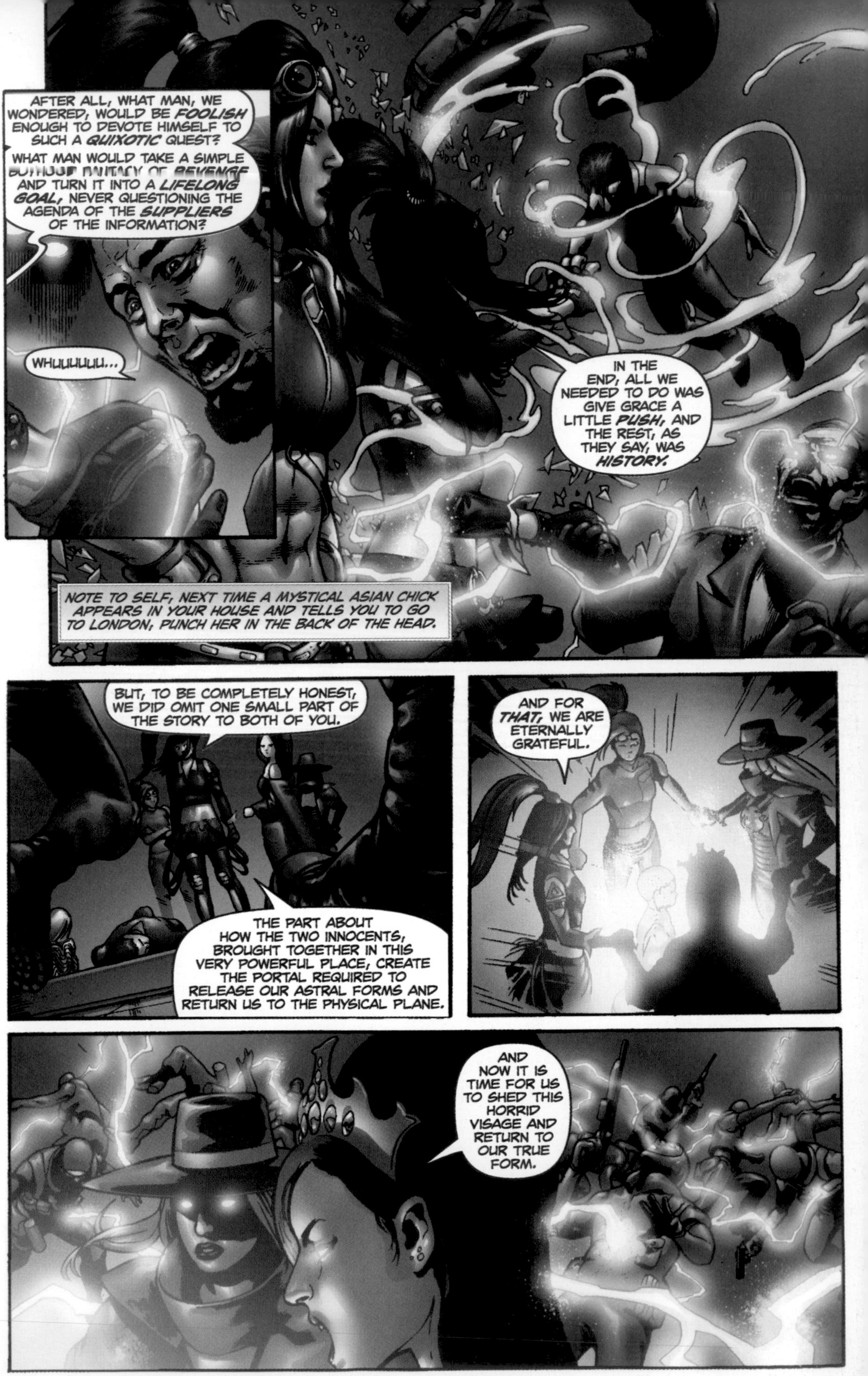
AFTER ALL, WHAT MAN, WE WONDERED, WOULD BE *FOOLISH* ENOUGH TO DEVOTE HIMSELF TO SUCH A *QUIXOTIC* QUEST?
WHAT MAN WOULD TAKE A SIMPLE OF *REVENGE* AND TURN IT INTO A *LIFELONG GOAL,* NEVER QUESTIONING THE AGENDA OF THE *SUPPLIERS* OF THE INFORMATION?
WHUUUUUU...
IN THE END, ALL WE NEEDED TO DO WAS GIVE GRACE A LITTLE *PUSH,* AND THE REST, AS THEY SAY, WAS *HISTORY.*
NOTE TO SELF, NEXT TIME A MYSTICAL ASIAN CHICK APPEARS IN YOUR HOUSE AND TELLS YOU TO GO TO LONDON, PUNCH HER IN THE BACK OF THE HEAD.
BUT, TO BE COMPLETELY HONEST, WE DID OMIT ONE SMALL PART OF THE STORY TO BOTH OF YOU.
THE PART ABOUT HOW THE TWO INNOCENTS, BROUGHT TOGETHER IN THIS VERY POWERFUL PLACE, CREATE THE PORTAL REQUIRED TO RELEASE OUR ASTRAL FORMS AND RETURN US TO THE PHYSICAL PLANE.
AND FOR *THAT,* WE ARE ETERNALLY GRATEFUL.
AND NOW IT IS TIME FOR US TO SHED THIS HORRID VISAGE AND RETURN TO OUR TRUE FORM.

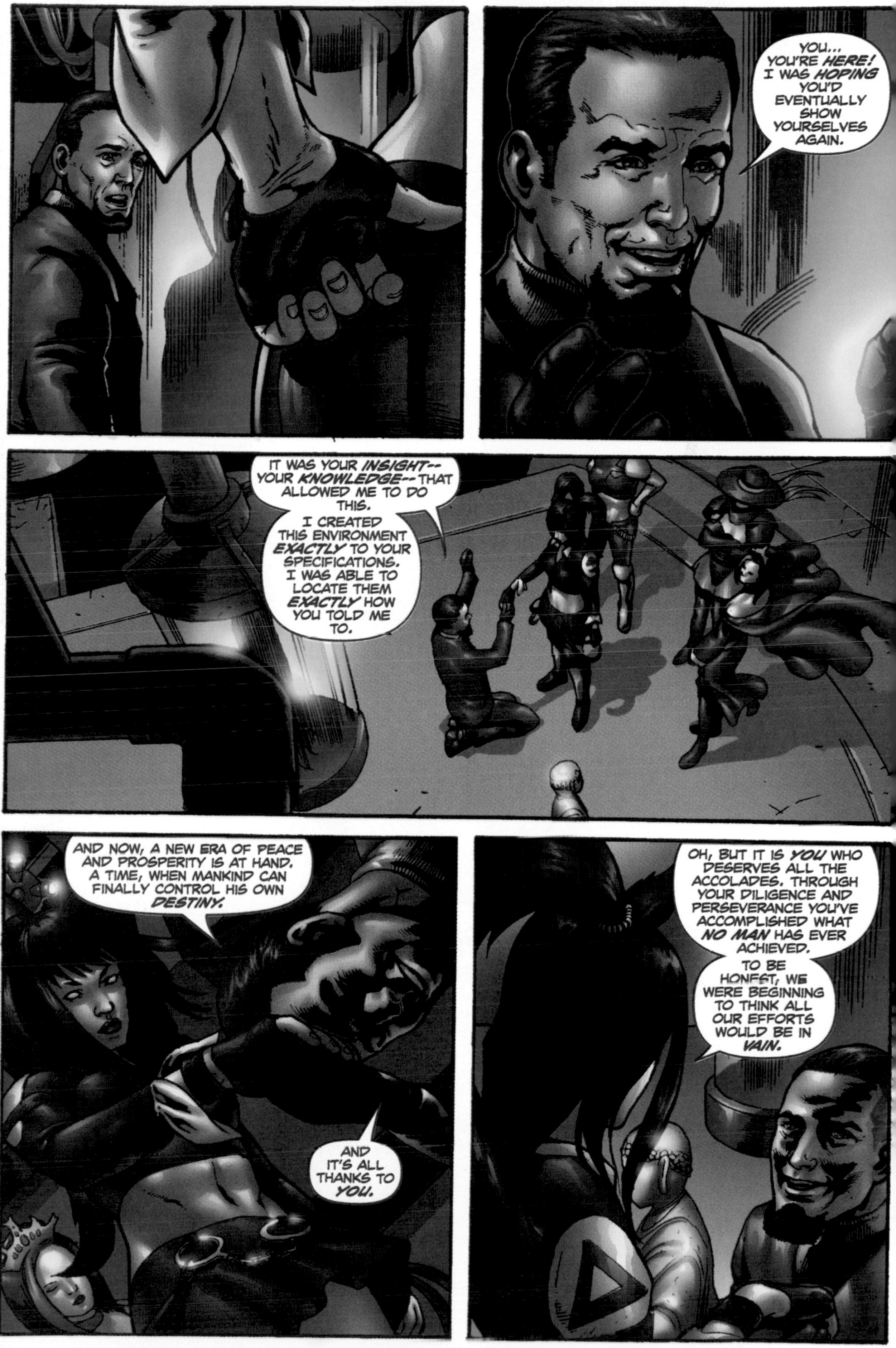
YOU... YOU'RE HERE! I WAS HOPING YOU'D EVENTUALLY SHOW YOURSELVES AGAIN.
IT WAS YOUR INSIGHT-- YOUR KNOWLEDGE-- THAT ALLOWED ME TO DO THIS.
I CREATED THIS ENVIRONMENT EXACTLY TO YOUR SPECIFICATIONS. I WAS ABLE TO LOCATE THEM EXACTLY HOW YOU TOLD ME TO.
AND NOW, A NEW ERA OF PEACE AND PROSPERITY IS AT HAND. A TIME, WHEN MANKIND CAN FINALLY CONTROL HIS OWN DESTINY.
AND IT'S ALL THANKS TO YOU.
OH, BUT IT IS YOU WHO DESERVES ALL THE ACCOLADES. THROUGH YOUR DILIGENCE AND PERSEVERANCE YOU'VE ACCOMPLISHED WHAT NO MAN HAS EVER ACHIEVED.
TO BE HONEST, WE WERE BEGINNING TO THINK ALL OUR EFFORTS WOULD BE IN VAIN.

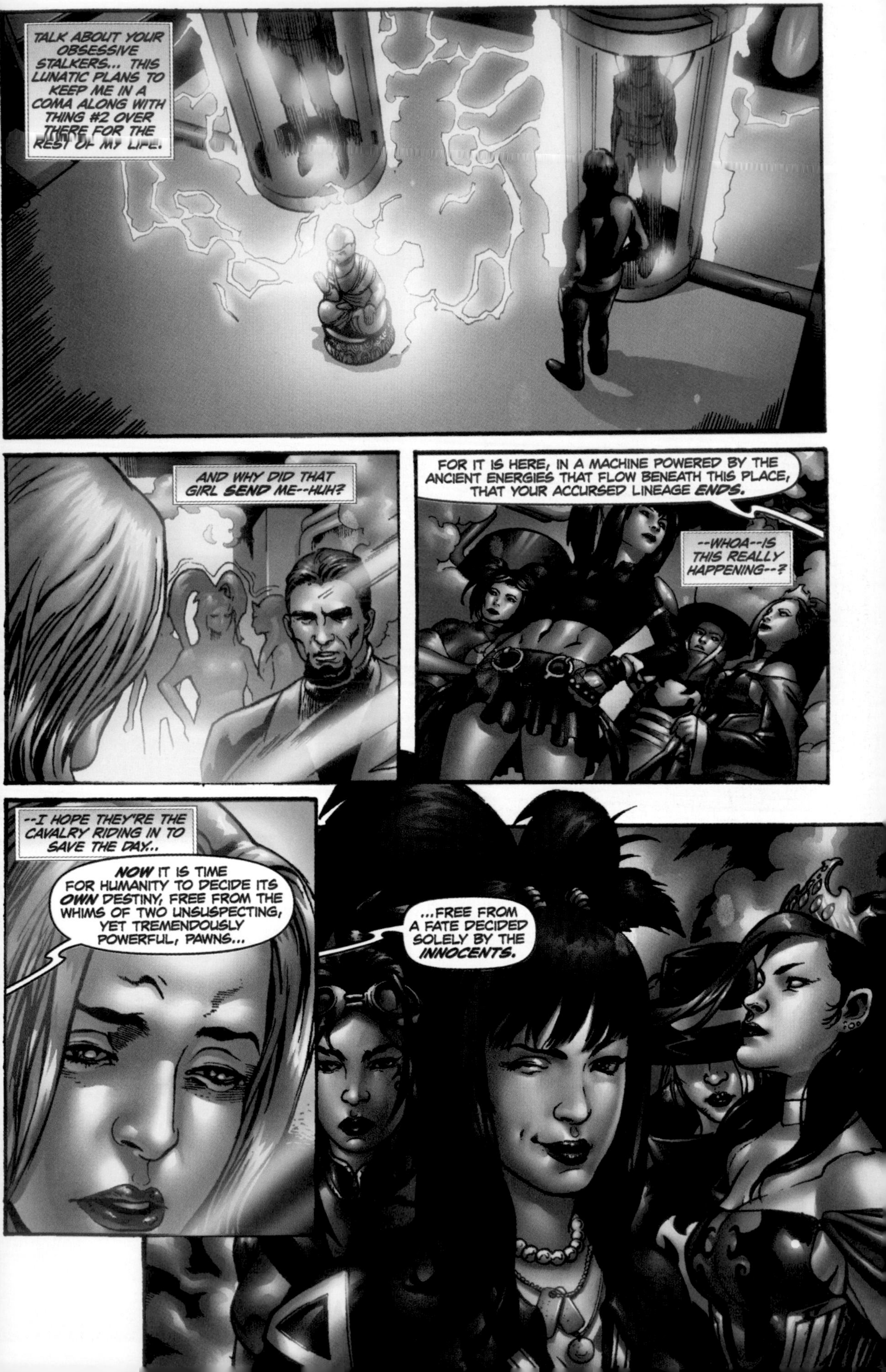
TALK ABOUT YOUR OBSESSIVE STALKERS... THIS LUNATIC PLANS TO KEEP ME IN A COMA ALONG WITH THING #2 OVER THERE FOR THE REST OF MY LIFE.
AND WHY DID THAT GIRL SEND ME--HUH?
FOR IT IS HERE, IN A MACHINE POWERED BY THE ANCIENT ENERGIES THAT FLOW BENEATH THIS PLACE, THAT YOUR ACCURSED LINEAGE ENDS.
--WHOA--IS THIS REALLY HAPPENING--?
--I HOPE THEY'RE THE CAVALRY RIDING IN TO SAVE THE DAY...
NOW IT IS TIME FOR HUMANITY TO DECIDE ITS OWN DESTINY, FREE FROM THE WHIMS OF TWO UNSUSPECTING, YET TREMENDOUSLY POWERFUL, PAWNS...
...FREE FROM A FATE DECIDED SOLELY BY THE INNOCENTS.

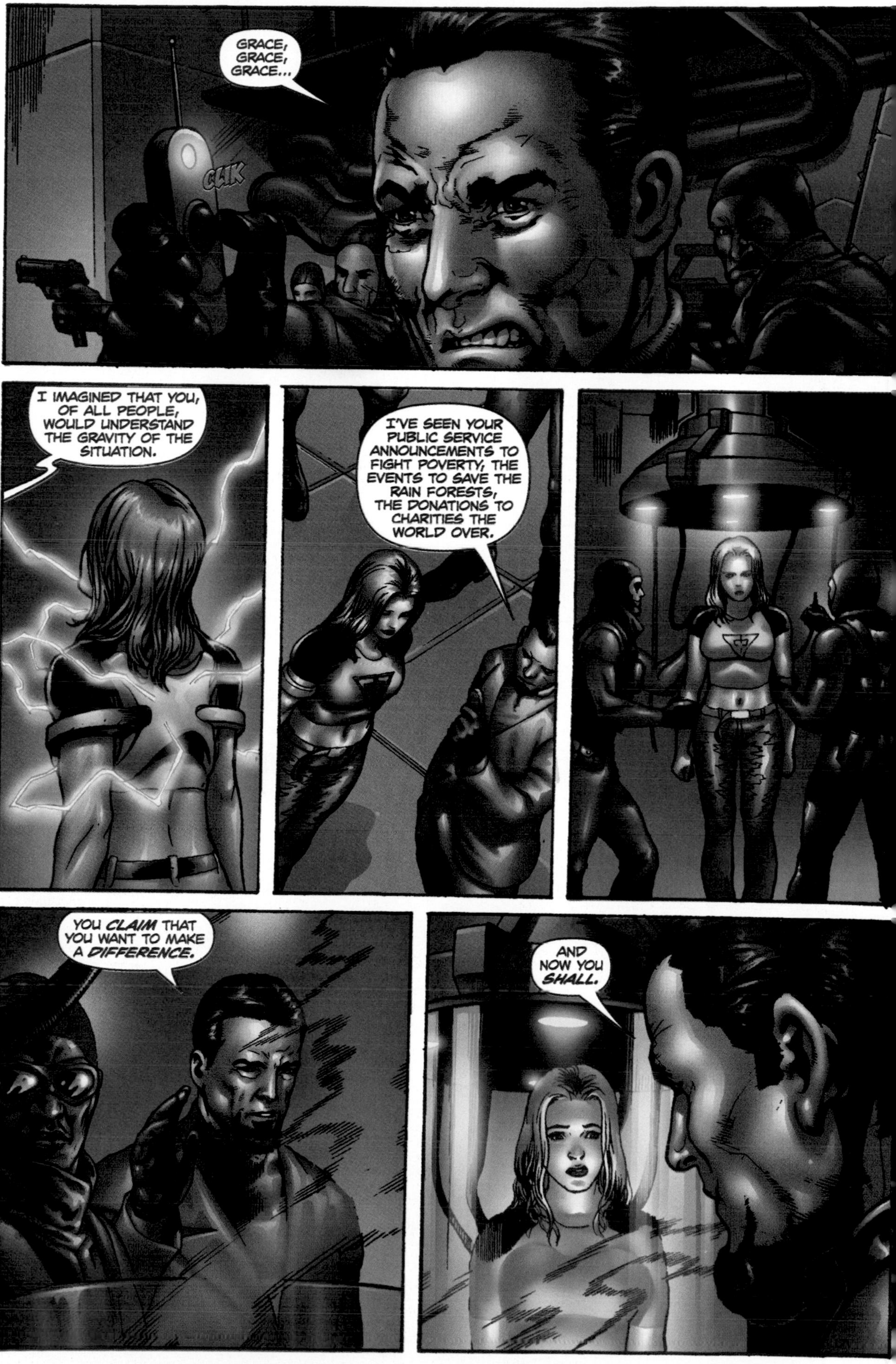
GRACE, GRACE, GRACE...
CLIK
I IMAGINED THAT YOU, OF ALL PEOPLE, WOULD UNDERSTAND THE GRAVITY OF THE SITUATION.
I'VE SEEN YOUR PUBLIC SERVICE ANNOUNCEMENTS TO FIGHT POVERTY, THE EVENTS TO SAVE THE RAIN FORESTS, THE DONATIONS TO CHARITIES THE WORLD OVER.
YOU CLAIM THAT YOU WANT TO MAKE A DIFFERENCE.
AND NOW YOU SHALL.

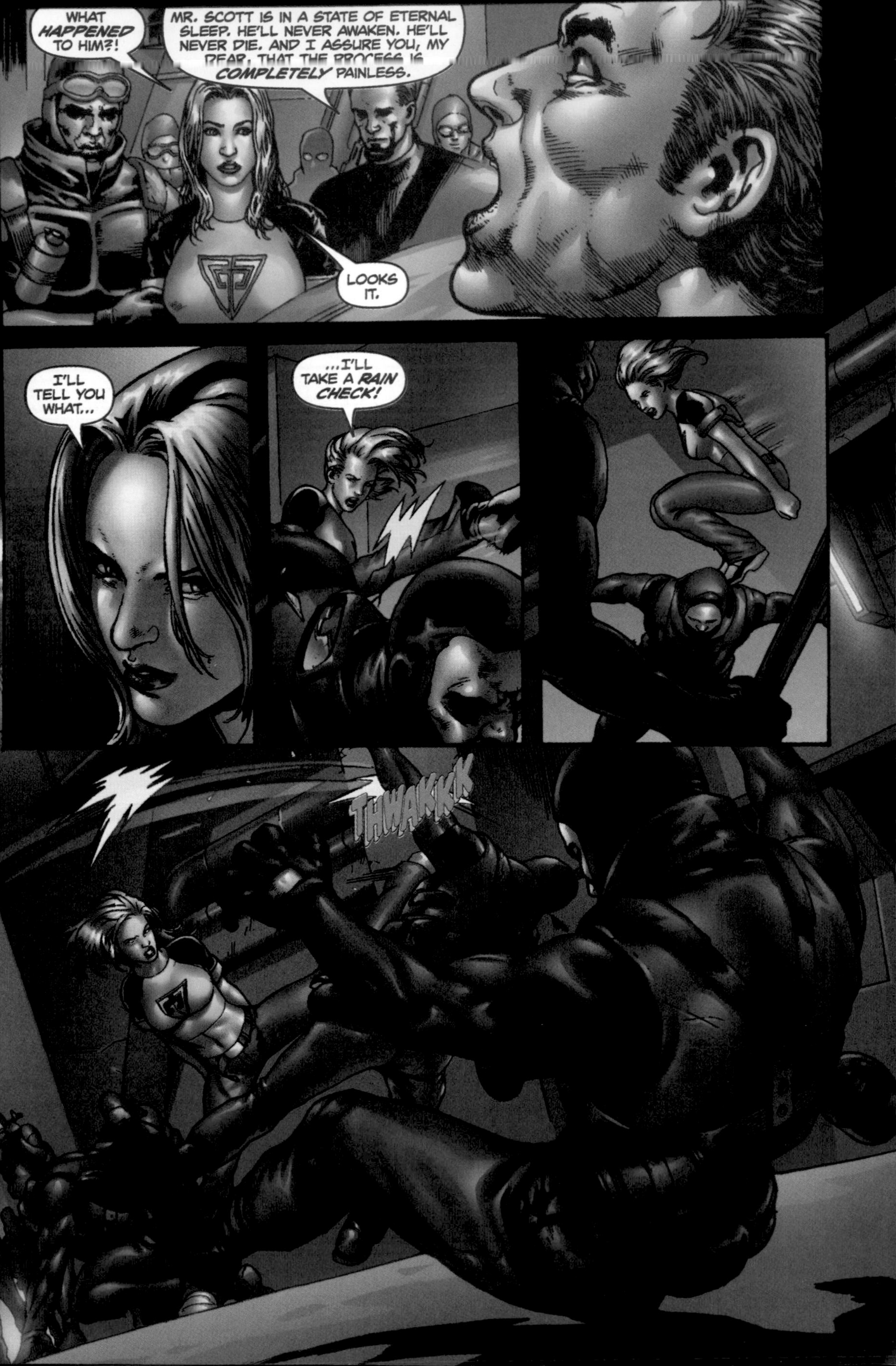
WHAT *HAPPENED* TO HIM?!
MR. SCOTT IS IN A STATE OF ETERNAL SLEEP. HE'LL NEVER AWAKEN. HE'LL NEVER DIE. AND I ASSURE YOU, MY DEAR, THAT THE PROCESS IS *COMPLETELY* PAINLESS.
LOOKS IT.
I'LL TELL YOU WHAT...
...I'LL TAKE A *RAIN CHECK!*
THWAKKK

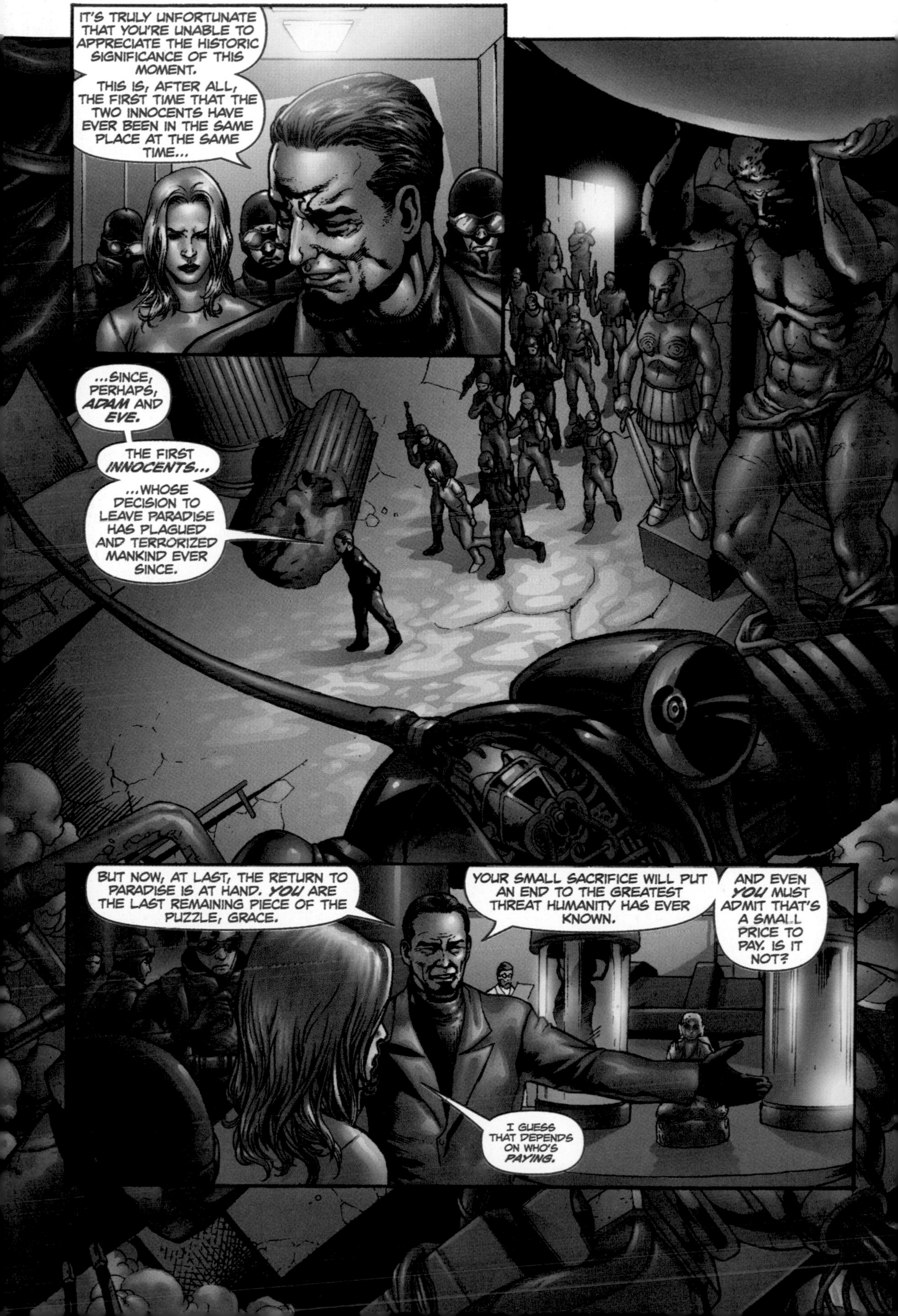
IT'S TRULY UNFORTUNATE THAT YOU'RE UNABLE TO APPRECIATE THE HISTORIC SIGNIFICANCE OF THIS MOMENT.
THIS IS, AFTER ALL, THE FIRST TIME THAT THE TWO INNOCENTS HAVE EVER BEEN IN THE SAME PLACE AT THE SAME TIME...
...SINCE, PERHAPS, ADAM AND EVE.
THE FIRST INNOCENTS...
...WHOSE DECISION TO LEAVE PARADISE HAS PLAGUED AND TERRORIZED MANKIND EVER SINCE.
BUT NOW, AT LAST, THE RETURN TO PARADISE IS AT HAND. YOU ARE THE LAST REMAINING PIECE OF THE PUZZLE, GRACE.
YOUR SMALL SACRIFICE WILL PUT AN END TO THE GREATEST THREAT HUMANITY HAS EVER KNOWN.
AND EVEN YOU MUST ADMIT THAT'S A SMALL PRICE TO PAY. IS IT NOT?
I GUESS THAT DEPENDS ON WHO'S PAYING.

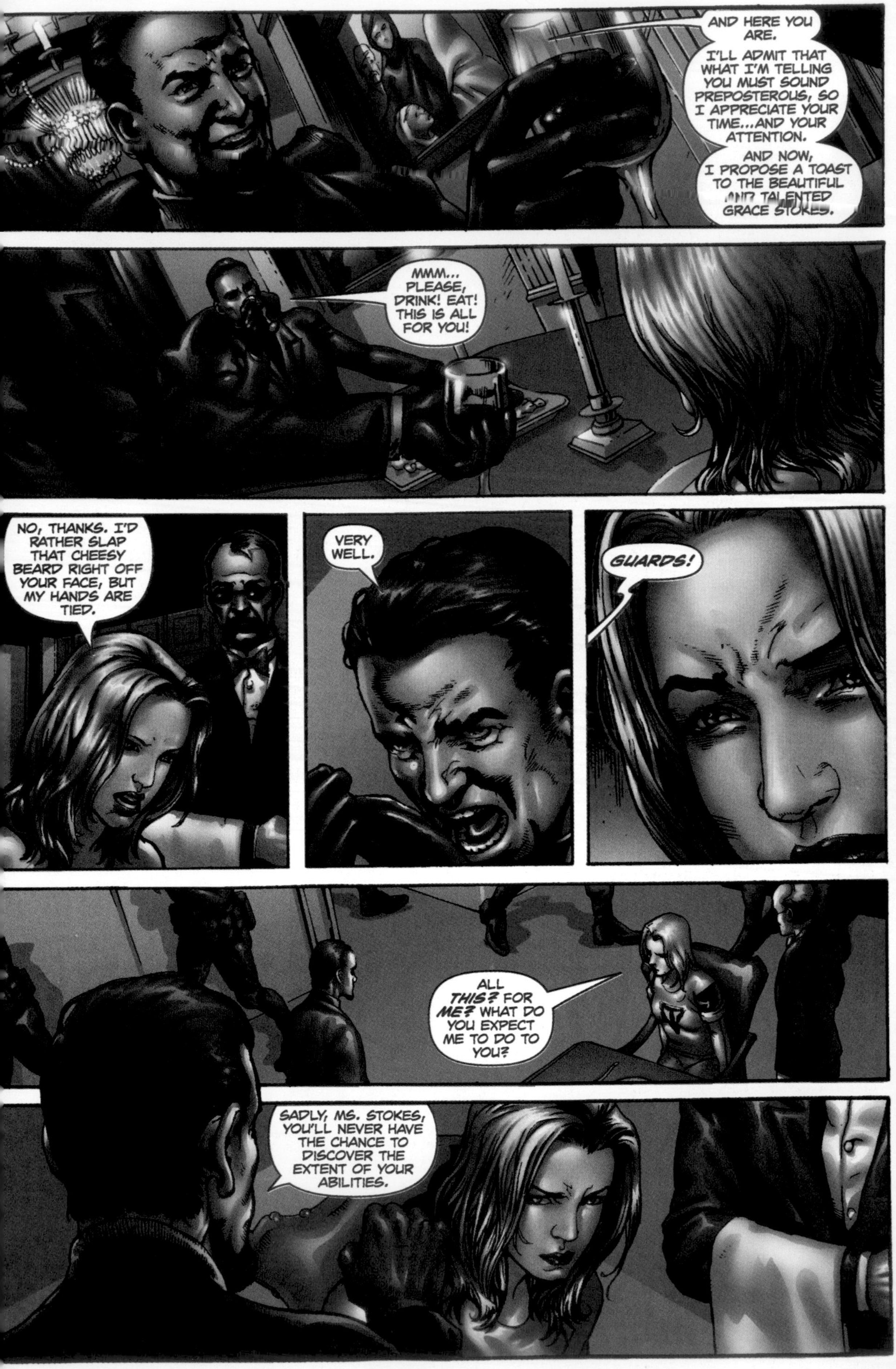
AND HERE YOU ARE.
I'LL ADMIT THAT WHAT I'M TELLING YOU MUST SOUND PREPOSTEROUS, SO I APPRECIATE YOUR TIME...AND YOUR ATTENTION.
AND NOW, I PROPOSE A TOAST TO THE BEAUTIFUL AND TALENTED GRACE STOKES.
MMM... PLEASE, DRINK! EAT! THIS IS ALL FOR YOU!
NO, THANKS. I'D RATHER SLAP THAT CHEESY BEARD RIGHT OFF YOUR FACE, BUT MY HANDS ARE TIED.
VERY WELL.
GUARDS!
ALL THIS? FOR ME? WHAT DO YOU EXPECT ME TO DO TO YOU?
SADLY, MS. STOKES, YOU'LL NEVER HAVE THE CHANCE TO DISCOVER THE EXTENT OF YOUR ABILITIES.

"WHEN I AWOKE, I HAD NO IDEA WHERE I WAS OR HOW I WAS SAVED.

"ALL I KNEW WAS THAT I WAS CERTAINLY ALIVE...

"...THANKS TO MY *GUARDIAN ANGELS.*

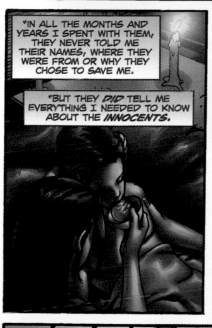

"IN ALL THE MONTHS AND YEARS I SPENT WITH THEM, THEY NEVER TOLD ME THEIR NAMES, WHERE THEY WERE FROM OR WHY THEY CHOSE TO SAVE ME.

"BUT THEY *DID* TELL ME EVERYTHING I NEEDED TO KNOW ABOUT THE *INNOCENTS.*

"HOW THEY DIDN'T *WILLINGLY* CAUSE THE DEATH OF MY PARENTS, BUT THEIR ACTIONS, WHATEVER THEY WERE, CAUSED IT NONETHELESS.

"FOR THAT IS THE ABILITY THAT THE INNOCENTS HAVE-- ANY ACTION THEY DO CAUSES SOME KIND OF EFFECT SOMEWHERE IN THE WORLD, LIKE A KARMIC TSUNAMI, AS IT WERE.

"THAT WAS THEIR FATE: TWO PEOPLE, WITH INCREDIBLE AND FAR-REACHING ABILITIES WERE BORN TO BE PHYSICAL MANIFESTATIONS OF YIN AND YANG.

"AND IN THEIR NAIVE HANDS, THE FATE OF THE WORLD WAS HELD, UNTIL THEY PASSED ON.

"AT WHICH TIME TWO OTHER UNSUSPECTING PEOPLE WOULD RECEIVE THE ABILITIES LIKE SOME SORT OF BIZARRE REINCARNATION.

"WHEN I INQUIRED WHAT WOULD HAPPEN IF I *CAPTURED* THESE PEOPLE AND KEPT THEM IN A PLACE WHERE THEY COULDN'T ACT, AND THEY COULDN'T DIE, MY GUARDIAN ANGELS REVEALED THAT THE LINEAGE WOULD BE BROKEN.

"I KNEW THEN THAT IT WAS TO BE MY ROLE TO ONE DAY DESTROY THE CHAOS AND RANDOMNESS THE INNOCENTS REIGNED UPON THE EARTH. BUT IT WOULD REQUIRE ALL THE TIME AND RESOURCES AT MY DISPOSAL.

"ALL I NEEDED TO LEARN WAS WHO THE INNOCENTS WERE AND WHERE I SHOULD TAKE THEM TO FULFILL THEIR DESTINY... AND MINE."

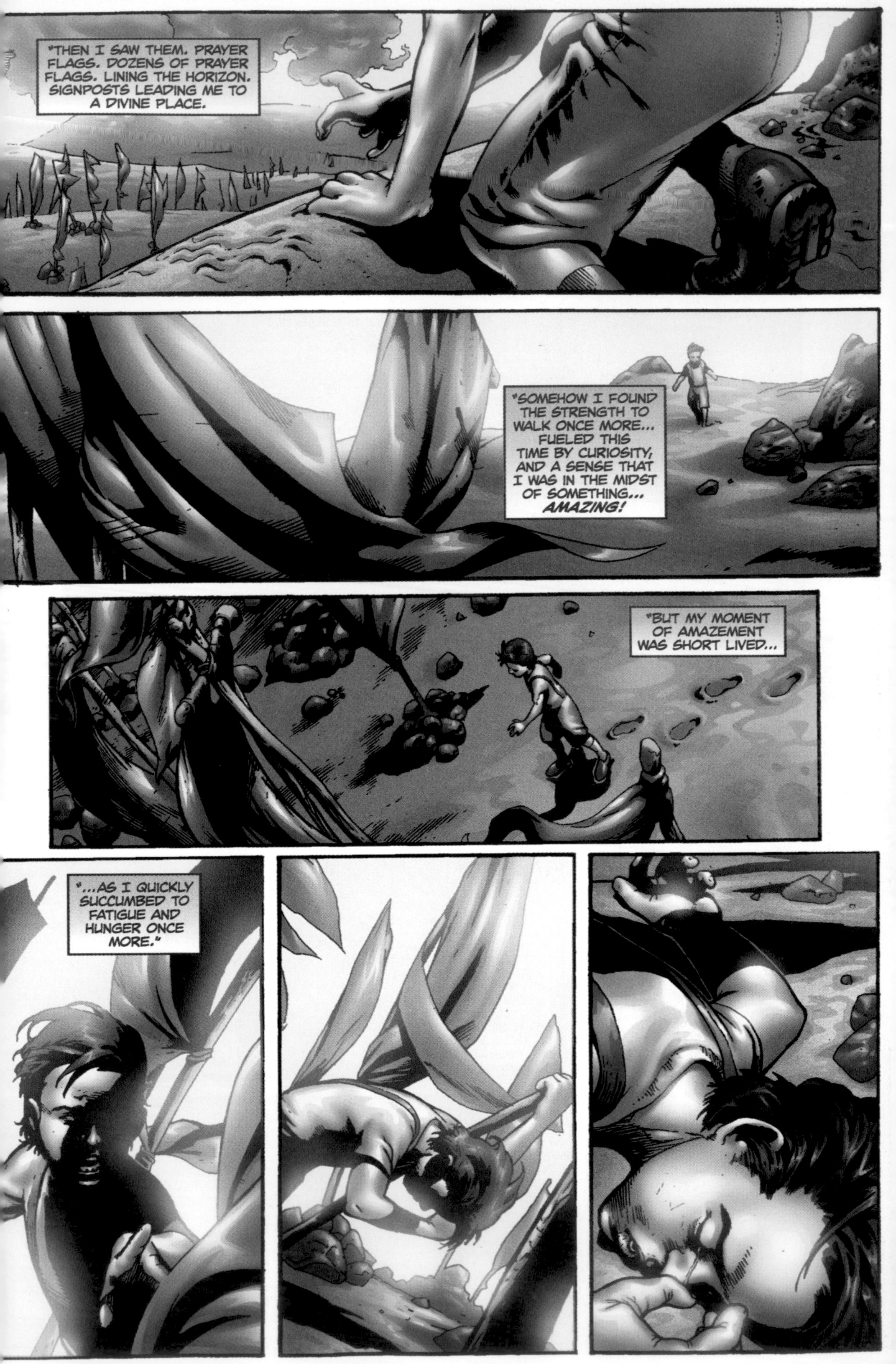
"THEN I SAW THEM. PRAYER FLAGS. DOZENS OF PRAYER FLAGS. LINING THE HORIZON. SIGNPOSTS LEADING ME TO A DIVINE PLACE.
"SOMEHOW I FOUND THE STRENGTH TO WALK ONCE MORE... FUELED THIS TIME BY CURIOSITY, AND A SENSE THAT I WAS IN THE MIDST OF SOMETHING... AMAZING!
"BUT MY MOMENT OF AMAZEMENT WAS SHORT LIVED...
"...AS I QUICKLY SUCCUMBED TO FATIGUE AND HUNGER ONCE MORE."

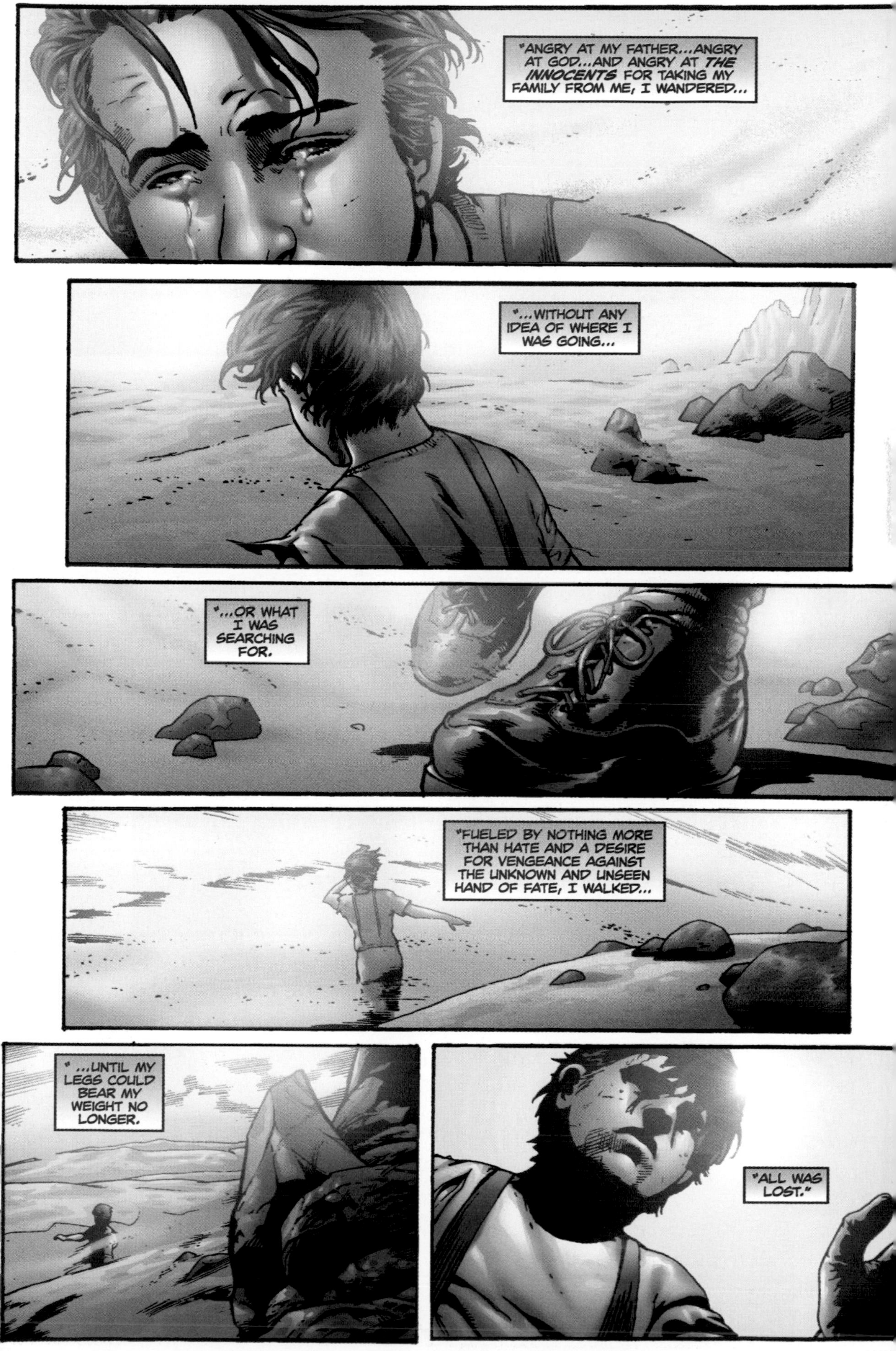
"ANGRY AT MY FATHER...ANGRY AT GOD...AND ANGRY AT *THE INNOCENTS* FOR TAKING MY FAMILY FROM ME, I WANDERED...
"...WITHOUT ANY IDEA OF WHERE I WAS GOING...
"...OR WHAT I WAS SEARCHING FOR.
"FUELED BY NOTHING MORE THAN HATE AND A DESIRE FOR VENGEANCE AGAINST THE UNKNOWN AND UNSEEN HAND OF FATE, I WALKED...
"...UNTIL MY LEGS COULD BEAR MY WEIGHT NO LONGER.
"ALL WAS LOST."

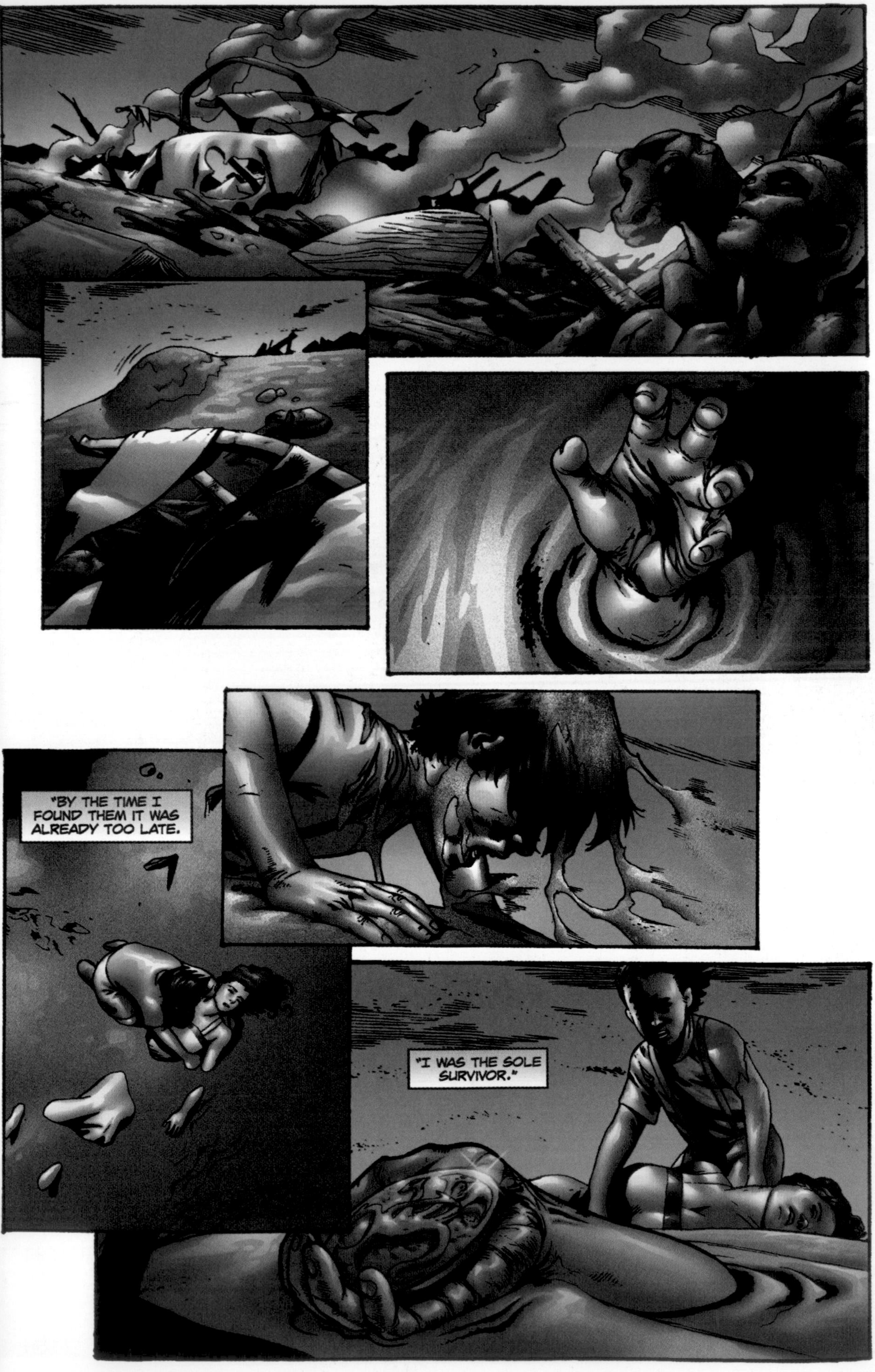
"BY THE TIME I FOUND THEM IT WAS ALREADY TOO LATE.
"I WAS THE SOLE SURVIVOR."

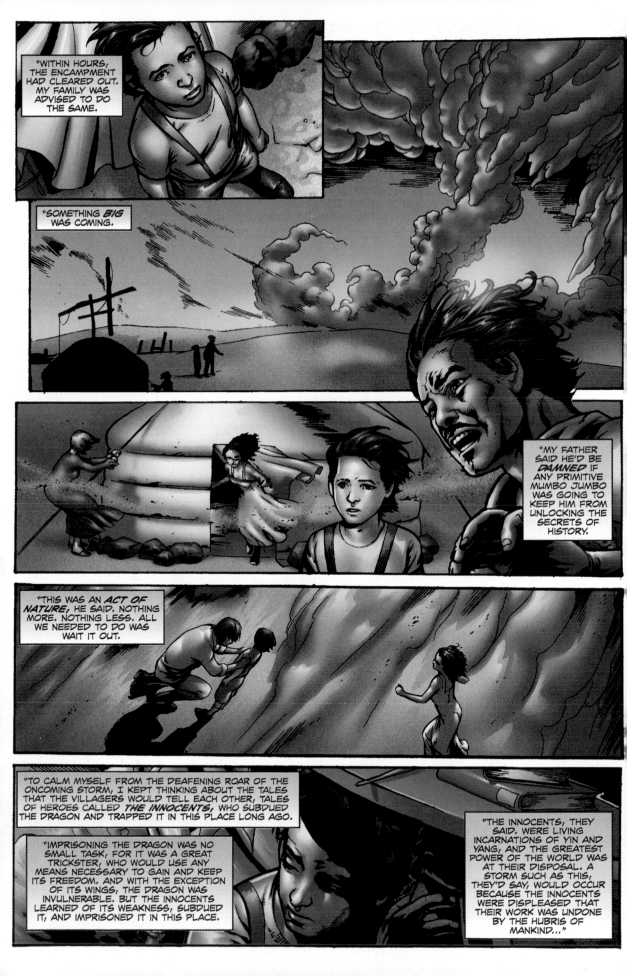

"WITHIN HOURS, THE ENCAMPMENT HAD CLEARED OUT. MY FAMILY WAS ADVISED TO DO THE SAME."

"SOMETHING *BIG* WAS COMING."

"MY FATHER SAID HE'D BE *DAMNED* IF ANY PRIMITIVE MUMBO JUMBO WAS GOING TO KEEP HIM FROM UNLOCKING THE SECRETS OF HISTORY."

"THIS WAS AN *ACT OF NATURE*, HE SAID. NOTHING MORE. NOTHING LESS. ALL WE NEEDED TO DO WAS WAIT IT OUT."

"TO CALM MYSELF FROM THE DEAFENING ROAR OF THE ONCOMING STORM, I KEPT THINKING ABOUT THE TALES THAT THE VILLAGERS WOULD TELL EACH OTHER, TALES OF HEROES CALLED *THE INNOCENTS*, WHO SUBDUED THE DRAGON AND TRAPPED IT IN THIS PLACE LONG AGO."

"IMPRISONING THE DRAGON WAS NO SMALL TASK, FOR IT WAS A GREAT TRICKSTER, WHO WOULD USE ANY MEANS NECESSARY TO GAIN AND KEEP ITS FREEDOM. AND WITH THE EXCEPTION OF ITS WINGS, THE DRAGON WAS INVULNERABLE. BUT THE INNOCENTS LEARNED OF ITS WEAKNESS, SUBDUED IT, AND IMPRISONED IT IN THIS PLACE."

"THE INNOCENTS, THEY SAID, WERE LIVING INCARNATIONS OF YIN AND YANG, AND THE GREATEST POWER OF THE WORLD WAS AT THEIR DISPOSAL. A STORM SUCH AS THIS, THEY'D SAY, WOULD OCCUR BECAUSE THE INNOCENTS WERE DISPLEASED THAT THEIR WORK WAS UNDONE BY THE HUBRIS OF MANKIND..."

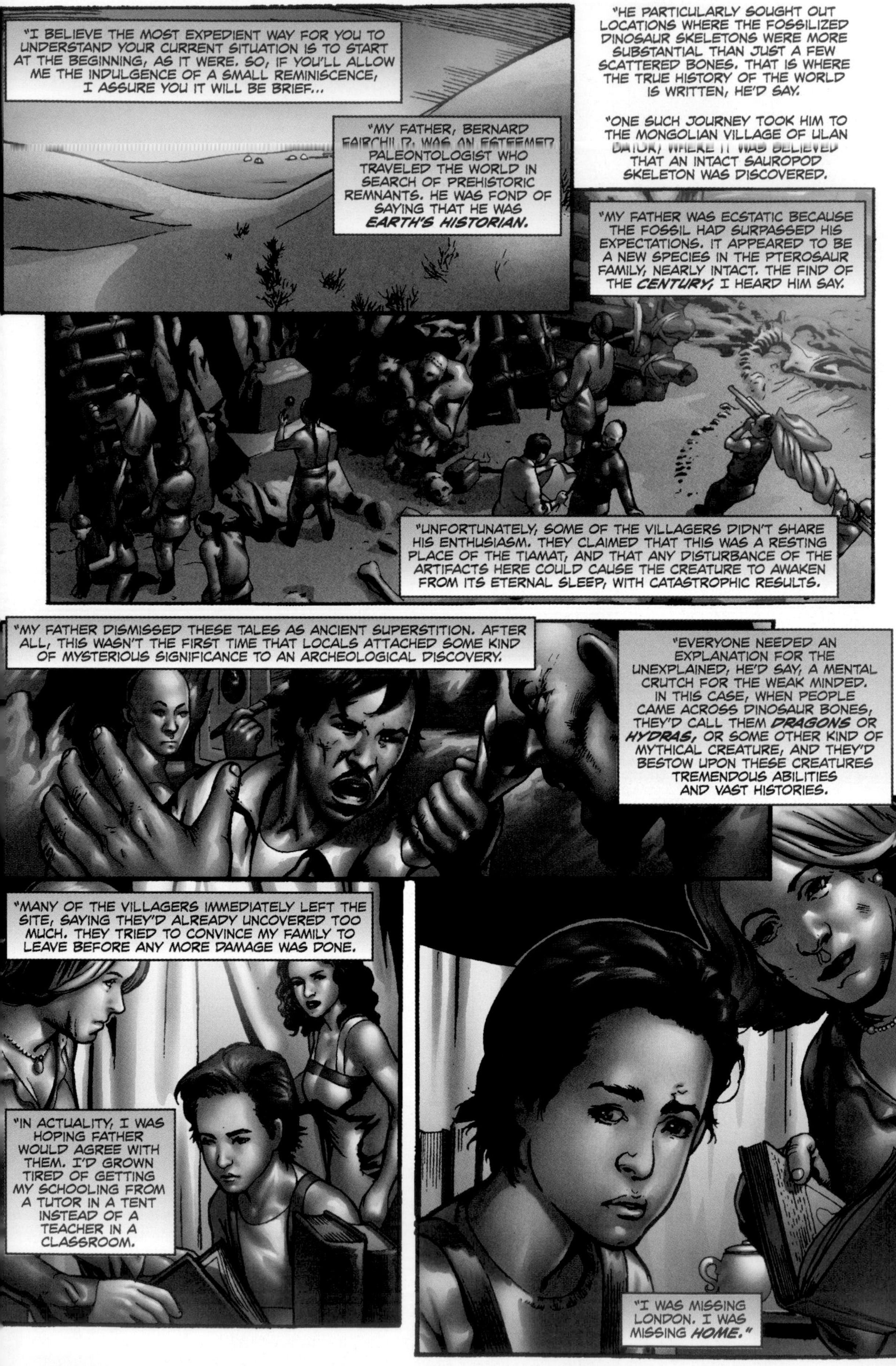
"I BELIEVE THE MOST EXPEDIENT WAY FOR YOU TO UNDERSTAND YOUR CURRENT SITUATION IS TO START AT THE BEGINNING, AS IT WERE. SO, IF YOU'LL ALLOW ME THE INDULGENCE OF A SMALL REMINISCENCE, I ASSURE YOU IT WILL BE BRIEF...
"MY FATHER, BERNARD FAIRCHILD, WAS AN ESTEEMED PALEONTOLOGIST WHO TRAVELED THE WORLD IN SEARCH OF PREHISTORIC REMNANTS. HE WAS FOND OF SAYING THAT HE WAS ***EARTH'S HISTORIAN.***
"HE PARTICULARLY SOUGHT OUT LOCATIONS WHERE THE FOSSILIZED DINOSAUR SKELETONS WERE MORE SUBSTANTIAL THAN JUST A FEW SCATTERED BONES. THAT IS WHERE THE TRUE HISTORY OF THE WORLD IS WRITTEN, HE'D SAY.
"ONE SUCH JOURNEY TOOK HIM TO THE MONGOLIAN VILLAGE OF ULAN BATOR, WHERE IT WAS BELIEVED THAT AN INTACT SAUROPOD SKELETON WAS DISCOVERED.
"MY FATHER WAS ECSTATIC BECAUSE THE FOSSIL HAD SURPASSED HIS EXPECTATIONS. IT APPEARED TO BE A NEW SPECIES IN THE PTEROSAUR FAMILY, NEARLY INTACT. THE FIND OF THE ***CENTURY,*** I HEARD HIM SAY.
"UNFORTUNATELY, SOME OF THE VILLAGERS DIDN'T SHARE HIS ENTHUSIASM. THEY CLAIMED THAT THIS WAS A RESTING PLACE OF THE TIAMAT, AND THAT ANY DISTURBANCE OF THE ARTIFACTS HERE COULD CAUSE THE CREATURE TO AWAKEN FROM ITS ETERNAL SLEEP, WITH CATASTROPHIC RESULTS.
"MY FATHER DISMISSED THESE TALES AS ANCIENT SUPERSTITION. AFTER ALL, THIS WASN'T THE FIRST TIME THAT LOCALS ATTACHED SOME KIND OF MYSTERIOUS SIGNIFICANCE TO AN ARCHEOLOGICAL DISCOVERY.
"EVERYONE NEEDED AN EXPLANATION FOR THE UNEXPLAINED, HE'D SAY, A MENTAL CRUTCH FOR THE WEAK MINDED. IN THIS CASE, WHEN PEOPLE CAME ACROSS DINOSAUR BONES, THEY'D CALL THEM ***DRAGONS*** OR ***HYDRAS,*** OR SOME OTHER KIND OF MYTHICAL CREATURE, AND THEY'D BESTOW UPON THESE CREATURES TREMENDOUS ABILITIES AND VAST HISTORIES.
"MANY OF THE VILLAGERS IMMEDIATELY LEFT THE SITE, SAYING THEY'D ALREADY UNCOVERED TOO MUCH. THEY TRIED TO CONVINCE MY FAMILY TO LEAVE BEFORE ANY MORE DAMAGE WAS DONE.
"IN ACTUALITY, I WAS HOPING FATHER WOULD AGREE WITH THEM. I'D GROWN TIRED OF GETTING MY SCHOOLING FROM A TUTOR IN A TENT INSTEAD OF A TEACHER IN A CLASSROOM.
"I WAS MISSING LONDON. I WAS MISSING ***HOME."***

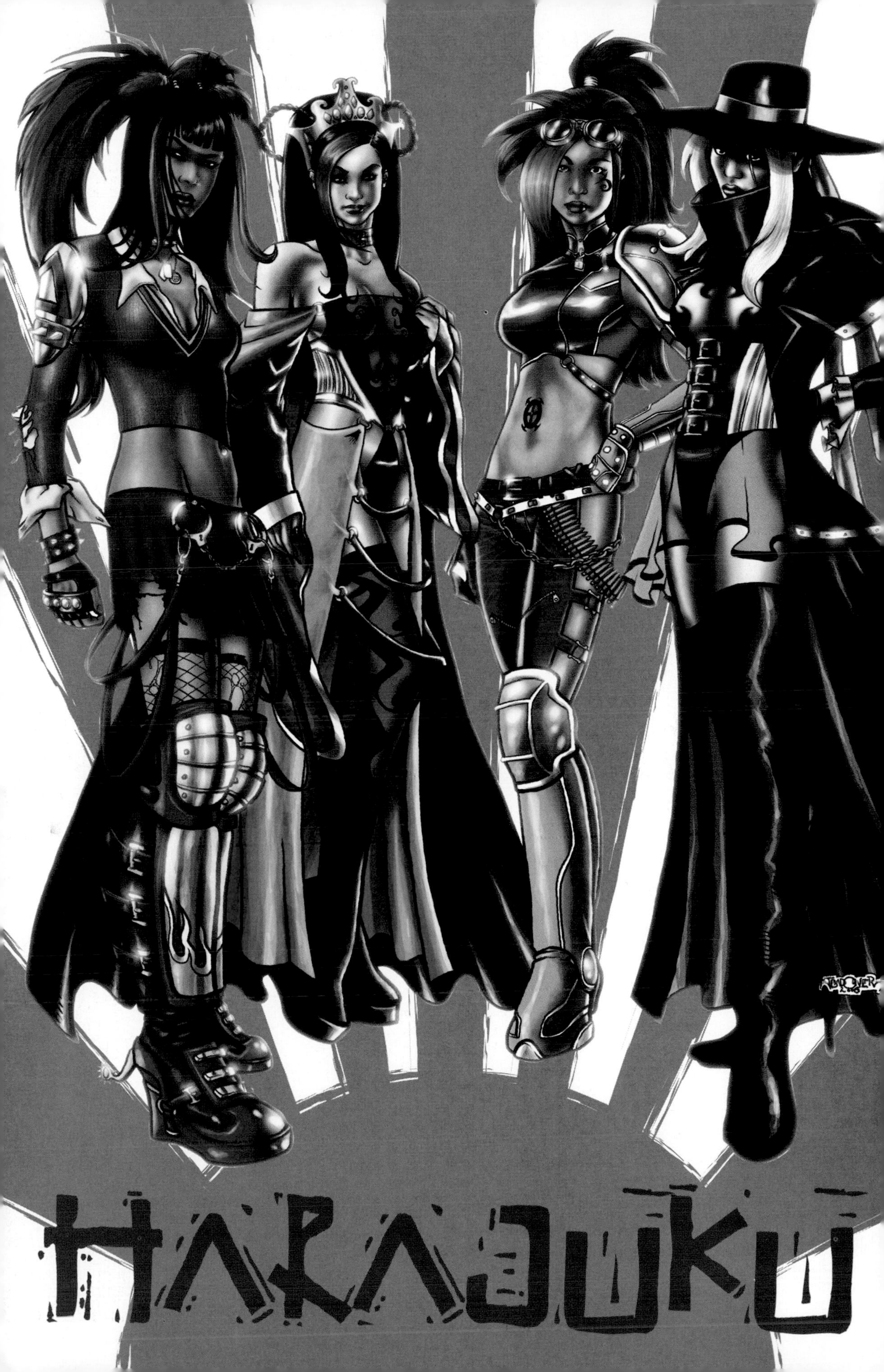
HARAJUKU

Man May Have Walked With Dinosaurs

ULAN BATUR, MONGOLIA - Archaeologists have recruited famed paleontologist Bernard Fairchild to conduct further research on skeletal remains recently unearthed on the plains of Mongolia which vaguely resemble the large winged species of flying lizard that existed in the time of dinosaurs known as Pteranodon. However, unlike Pteranodon, which scientists speculate was extinct by the end of the Jurassic period 144 million years ago, initial carbon dating on the bones suggest that this as yet unnamed relative of the dinosaurs may have soared the skies less then 2,000 years ago when our ancestors walked the earth. Though widespread skepticism has marred this claim, paleontologists are thrilled about the possibility of a new species being discovered. Said Fairchild, "it is potentially the biggest discovery in our field of the last fifty years."

Though he went on to say he "doubted" the veracity of the dating process, speculating that our early ancestors of the period may have initially uncovered the bones and "contaminated" the carbon by mixing in elements from one much later period with that of the bones. Fairchild says clarifying the date of the bones will be the first order of business for his team.

initial models of how the large, winged reptile may have looked are being created using MRI and advanced computer enhanced kinesthetic technology. One technician joked, "the thing looks more like Milla's Dragon than a T-Rex."

"We know it's tough," said Dupree, "but we also created so it off, we'd have created so before seen on film."

It appears that audiences will be the final judge of FX Wessel's special effects when Knights of Glory opens this weekend.

When Manager W. ment.

Enter Corey Sosner. Sosner the Manheim Group, was more this endeavor. No stranger to taking company in the throes of a turbulent ch guard, Sosner brought the Manheim Group fr depths of bankruptcy to the top of the pharmaceutic industries' food chain, making it the number one pr ducer of consumer drugs in the United States and Canada, a move that some said was impossible. Sosner in place, Gravitas Inc. was staged for back.

But bringing a corporation back from th ter was going to take more than bringi There was still the matter of replaci & Development team. After its u in early Spring, all five member including head chemist, Laure dropped 17 points on the NA pulled their funding, a blo yet fully recovered. The layoffs of hundreds of some of their projec into the cures and AIDS, and Alzhe

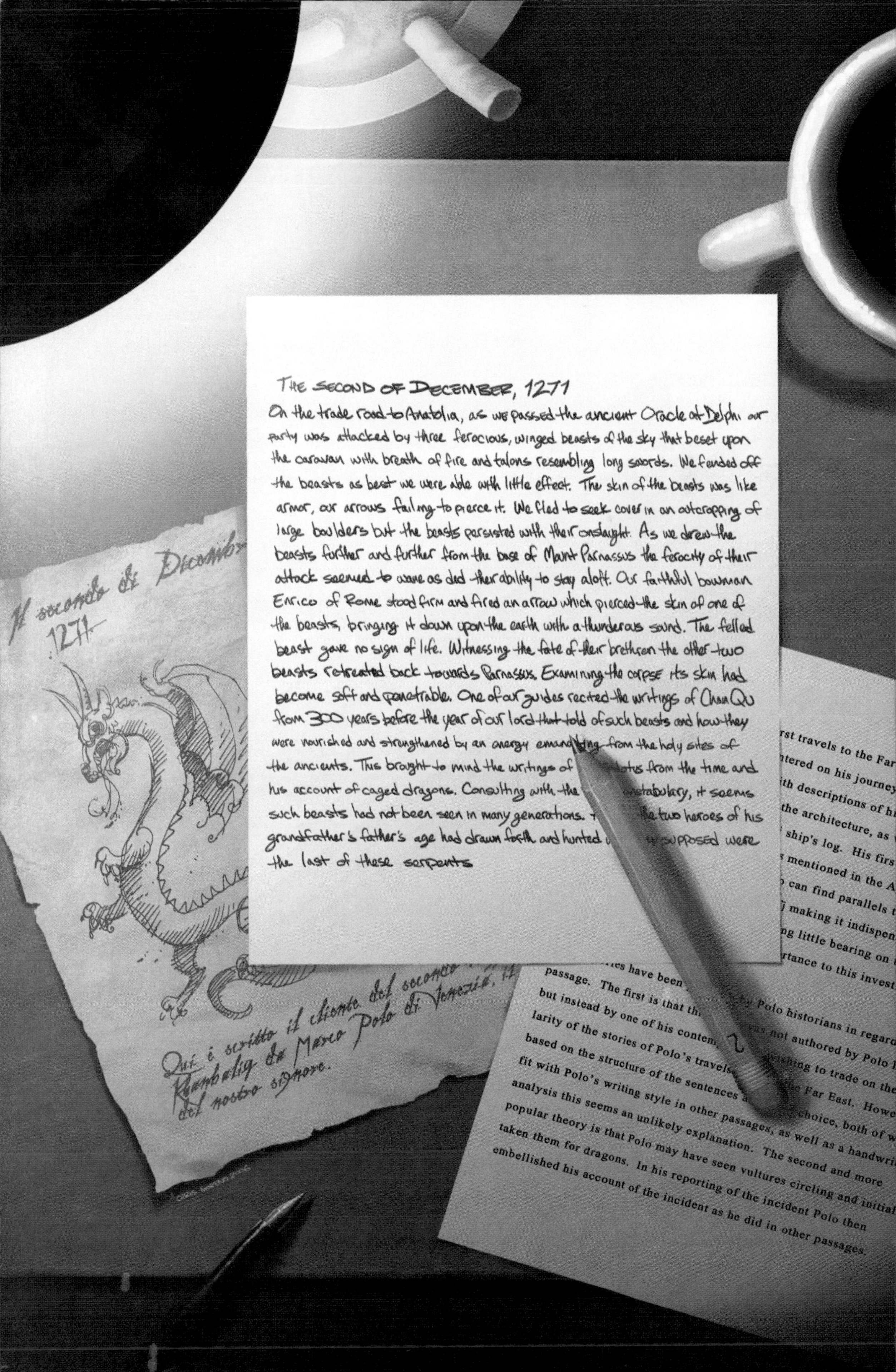
The second of December, 1271
On the trade road to Anatolia, as we passed the ancient Oracle at Delphi our party was attacked by three ferocious, winged beasts of the sky that beset upon the caravan with breath of fire and talons resembling long swords. We fended off the beasts as best we were able with little effect. The skin of the beasts was like armor, our arrows failing to pierce it. We fled to seek cover in an outcropping of large boulders but the beasts persisted with their onslaught. As we drew the beasts further and further from the base of Mount Parnassus the ferocity of their attack seemed to wane as did their ability to stay aloft. Our faithful bowman Enrico of Rome stood firm and fired an arrow which pierced the skin of one of the beasts, bringing it down upon the earth with a thunderous sound. The felled beast gave no sign of life. Witnessing the fate of their brethren the other two beasts retreated back towards Parnassus. Examining the corpse its skin had become soft and penetrable. One of our guides recited the writings of Chan Qu from 300 years before the year of our lord that told of such beasts and how they were nourished and strengthened by an energy emanating from the holy sites of the ancients. This brought to mind the writings of dotus from the time and his account of caged dragons. Consulting with the constabulary, it seems such beasts had not been seen in many generations. the two heroes of his grandfather's father's age had drawn forth and hunted supposed were the last of these serpents
Il secondo di Decembre 1271
Qui è scritto il cliente del secondo Khanbalig de Marco Polo di Venezia, il del nostro signore.
rst travels to the Far
ntered on his journey
ith descriptions of hi
the architecture, as
ship's log. His firs
s mentioned in the A
can find parallels t
making it indispen
ng little bearing on
rtance to this invest
es have been
passage. The first is that th
by Polo historians in regard
but instead by one of his contem
not authored by Polo
larity of the stories of Polo's travels
shing to trade on the
based on the structure of the sentences
e Far East. Howe
fit with Polo's writing style in other passages,
choice, both of w
analysis this seems an unlikely explanation. The second and more
as well as a handwri
popular theory is that Polo may have seen vultures circling and initia
taken them for dragons. In his reporting of the incident Polo then
embellished his account of the incident as he did in other passages.

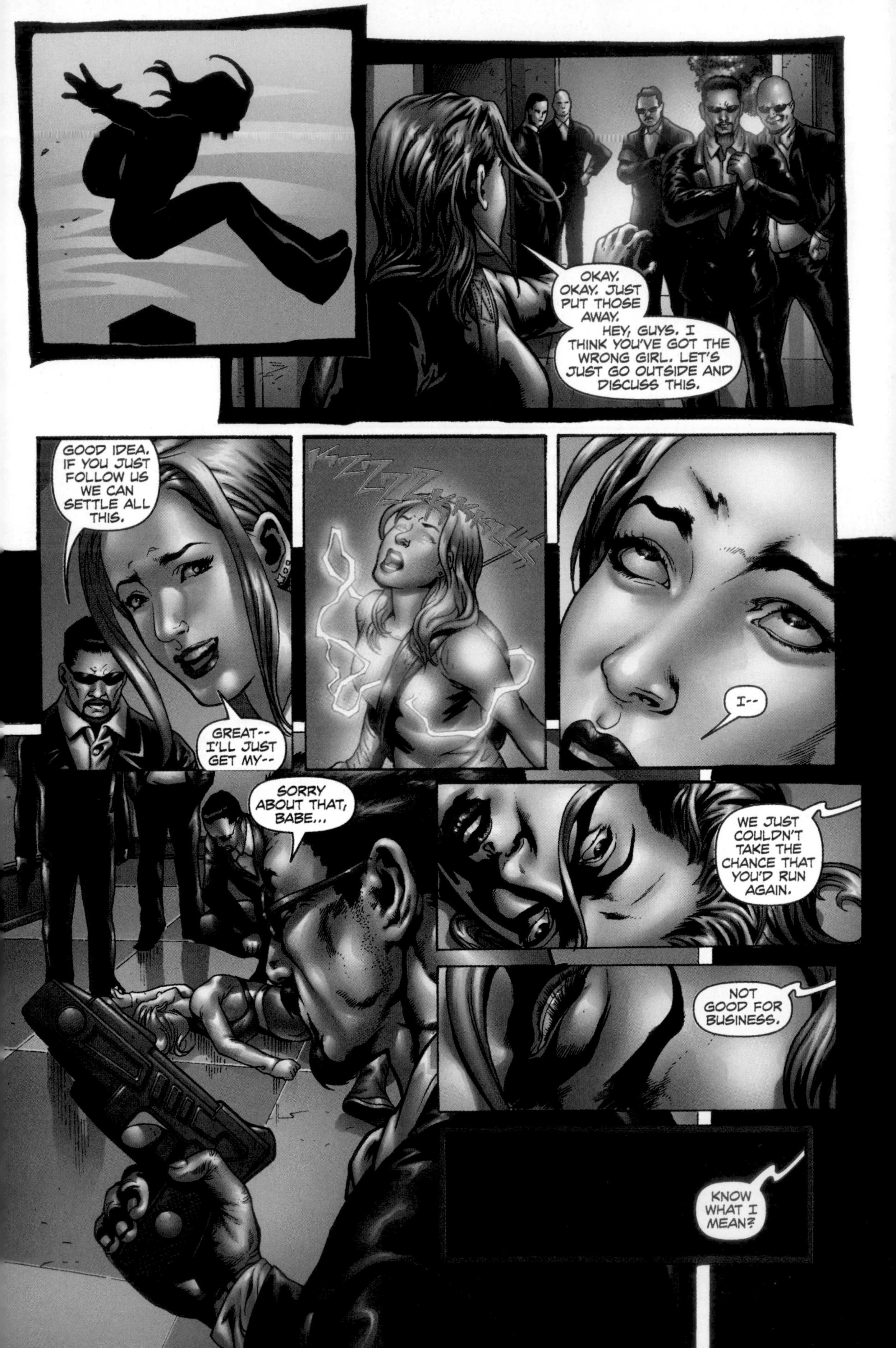
OKAY. OKAY. JUST PUT THOSE AWAY.
HEY, GUYS. I THINK YOU'VE GOT THE WRONG GIRL. LET'S JUST GO OUTSIDE AND DISCUSS THIS.
GOOD IDEA. IF YOU JUST FOLLOW US WE CAN SETTLE ALL THIS.
GREAT-- I'LL JUST GET MY--
I--
SORRY ABOUT THAT, BABE...
WE JUST COULDN'T TAKE THE CHANCE THAT YOU'D RUN AGAIN.
NOT GOOD FOR BUSINESS.
KNOW WHAT I MEAN?

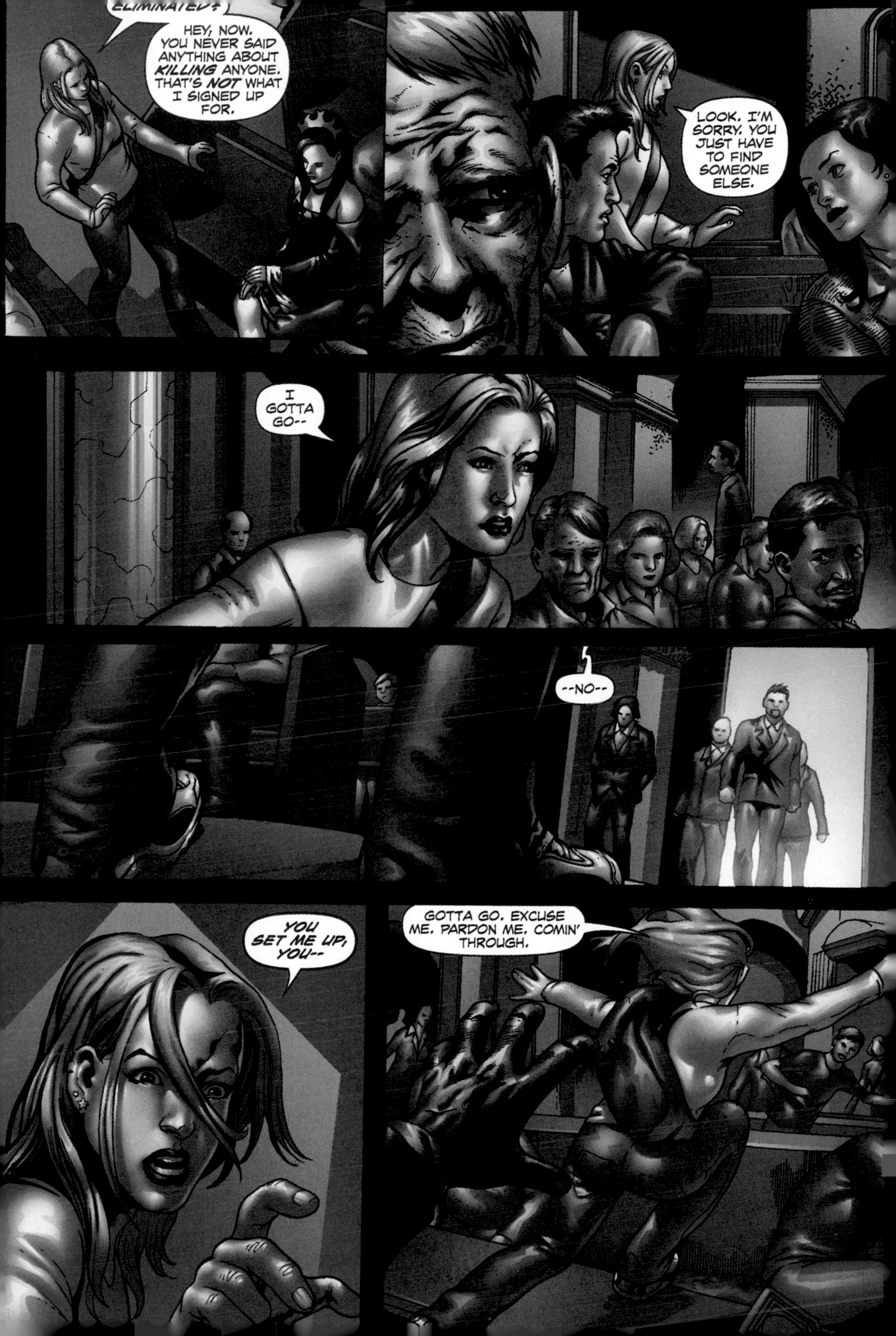
HEY, NOW. YOU NEVER SAID ANYTHING ABOUT KILLING ANYONE. THAT'S NOT WHAT I SIGNED UP FOR.
LOOK. I'M SORRY. YOU JUST HAVE TO FIND SOMEONE ELSE.
I GOTTA GO--
--NO--
YOU SET ME UP, YOU--
GOTTA GO. EXCUSE ME. PARDON ME. COMIN' THROUGH.

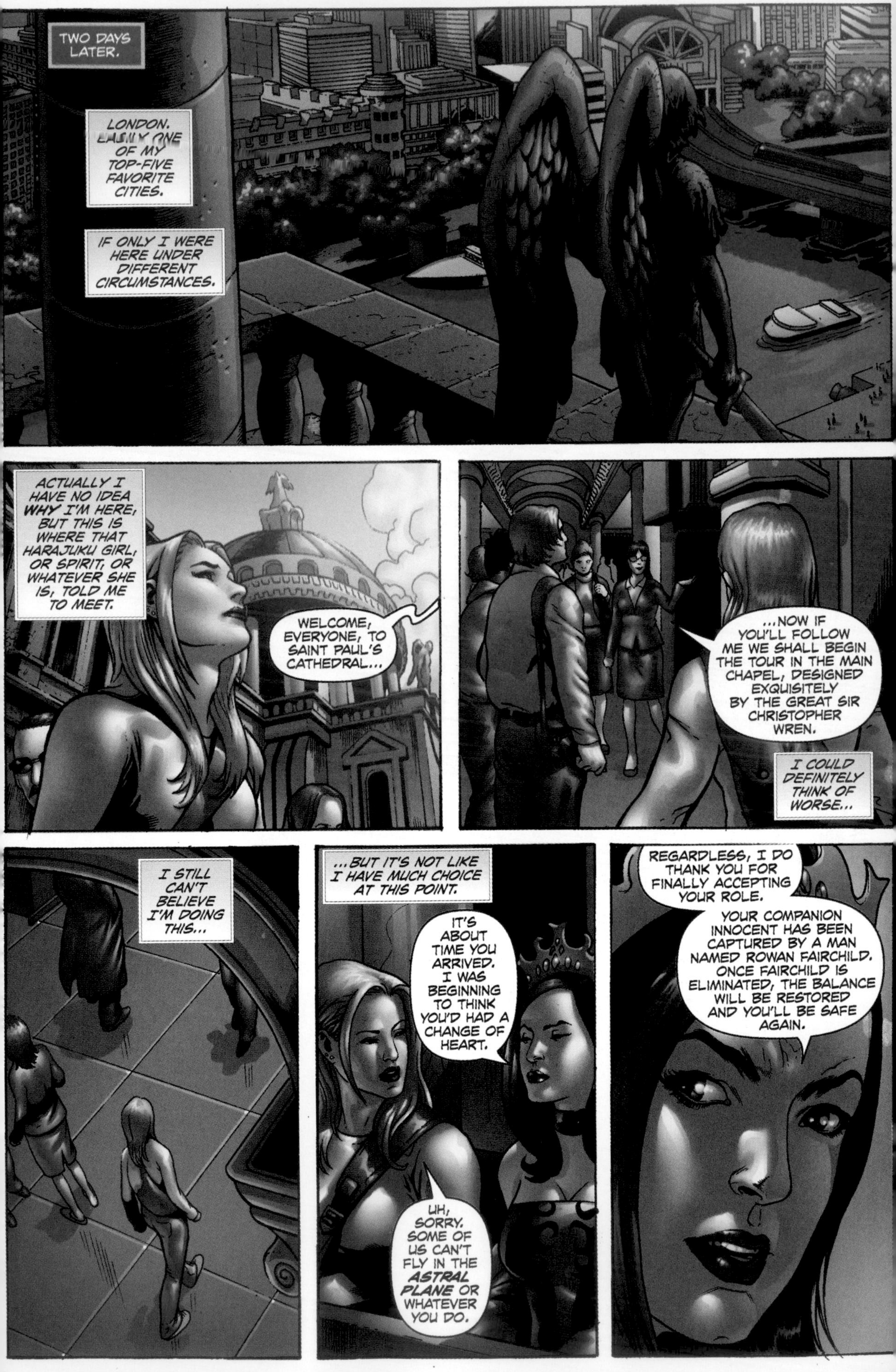
TWO DAYS LATER.
LONDON. EASILY ONE OF MY TOP-FIVE FAVORITE CITIES.
IF ONLY I WERE HERE UNDER DIFFERENT CIRCUMSTANCES.
ACTUALLY I HAVE NO IDEA WHY I'M HERE, BUT THIS IS WHERE THAT HARAJUKU GIRL, OR SPIRIT, OR WHATEVER SHE IS, TOLD ME TO MEET.
WELCOME, EVERYONE, TO SAINT PAUL'S CATHEDRAL...
...NOW IF YOU'LL FOLLOW ME WE SHALL BEGIN THE TOUR IN THE MAIN CHAPEL, DESIGNED EXQUISITELY BY THE GREAT SIR CHRISTOPHER WREN.
I COULD DEFINITELY THINK OF WORSE...
I STILL CAN'T BELIEVE I'M DOING THIS...
...BUT IT'S NOT LIKE I HAVE MUCH CHOICE AT THIS POINT.
IT'S ABOUT TIME YOU ARRIVED. I WAS BEGINNING TO THINK YOU'D HAD A CHANGE OF HEART.
UH, SORRY. SOME OF US CAN'T FLY IN THE ASTRAL PLANE OR WHATEVER YOU DO.
REGARDLESS, I DO THANK YOU FOR FINALLY ACCEPTING YOUR ROLE.
YOUR COMPANION INNOCENT HAS BEEN CAPTURED BY A MAN NAMED ROWAN FAIRCHILD. ONCE FAIRCHILD IS ELIMINATED, THE BALANCE WILL BE RESTORED AND YOU'LL BE SAFE AGAIN.

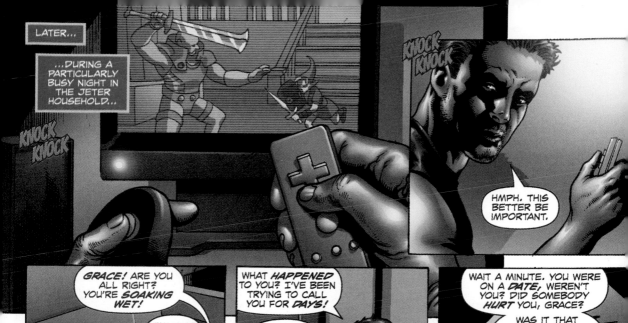

LATER...

...DURING A PARTICULARLY BUSY NIGHT IN THE JETER HOUSEHOLD...

KNOCK KNOCK

KNOCK KNOCK

HMPH. THIS BETTER BE IMPORTANT.

GRACE! ARE YOU ALL RIGHT? YOU'RE *SOAKING WET!*

I'M FINE ROSS. I NEED TO TALK TO YOU, THOUGH.

WHAT *HAPPENED* TO YOU? I'VE BEEN TRYING TO CALL YOU FOR *DAYS!*

ROSS-- SOMETHING'S COME UP. I NEED YOU TO CANCEL MY PLANS FOR THE NEXT COUPLE OF WEEKS AND GET ME IN CONTACT WITH THAT TRAVEL AGENT WE USE. I NEED TO GET A FLIGHT TO LONDON *ASAP.*

WAIT A MINUTE. YOU WERE ON A *DATE*, WEREN'T YOU? DID SOMEBODY *HURT* YOU, GRACE?

WAS IT THAT CARLSON GUY? I *HEARD* HIM MAKING PLANS WITH YOU. I *KNEW* HE WAS BAD NEWS. I'LL *KILL* THE GUY!

ROSS! I NEED YOU TO JUST SHUT UP AND *LISTEN* TO ME!

OKAY. SORRY, GRACE. LOOK, I'LL TAKE CARE OF IT.

BUT I JUST NEED TO KNOW, HAVE YOU GOTTEN INTO TROUBLE? ARE YOU GONNA BE OKAY?

I--DON'T KNOW YET. I--I'LL TALK TO YOU SOON.

LATE.

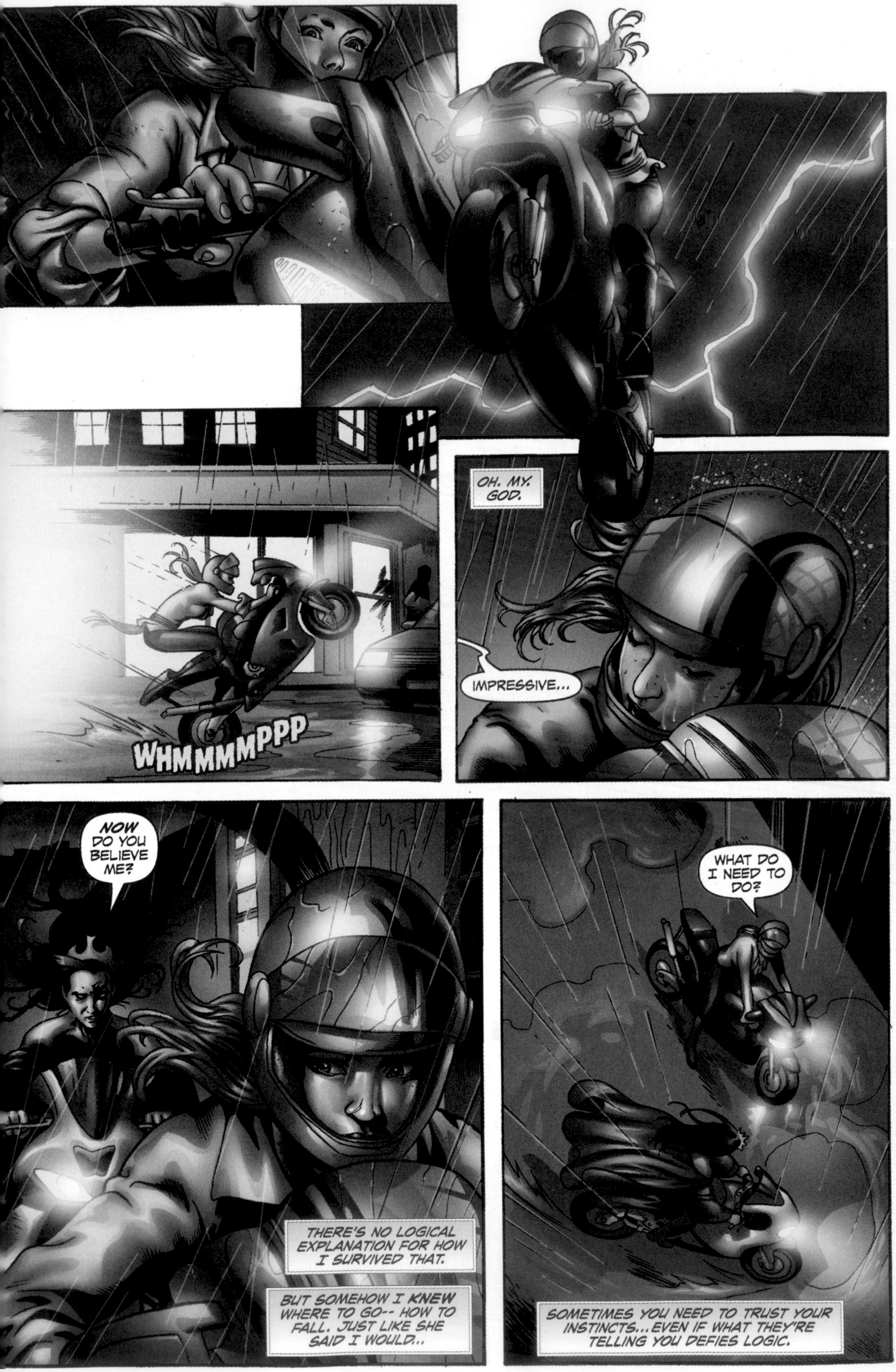
OH. MY. GOD.
IMPRESSIVE...
WHMMMMPPP
NOW DO YOU BELIEVE ME?
THERE'S NO LOGICAL EXPLANATION FOR HOW I SURVIVED THAT.
BUT SOMEHOW I KNEW WHERE TO GO-- HOW TO FALL. JUST LIKE SHE SAID I WOULD...
WHAT DO I NEED TO DO?
SOMETIMES YOU NEED TO TRUST YOUR INSTINCTS...EVEN IF WHAT THEY'RE TELLING YOU DEFIES LOGIC.

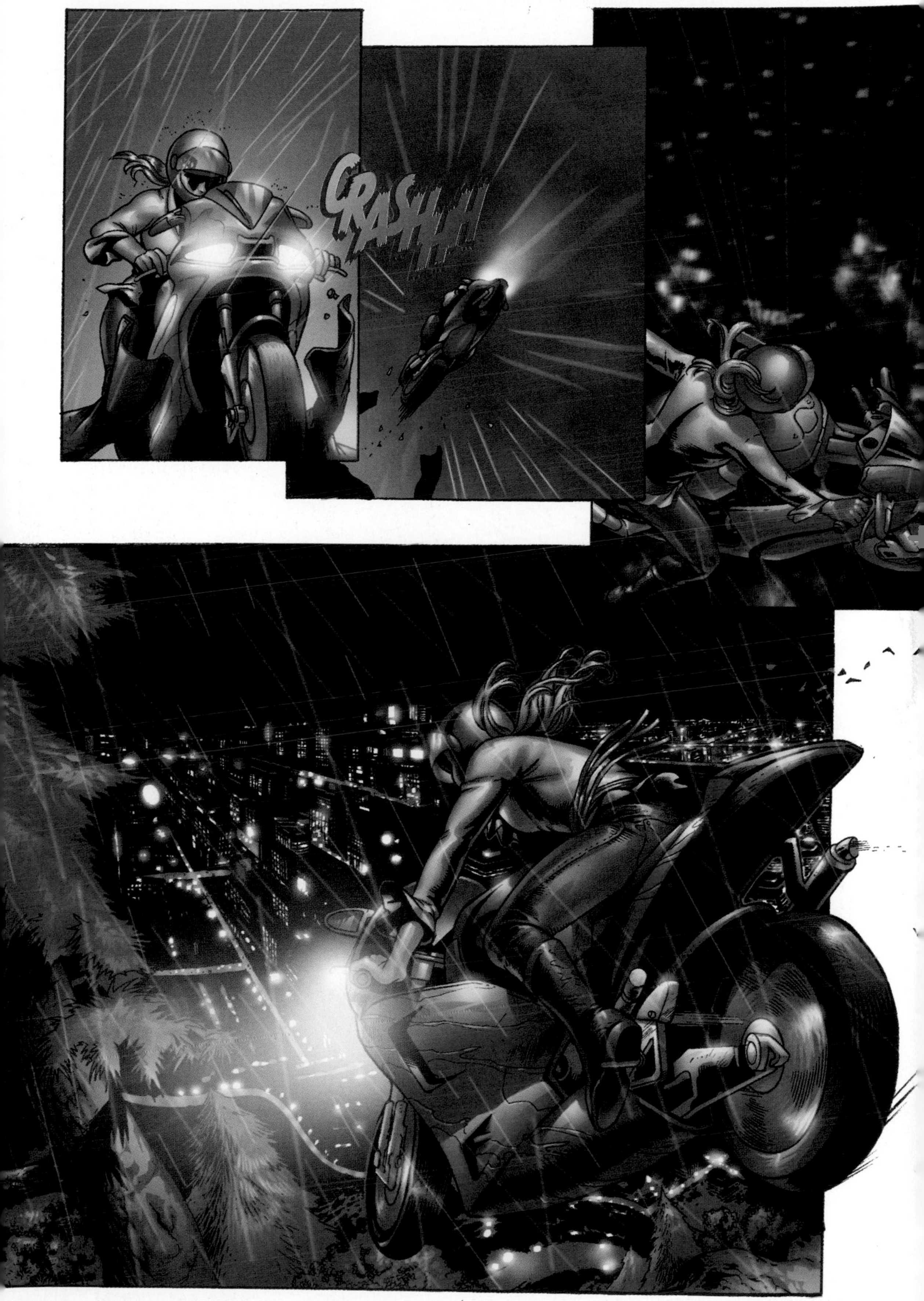
CRASHHH

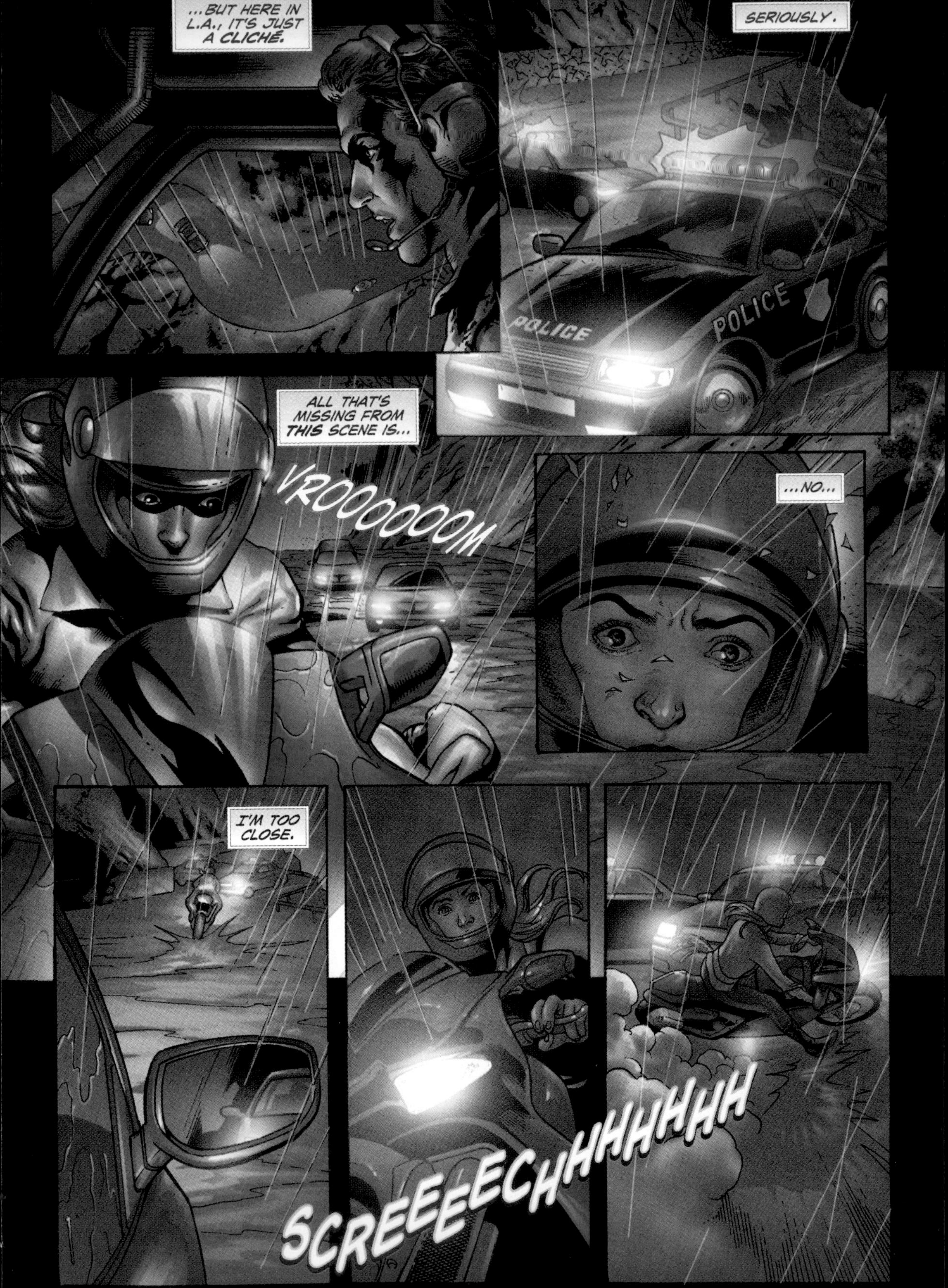
...BUT HERE IN L.A., IT'S JUST A CLICHÉ.
SERIOUSLY.
POLICE
POLICE
ALL THAT'S MISSING FROM THIS SCENE IS...
VROOOOOOM
...NO...
I'M TOO CLOSE.
SCREEEEECHHHHHHH

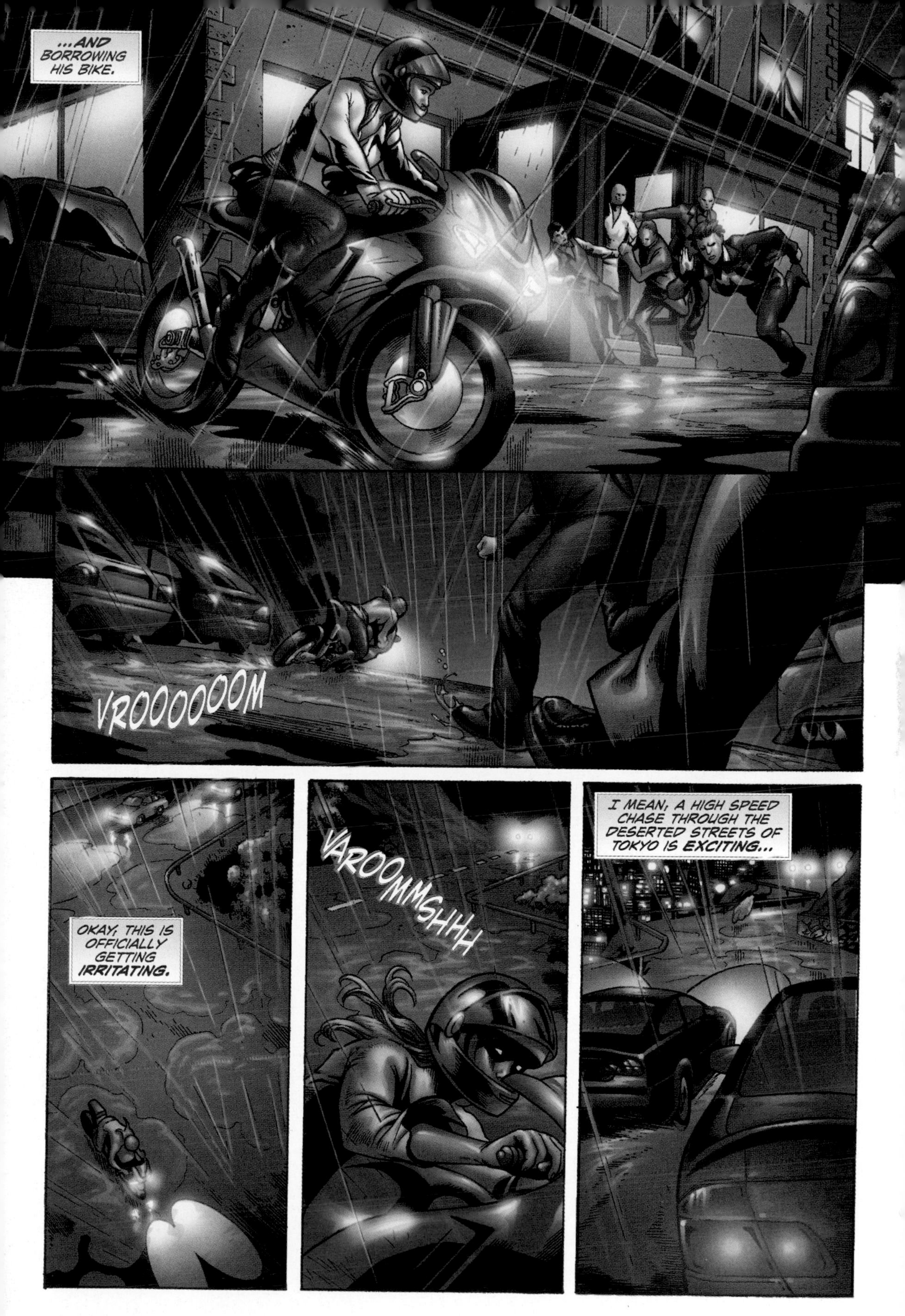
...AND BORROWING HIS BIKE.
VROOOOOOM
OKAY, THIS IS OFFICIALLY GETTING IRRITATING.
VAROOMMSHHH
I MEAN, A HIGH SPEED CHASE THROUGH THE DESERTED STREETS OF TOKYO IS EXCITING...

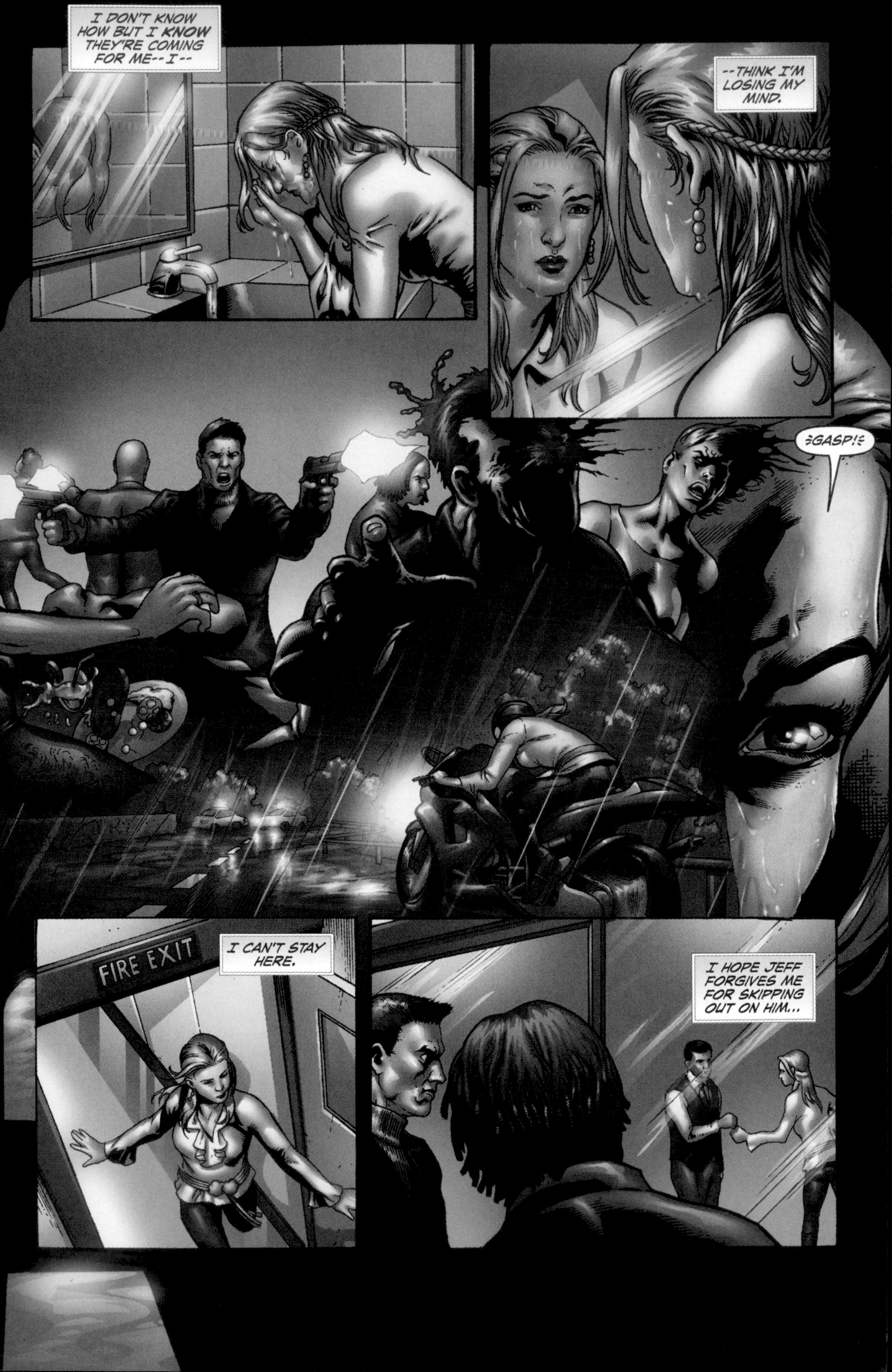
I DON'T KNOW HOW BUT I KNOW THEY'RE COMING FOR ME-- I--
--THINK I'M LOSING MY MIND.
GASP!
FIRE EXIT
I CAN'T STAY HERE.
I HOPE JEFF FORGIVES ME FOR SKIPPING OUT ON HIM...

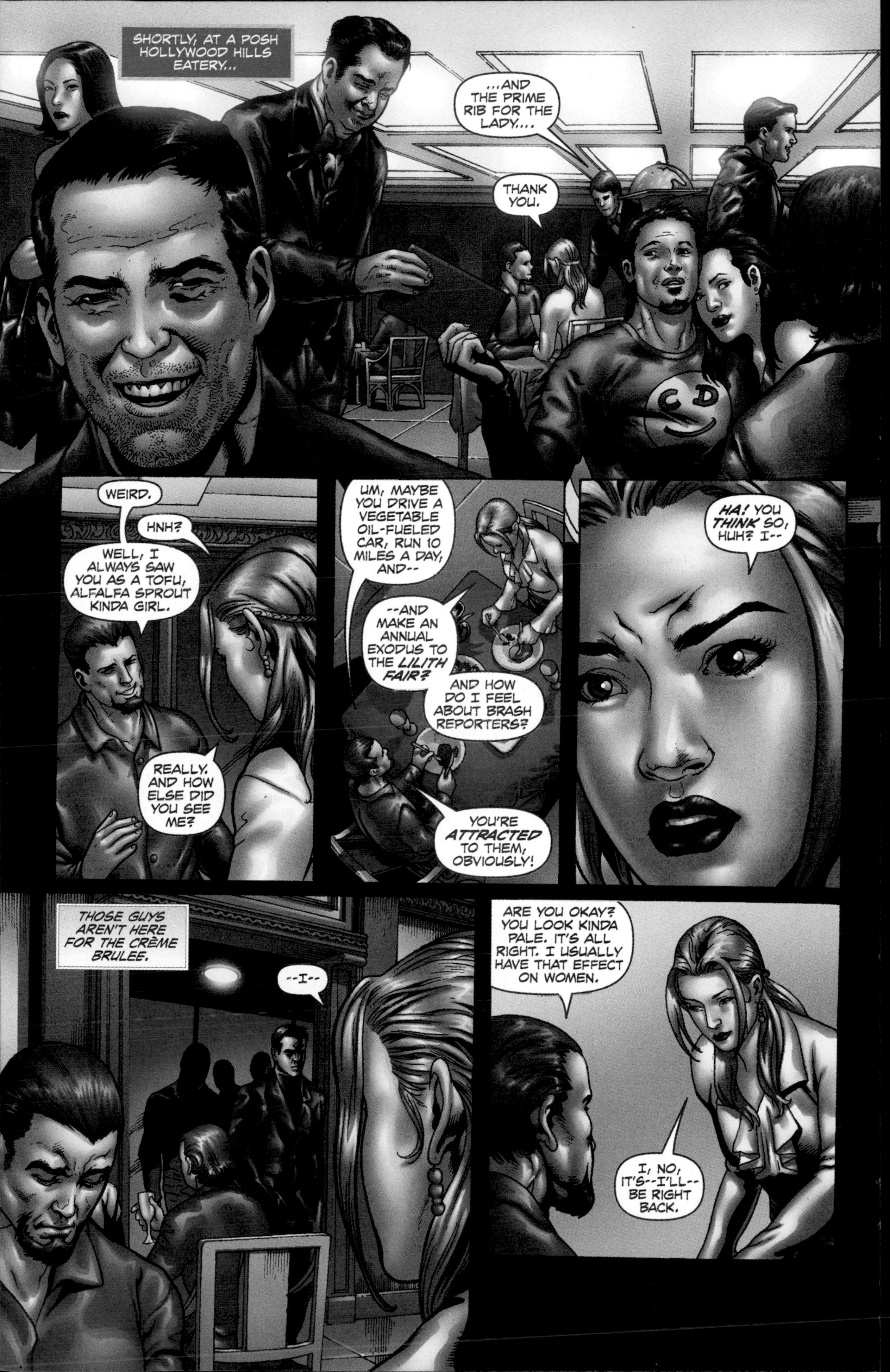

SHORTLY, AT A POSH HOLLYWOOD HILLS EATERY...
...AND THE PRIME RIB FOR THE LADY....
THANK YOU.
WEIRD.
HNH?
WELL, I ALWAYS SAW YOU AS A TOFU, ALFALFA SPROUT KINDA GIRL.
REALLY. AND HOW ELSE DID YOU SEE ME?
UM, MAYBE YOU DRIVE A VEGETABLE OIL-FUELED CAR, RUN 10 MILES A DAY, AND--
--AND MAKE AN ANNUAL EXODUS TO THE LILITH FAIR?
AND HOW DO I FEEL ABOUT BRASH REPORTERS?
YOU'RE ATTRACTED TO THEM, OBVIOUSLY!
HA! YOU THINK SO, HUH? I--
THOSE GUYS AREN'T HERE FOR THE CRÈME BRULEE.
--I--
ARE YOU OKAY? YOU LOOK KINDA PALE. IT'S ALL RIGHT. I USUALLY HAVE THAT EFFECT ON WOMEN.
I, NO, IT'S--I'LL--BE RIGHT BACK.

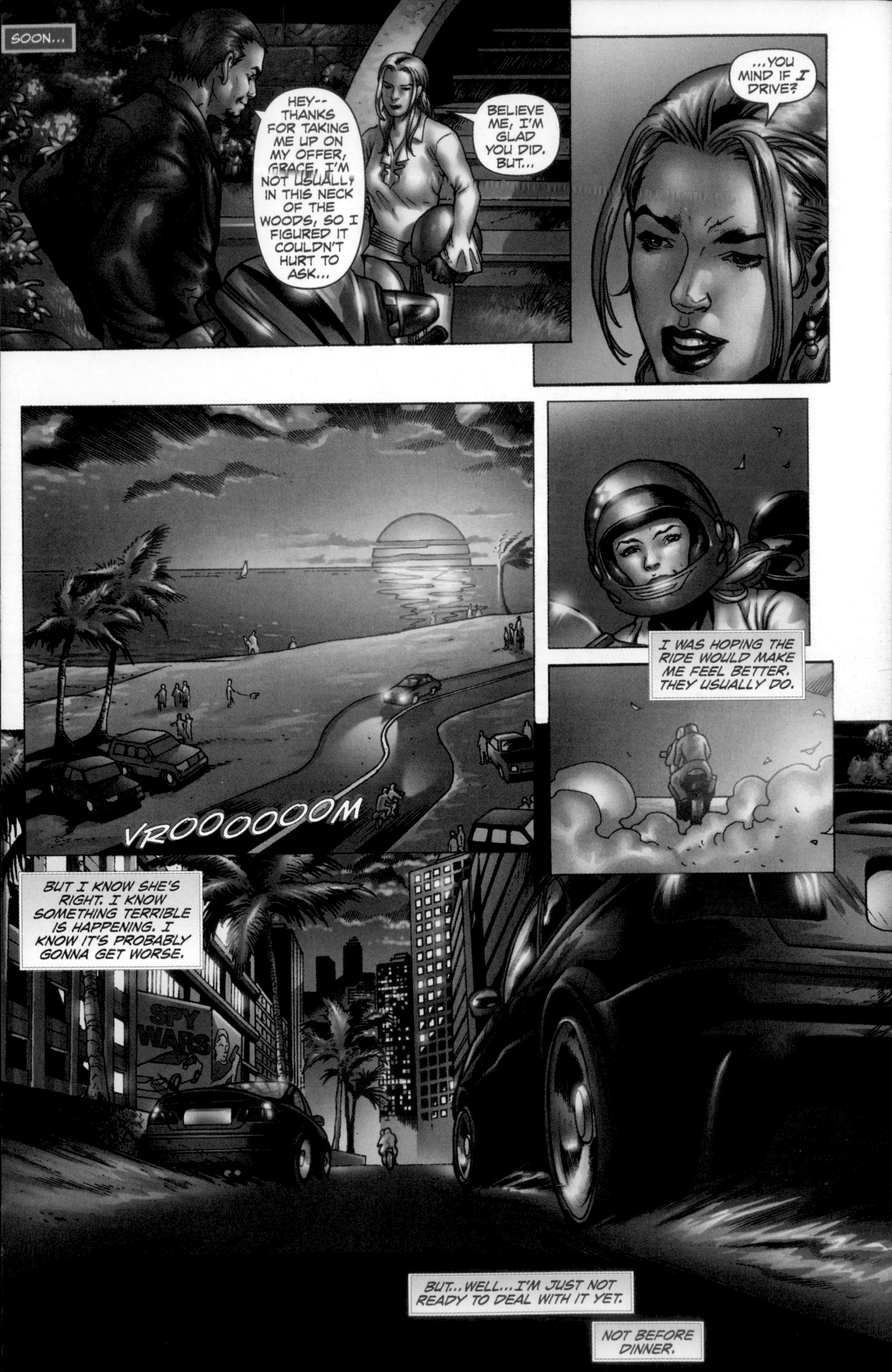
SOON...
HEY-- THANKS FOR TAKING ME UP ON MY OFFER, GRACE. I'M NOT USUALLY IN THIS NECK OF THE WOODS, SO I FIGURED IT COULDN'T HURT TO ASK...
BELIEVE ME, I'M GLAD YOU DID. BUT...
...YOU MIND IF I DRIVE?
VROOOOOOM
I WAS HOPING THE RIDE WOULD MAKE ME FEEL BETTER. THEY USUALLY DO.
BUT I KNOW SHE'S RIGHT. I KNOW SOMETHING TERRIBLE IS HAPPENING. I KNOW IT'S PROBABLY GONNA GET WORSE.
SPY WARS
BUT...WELL...I'M JUST NOT READY TO DEAL WITH IT YET.
NOT BEFORE DINNER.

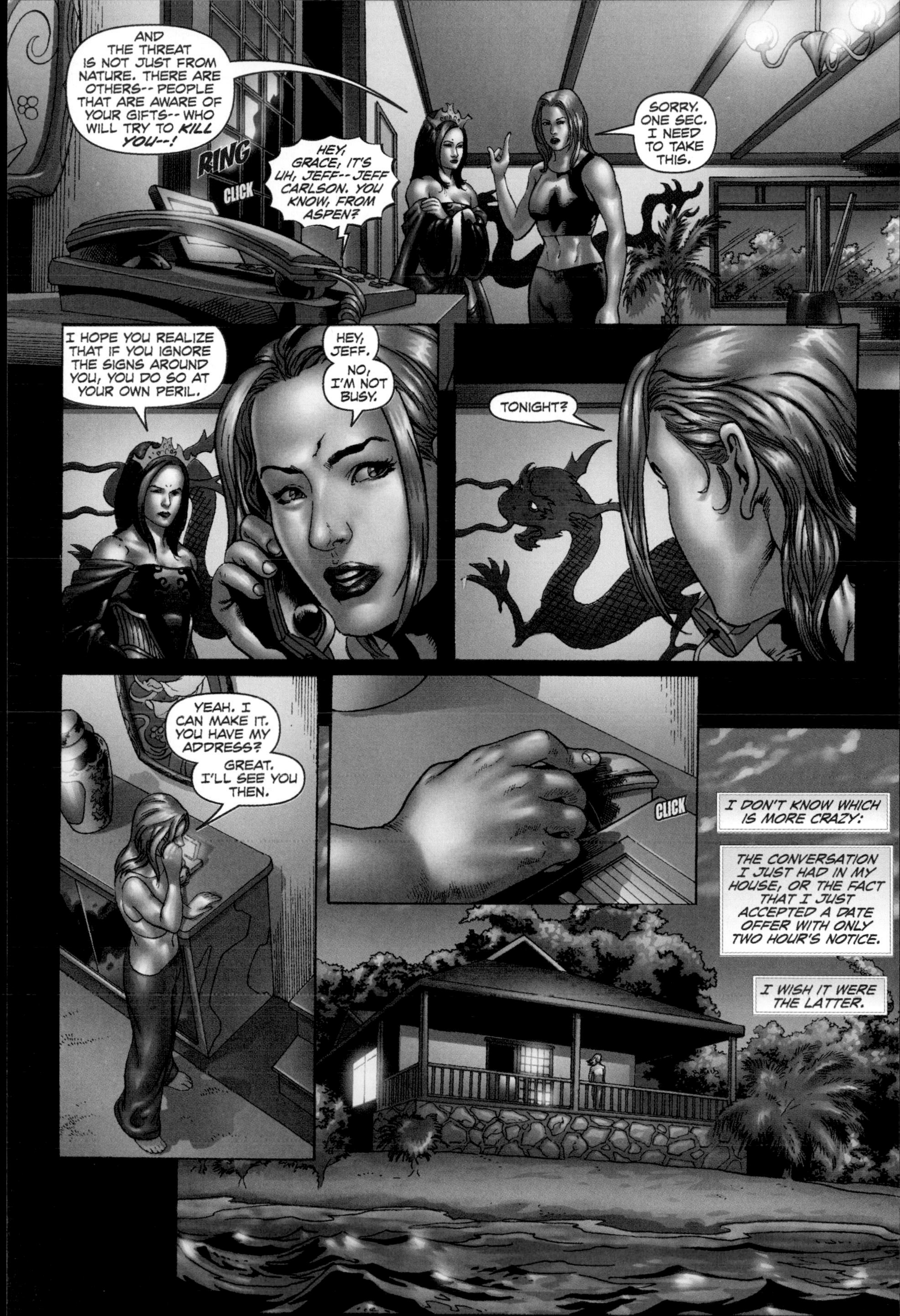
AND THE THREAT IS NOT JUST FROM NATURE. THERE ARE OTHERS-- PEOPLE THAT ARE AWARE OF YOUR GIFTS-- WHO WILL TRY TO KILL YOU--!
RING
CLICK
HEY, GRACE, IT'S UH, JEFF-- JEFF CARLSON. YOU KNOW, FROM ASPEN?
SORRY. ONE SEC. I NEED TO TAKE THIS.
I HOPE YOU REALIZE THAT IF YOU IGNORE THE SIGNS AROUND YOU, YOU DO SO AT YOUR OWN PERIL.
HEY, JEFF.
NO, I'M NOT BUSY.
TONIGHT?
YEAH. I CAN MAKE IT. YOU HAVE MY ADDRESS?
GREAT. I'LL SEE YOU THEN.
CLICK
I DON'T KNOW WHICH IS MORE CRAZY:
THE CONVERSATION I JUST HAD IN MY HOUSE, OR THE FACT THAT I JUST ACCEPTED A DATE OFFER WITH ONLY TWO HOUR'S NOTICE.
I WISH IT WERE THE LATTER.

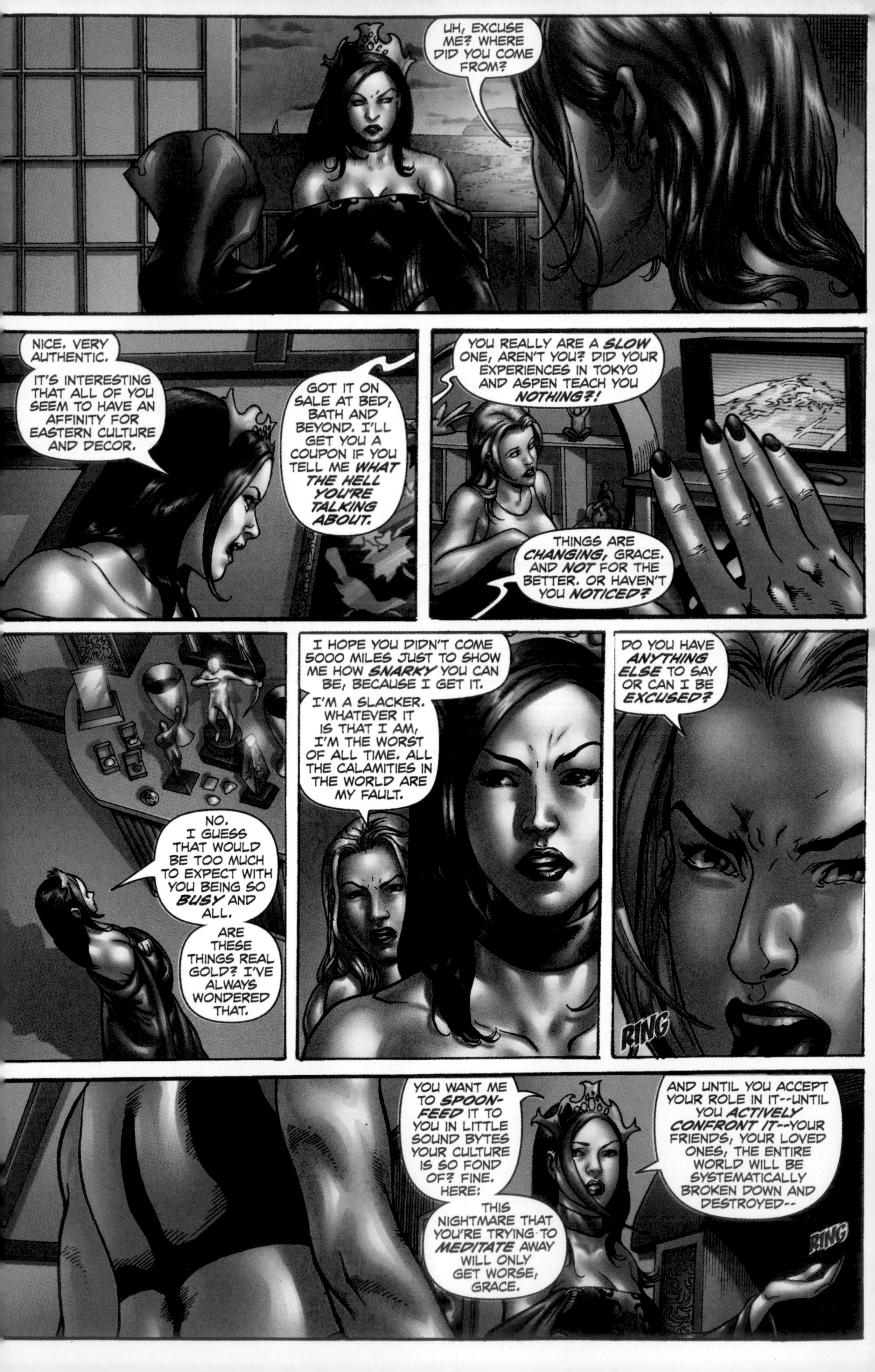
UH, EXCUSE ME? WHERE DID YOU COME FROM?
NICE. VERY AUTHENTIC.
IT'S INTERESTING THAT ALL OF YOU SEEM TO HAVE AN AFFINITY FOR EASTERN CULTURE AND DECOR.
GOT IT ON SALE AT BED, BATH AND BEYOND. I'LL GET YOU A COUPON IF YOU TELL ME *WHAT THE HELL YOU'RE TALKING ABOUT.*
YOU REALLY ARE A *SLOW* ONE, AREN'T YOU? DID YOUR EXPERIENCES IN TOKYO AND ASPEN TEACH YOU *NOTHING?!*
THINGS ARE *CHANGING,* GRACE. AND *NOT* FOR THE BETTER. OR HAVEN'T YOU *NOTICED?*
NO. I GUESS THAT WOULD BE TOO MUCH TO EXPECT WITH YOU BEING SO *BUSY* AND ALL.
ARE THESE THINGS REAL GOLD? I'VE ALWAYS WONDERED THAT.
I HOPE YOU DIDN'T COME 5000 MILES JUST TO SHOW ME HOW *SNARKY* YOU CAN BE, BECAUSE I GET IT.
I'M A SLACKER. WHATEVER IT IS THAT I AM, I'M THE WORST OF ALL TIME. ALL THE CALAMITIES IN THE WORLD ARE MY FAULT.
DO YOU HAVE *ANYTHING ELSE* TO SAY OR CAN I BE *EXCUSED?*
RING
YOU WANT ME TO *SPOON-FEED* IT TO YOU IN LITTLE SOUND BYTES YOUR CULTURE IS SO FOND OF? FINE. HERE:
THIS NIGHTMARE THAT YOU'RE TRYING TO *MEDITATE* AWAY WILL ONLY GET WORSE, GRACE.
AND UNTIL YOU ACCEPT YOUR ROLE IN IT--UNTIL YOU *ACTIVELY CONFRONT IT*--YOUR FRIENDS, YOUR LOVED ONES, THE ENTIRE WORLD WILL BE SYSTEMATICALLY BROKEN DOWN AND DESTROYED--
RING

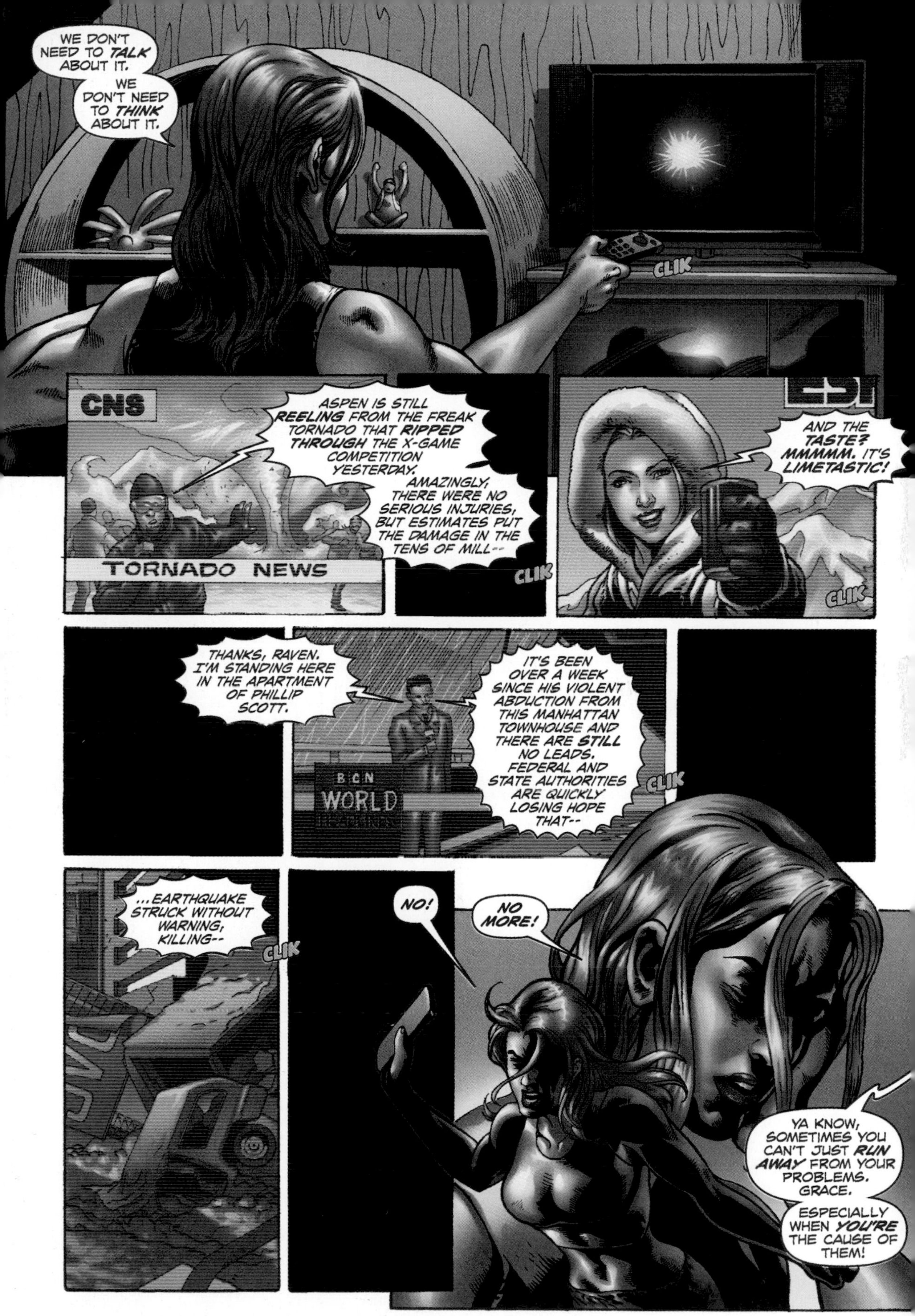
WE DON'T NEED TO TALK ABOUT IT.
WE DON'T NEED TO THINK ABOUT IT.
CLIK
CNS
ASPEN IS STILL REELING FROM THE FREAK TORNADO THAT RIPPED THROUGH THE X-GAME COMPETITION YESTERDAY.
AMAZINGLY, THERE WERE NO SERIOUS INJURIES, BUT ESTIMATES PUT THE DAMAGE IN THE TENS OF MILL--
TORNADO NEWS
CLIK
AND THE TASTE? MMMMM. IT'S LIMETASTIC!
CLIK
THANKS, RAVEN. I'M STANDING HERE IN THE APARTMENT OF PHILLIP SCOTT.
IT'S BEEN OVER A WEEK SINCE HIS VIOLENT ABDUCTION FROM THIS MANHATTAN TOWNHOUSE AND THERE ARE STILL NO LEADS. FEDERAL AND STATE AUTHORITIES ARE QUICKLY LOSING HOPE THAT--
BCN
WORLD
CLIK
...EARTHQUAKE STRUCK WITHOUT WARNING, KILLING--
CLIK
NO!
NO MORE!
YA KNOW, SOMETIMES YOU CAN'T JUST RUN AWAY FROM YOUR PROBLEMS. GRACE.
ESPECIALLY WHEN YOU'RE THE CAUSE OF THEM!

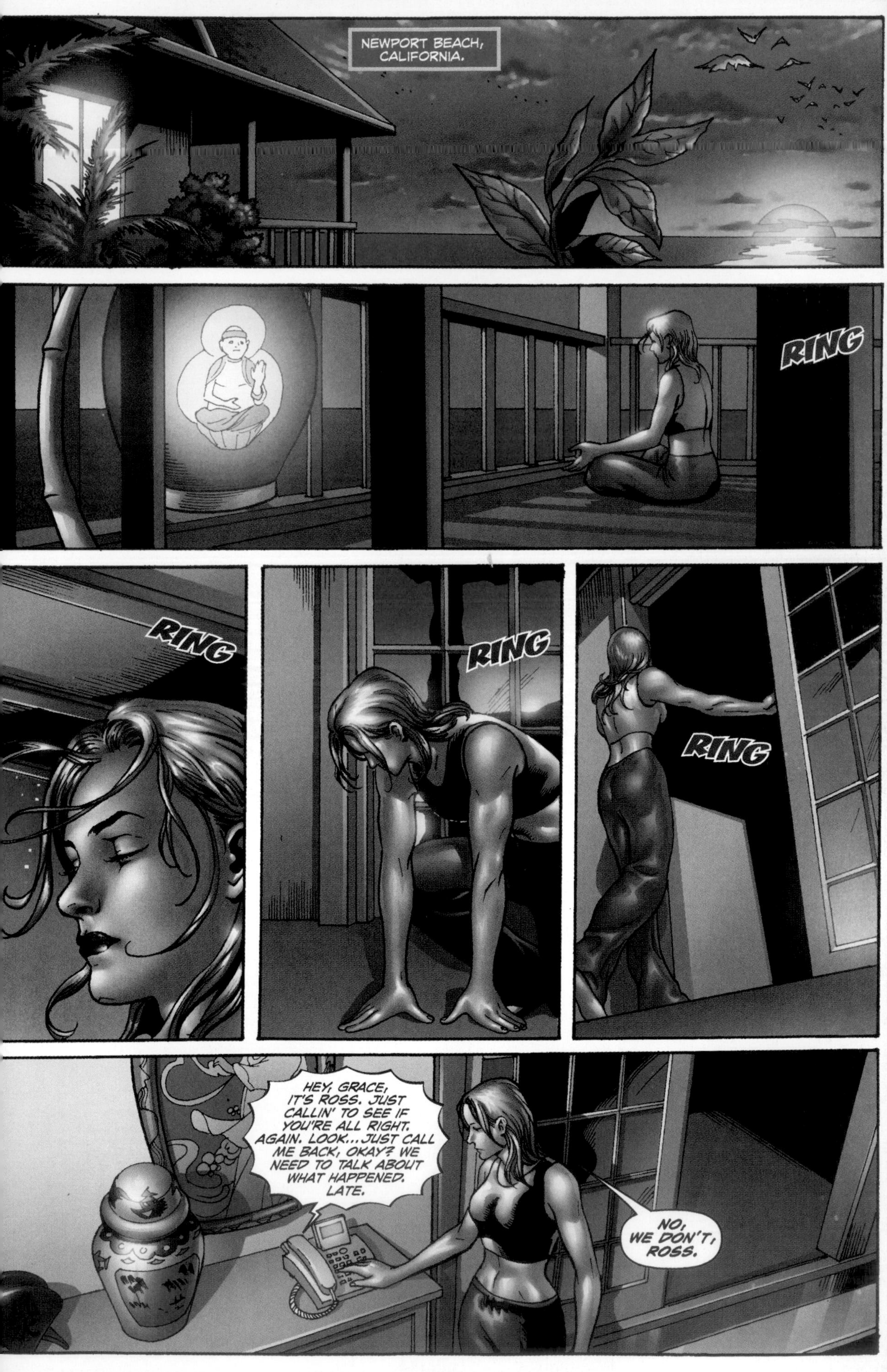
NEWPORT BEACH, CALIFORNIA.
RING
RING
RING
RING
HEY, GRACE, IT'S ROSS. JUST CALLIN' TO SEE IF YOU'RE ALL RIGHT. AGAIN. LOOK...JUST CALL ME BACK, OKAY? WE NEED TO TALK ABOUT WHAT HAPPENED. LATE.
NO, WE DON'T, ROSS.

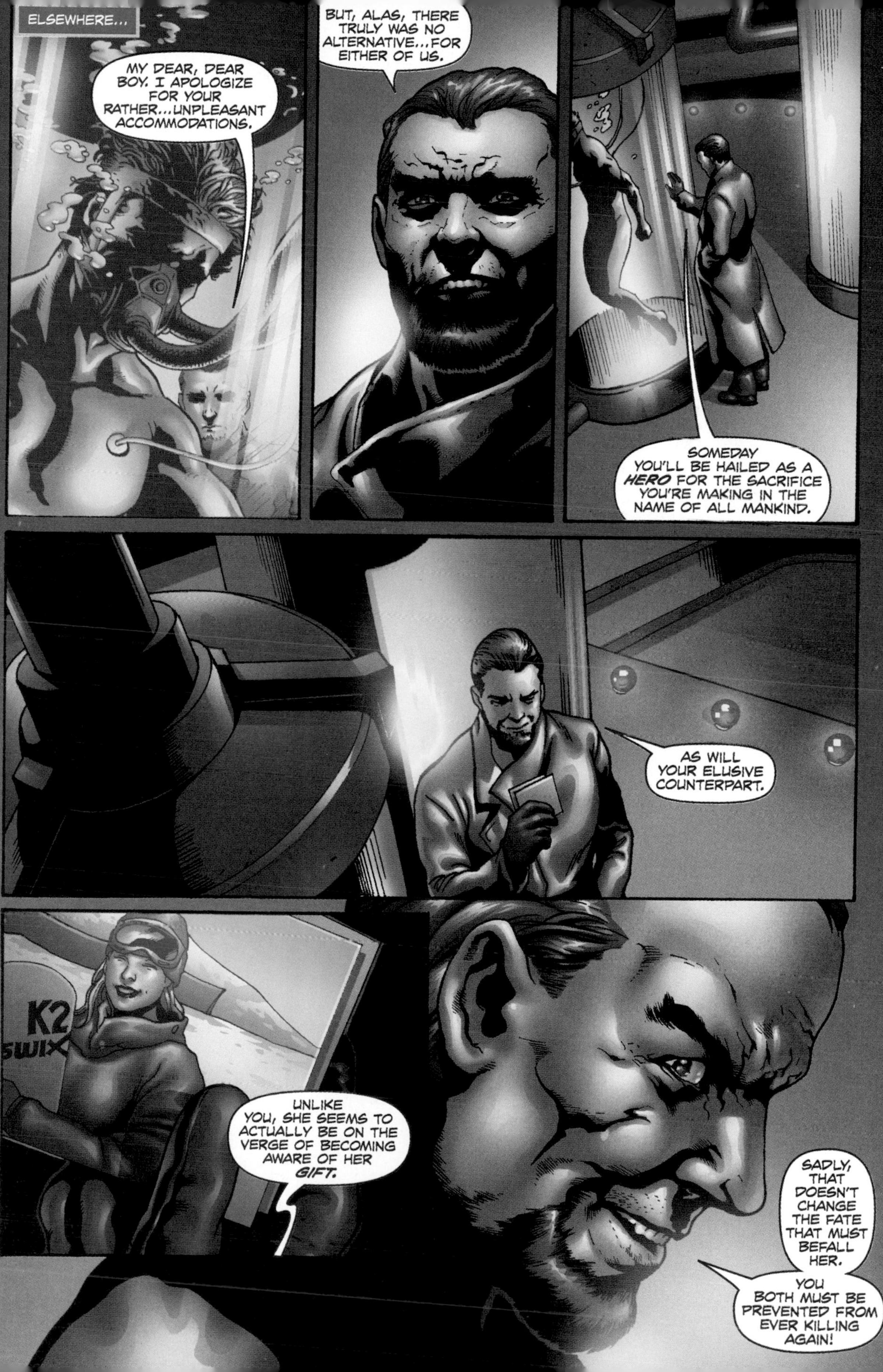
ELSEWHERE...
MY DEAR, DEAR BOY. I APOLOGIZE FOR YOUR RATHER...UNPLEASANT ACCOMMODATIONS.
BUT, ALAS, THERE TRULY WAS NO ALTERNATIVE...FOR EITHER OF US.
SOMEDAY YOU'LL BE HAILED AS A HERO FOR THE SACRIFICE YOU'RE MAKING IN THE NAME OF ALL MANKIND.
AS WILL YOUR ELUSIVE COUNTERPART.
K2
SWIX
UNLIKE YOU, SHE SEEMS TO ACTUALLY BE ON THE VERGE OF BECOMING AWARE OF HER GIFT.
SADLY, THAT DOESN'T CHANGE THE FATE THAT MUST BEFALL HER.
YOU BOTH MUST BE PREVENTED FROM EVER KILLING AGAIN!

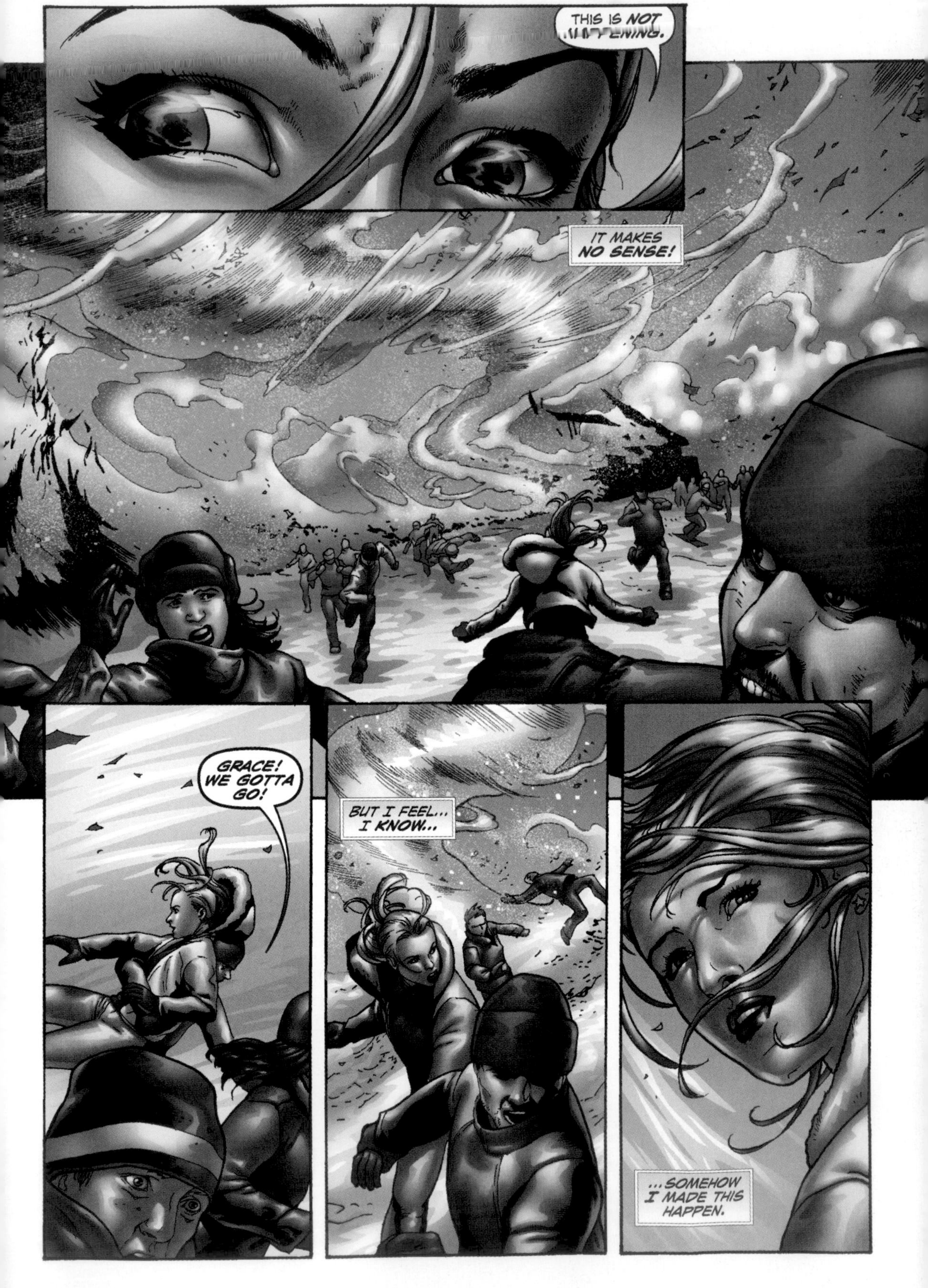
THIS IS NOT
IT MAKES NO SENSE!
GRACE! WE GOTTA GO!
BUT I FEEL... I KNOW...
...SOMEHOW I MADE THIS HAPPEN.

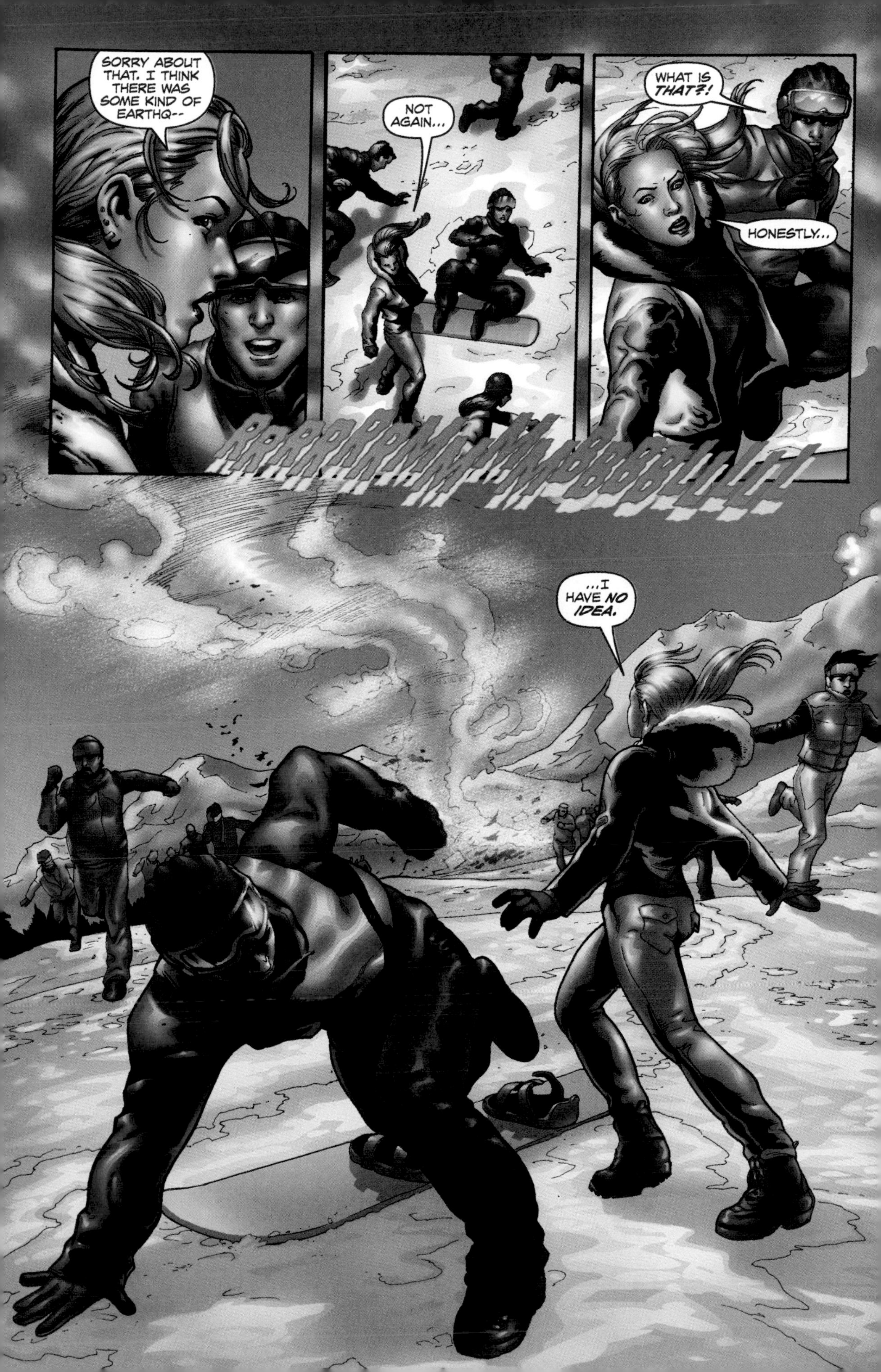
SORRY ABOUT THAT. I THINK THERE WAS SOME KIND OF EARTHQ--
NOT AGAIN...
WHAT IS *THAT?!*
HONESTLY...
RRRRRRMMMMMBBBLLL!!
...I HAVE *NO IDEA.*

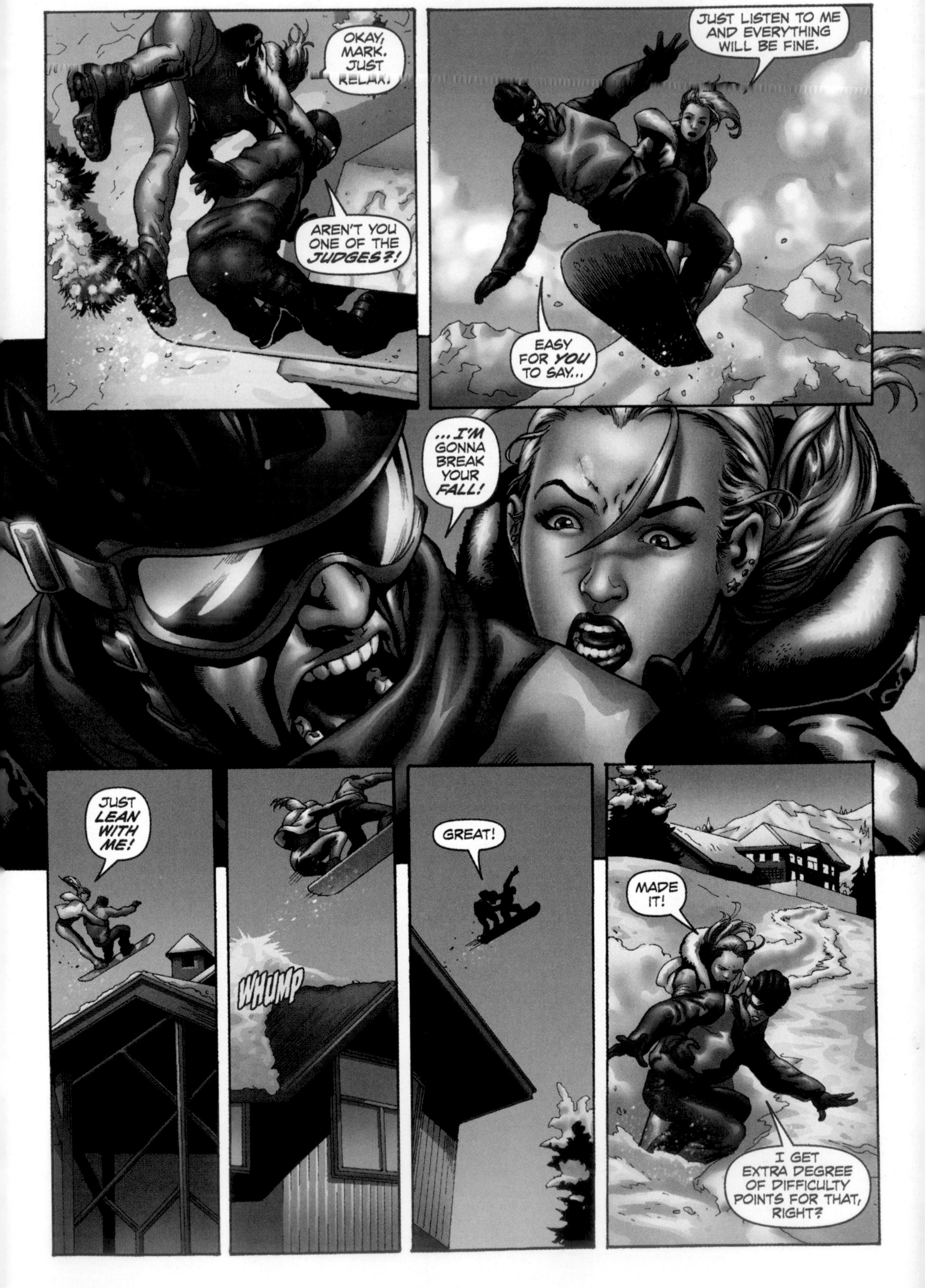
OKAY, MARK. JUST RELAX!
AREN'T YOU ONE OF THE JUDGES?!
JUST LISTEN TO ME AND EVERYTHING WILL BE FINE.
EASY FOR YOU TO SAY...
...I'M GONNA BREAK YOUR FALL!
JUST LEAN WITH ME!
WHUMP
GREAT!
MADE IT!
I GET EXTRA DEGREE OF DIFFICULTY POINTS FOR THAT, RIGHT?

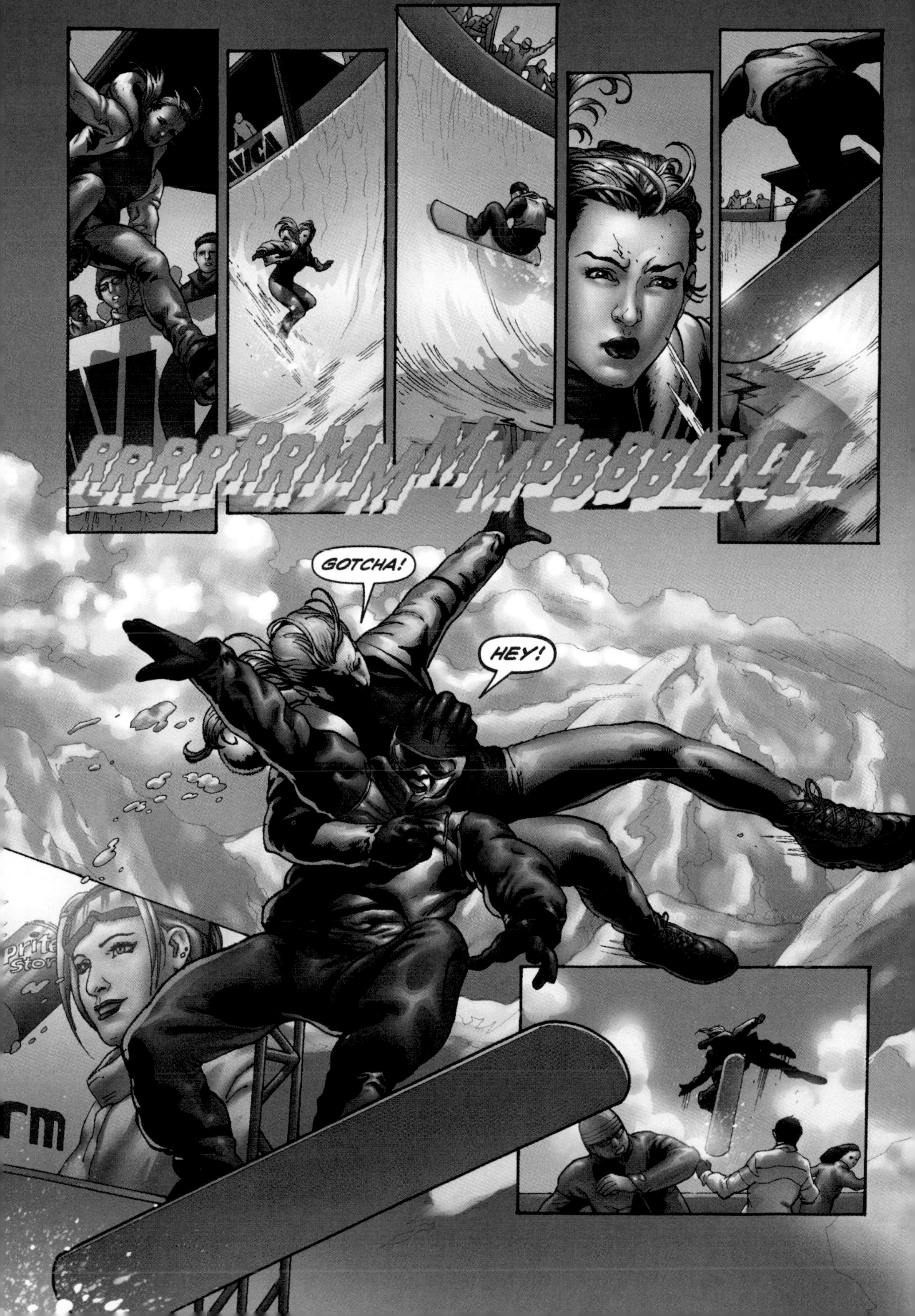
RRRRRRRMMMMMBBBBLLLLL
GOTCHA!
HEY!

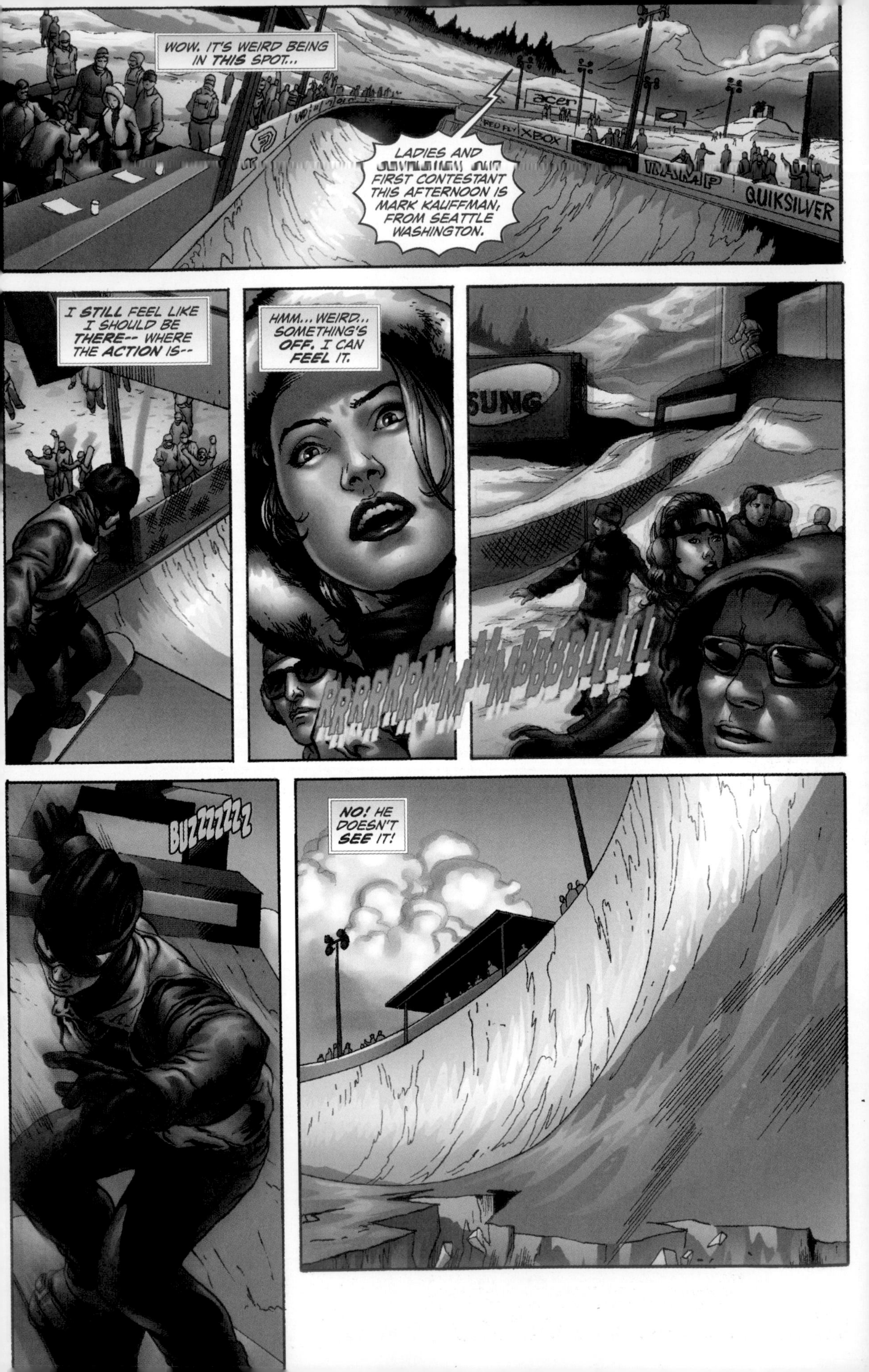

WOW. IT'S WEIRD BEING IN THIS SPOT...
LADIES AND
FIRST CONTESTANT THIS AFTERNOON IS MARK KAUFFMAN, FROM SEATTLE WASHINGTON.
acer
XBOX
QUIKSILVER
I STILL FEEL LIKE I SHOULD BE THERE-- WHERE THE ACTION IS--
HMM... WEIRD... SOMETHING'S OFF. I CAN FEEL IT.
SUNG
RRRRRRMMMMMBBBBLLLL
BUZZZZZZZ
NO! HE DOESN'T SEE IT!

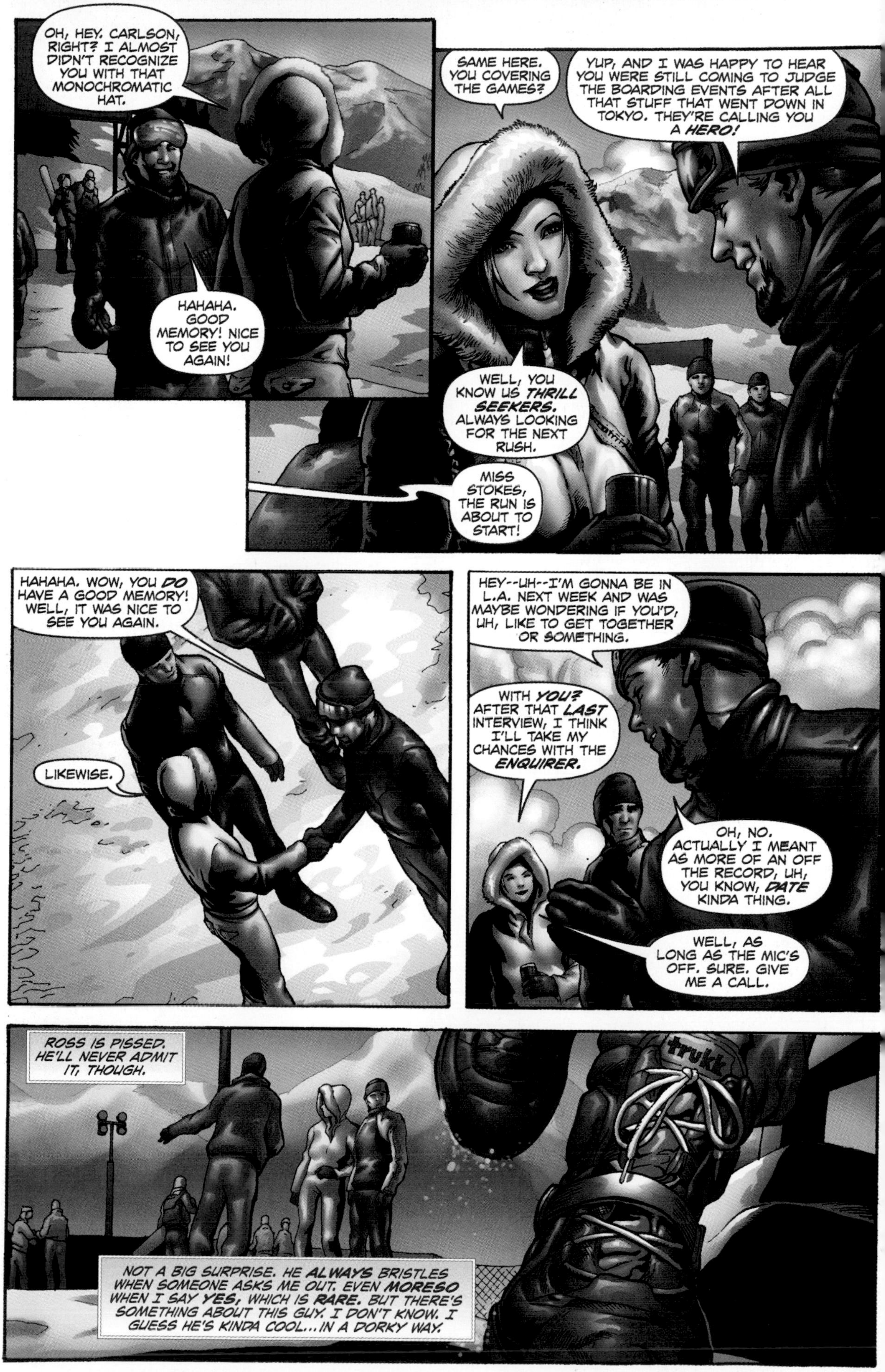
OH, HEY. CARLSON, RIGHT? I ALMOST DIDN'T RECOGNIZE YOU WITH THAT MONOCHROMATIC HAT.
HAHAHA. GOOD MEMORY! NICE TO SEE YOU AGAIN!
SAME HERE. YOU COVERING THE GAMES?
YUP, AND I WAS HAPPY TO HEAR YOU WERE STILL COMING TO JUDGE THE BOARDING EVENTS AFTER ALL THAT STUFF THAT WENT DOWN IN TOKYO. THEY'RE CALLING YOU A HERO!
WELL, YOU KNOW US THRILL SEEKERS. ALWAYS LOOKING FOR THE NEXT RUSH.
MISS STOKES, THE RUN IS ABOUT TO START!
HAHAHA. WOW, YOU DO HAVE A GOOD MEMORY! WELL, IT WAS NICE TO SEE YOU AGAIN.
LIKEWISE.
HEY--UH--I'M GONNA BE IN L.A. NEXT WEEK AND WAS MAYBE WONDERING IF YOU'D, UH, LIKE TO GET TOGETHER OR SOMETHING.
WITH YOU? AFTER THAT LAST INTERVIEW, I THINK I'LL TAKE MY CHANCES WITH THE ENQUIRER.
OH, NO. ACTUALLY I MEANT AS MORE OF AN OFF THE RECORD, UH, YOU KNOW, DATE KINDA THING.
WELL, AS LONG AS THE MIC'S OFF. SURE. GIVE ME A CALL.
ROSS IS PISSED. HE'LL NEVER ADMIT IT, THOUGH.
trukk
NOT A BIG SURPRISE. HE ALWAYS BRISTLES WHEN SOMEONE ASKS ME OUT. EVEN MORESO WHEN I SAY YES, WHICH IS RARE. BUT THERE'S SOMETHING ABOUT THIS GUY. I DON'T KNOW. I GUESS HE'S KINDA COOL...IN A DORKY WAY.

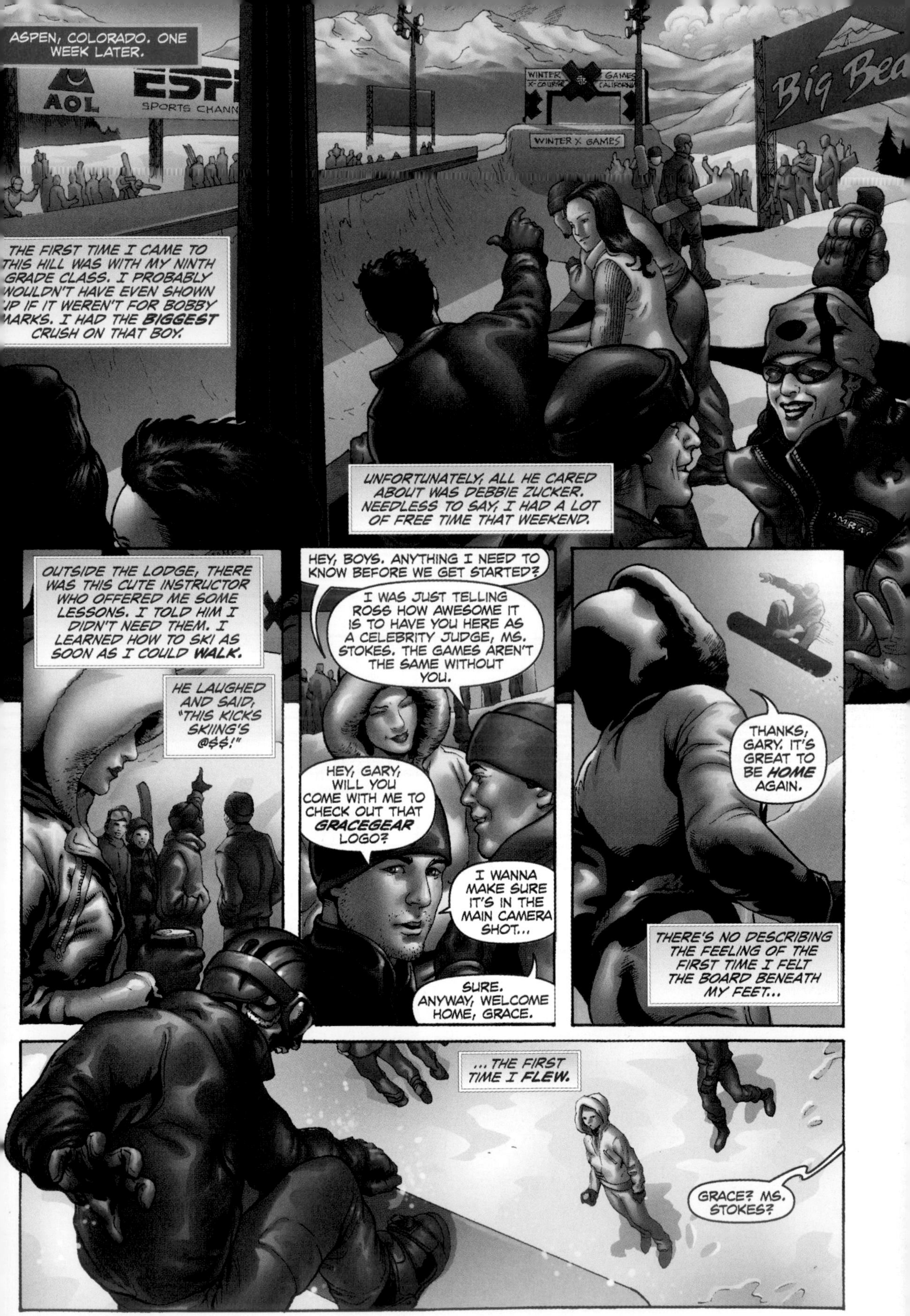
ASPEN, COLORADO. ONE WEEK LATER.
AOL
ESPN SPORTS CHANN
WINTER X GAMES
Big Bea
THE FIRST TIME I CAME TO THIS HILL WAS WITH MY NINTH GRADE CLASS. I PROBABLY WOULDN'T HAVE EVEN SHOWN UP IF IT WEREN'T FOR BOBBY MARKS. I HAD THE BIGGEST CRUSH ON THAT BOY.
UNFORTUNATELY, ALL HE CARED ABOUT WAS DEBBIE ZUCKER. NEEDLESS TO SAY, I HAD A LOT OF FREE TIME THAT WEEKEND.
OUTSIDE THE LODGE, THERE WAS THIS CUTE INSTRUCTOR WHO OFFERED ME SOME LESSONS. I TOLD HIM I DIDN'T NEED THEM. I LEARNED HOW TO SKI AS SOON AS I COULD WALK.
HE LAUGHED AND SAID, "THIS KICKS SKIING'S @$$!"
HEY, BOYS. ANYTHING I NEED TO KNOW BEFORE WE GET STARTED?
I WAS JUST TELLING ROSS HOW AWESOME IT IS TO HAVE YOU HERE AS A CELEBRITY JUDGE, MS. STOKES. THE GAMES AREN'T THE SAME WITHOUT YOU.
HEY, GARY, WILL YOU COME WITH ME TO CHECK OUT THAT GRACEGEAR LOGO?
I WANNA MAKE SURE IT'S IN THE MAIN CAMERA SHOT...
SURE. ANYWAY, WELCOME HOME, GRACE.
THANKS, GARY. IT'S GREAT TO BE HOME AGAIN.
THERE'S NO DESCRIBING THE FEELING OF THE FIRST TIME I FELT THE BOARD BENEATH MY FEET...
...THE FIRST TIME I FLEW.
GRACE? MS. STOKES?

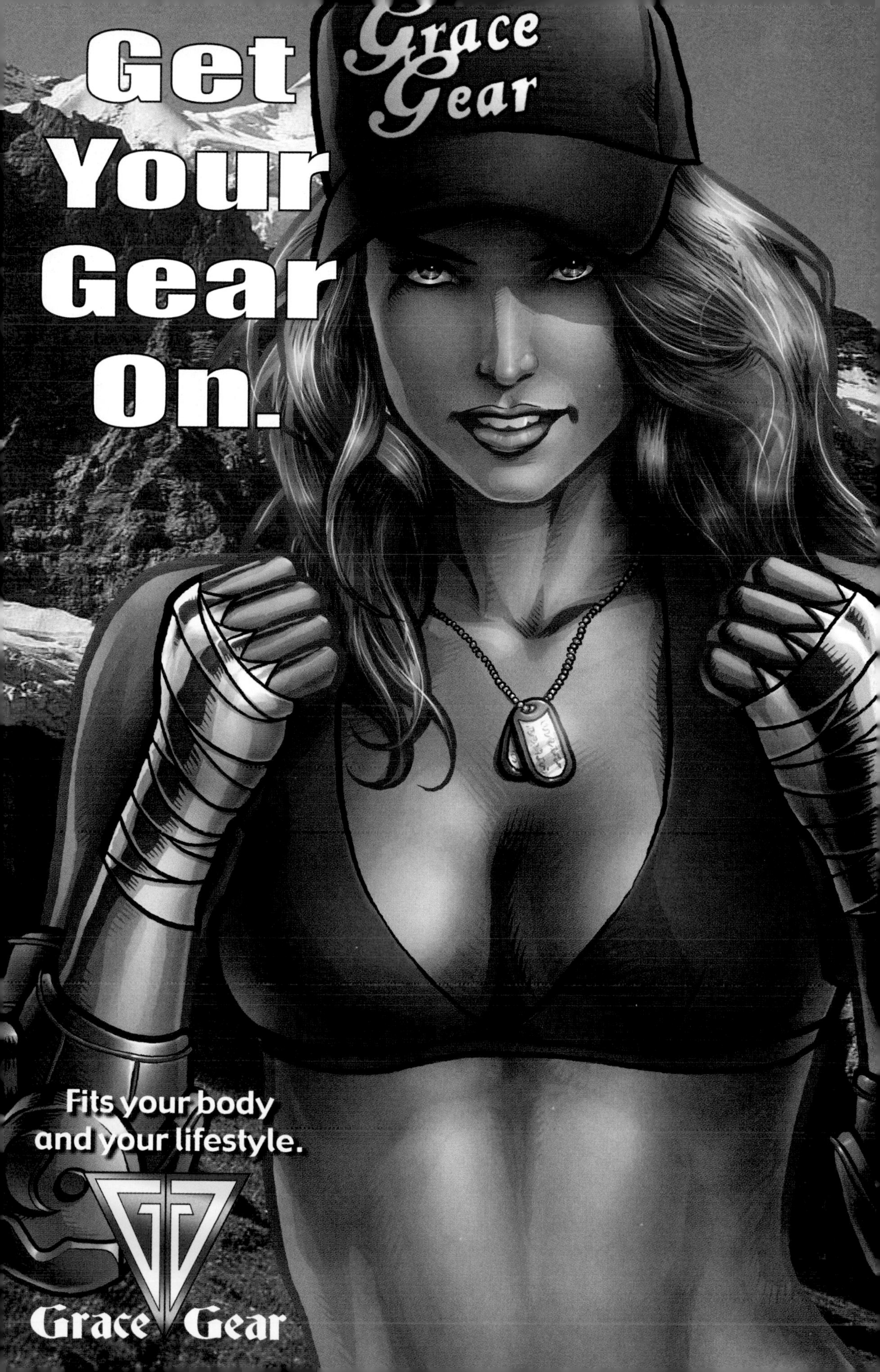
Get
Your
Gear
On.
Grace
Gear
Fits your body
and your lifestyle.
Grace Gear

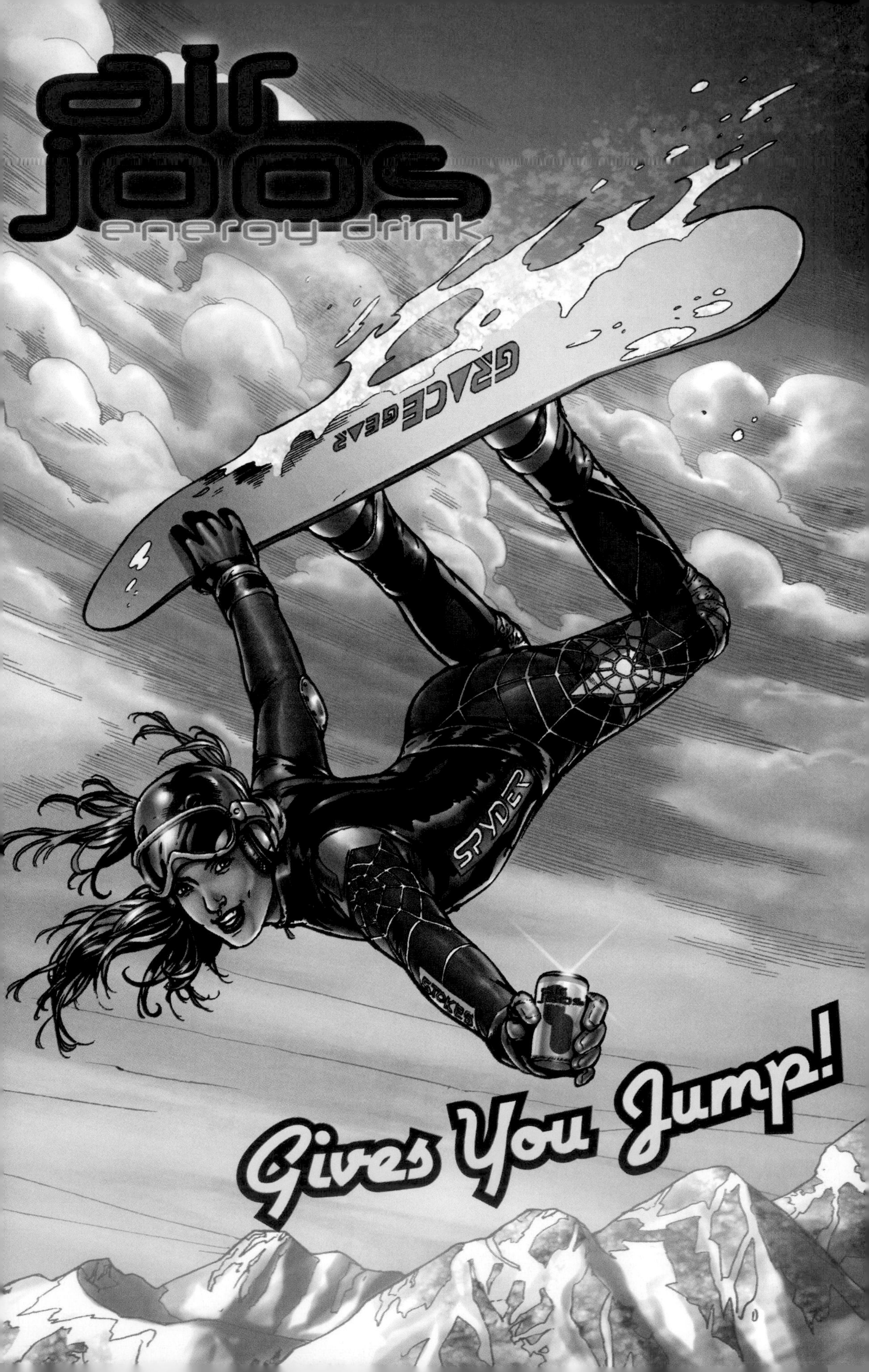
air joos
energy drink
GRACE GEAR
SPYDER
STOKES
Gives You Jump!

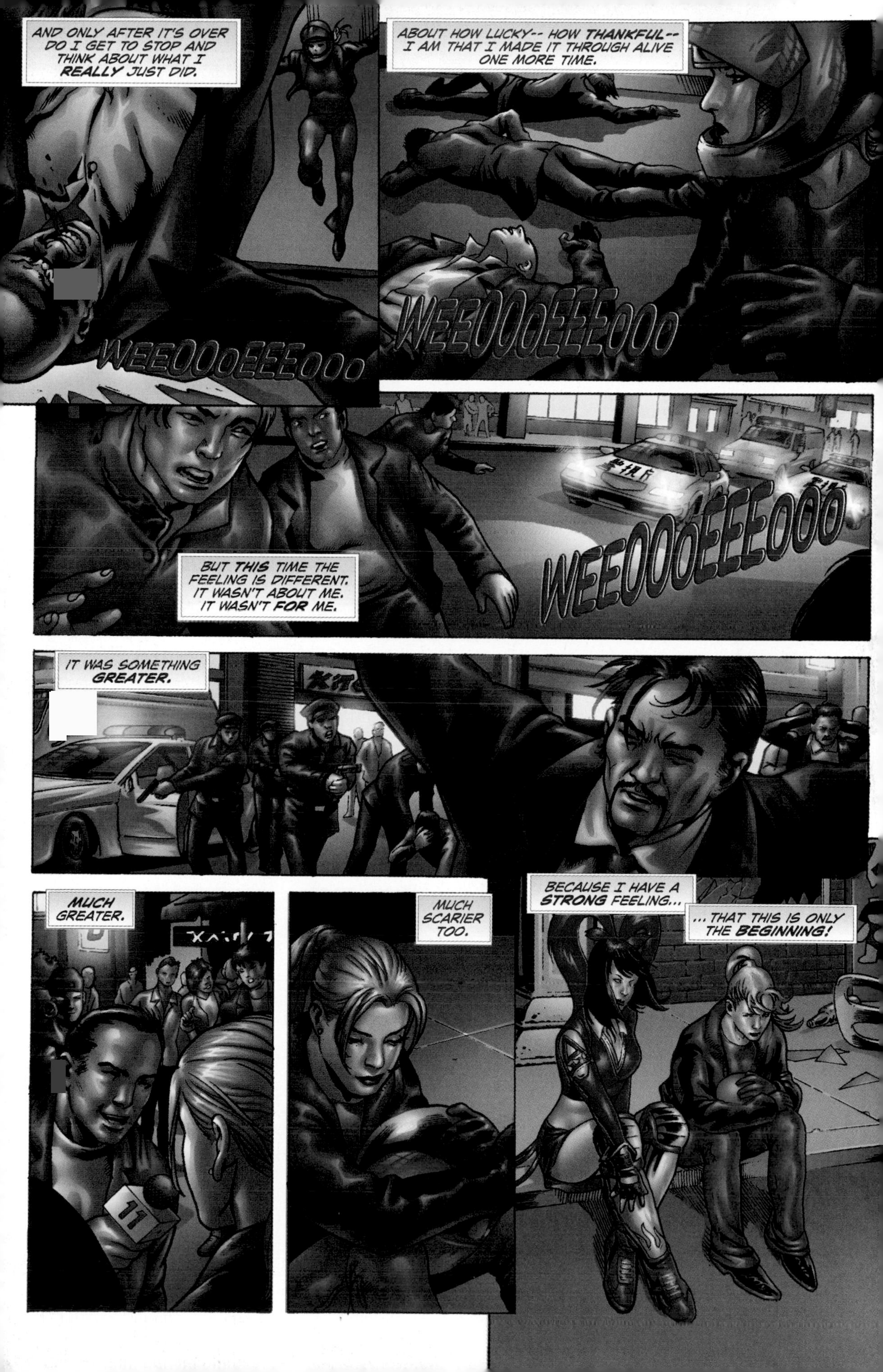
AND ONLY AFTER IT'S OVER DO I GET TO STOP AND THINK ABOUT WHAT I REALLY JUST DID.
WEEOOOoEEEooo
ABOUT HOW LUCKY-- HOW THANKFUL-- I AM THAT I MADE IT THROUGH ALIVE ONE MORE TIME.
WEEOOOoEEEooo
BUT THIS TIME THE FEELING IS DIFFERENT. IT WASN'T ABOUT ME. IT WASN'T FOR ME.
WEEOOOoEEEOOO
IT WAS SOMETHING GREATER.
MUCH GREATER.
11
MUCH SCARIER TOO.
BECAUSE I HAVE A STRONG FEELING...
...THAT THIS IS ONLY THE BEGINNING!

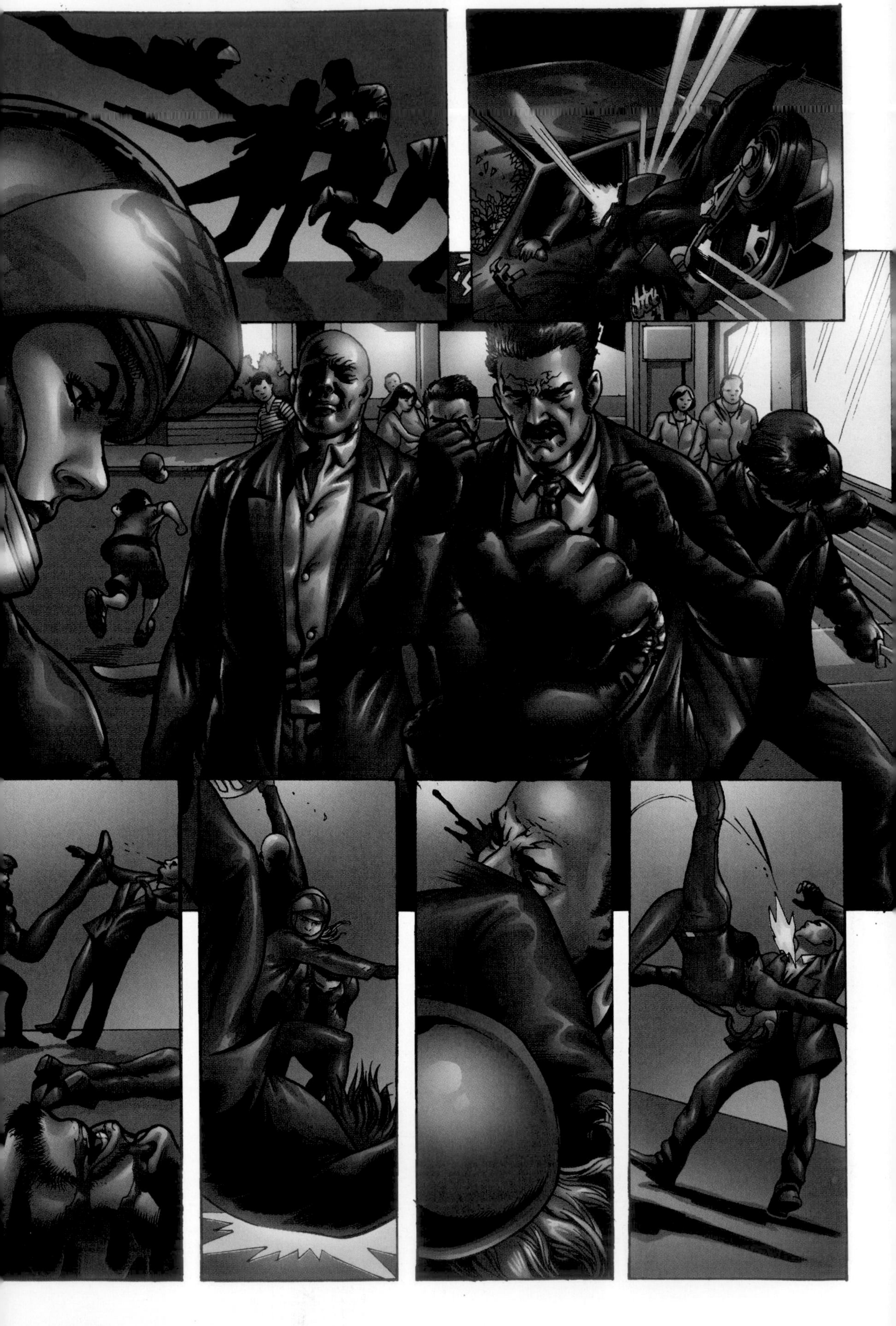

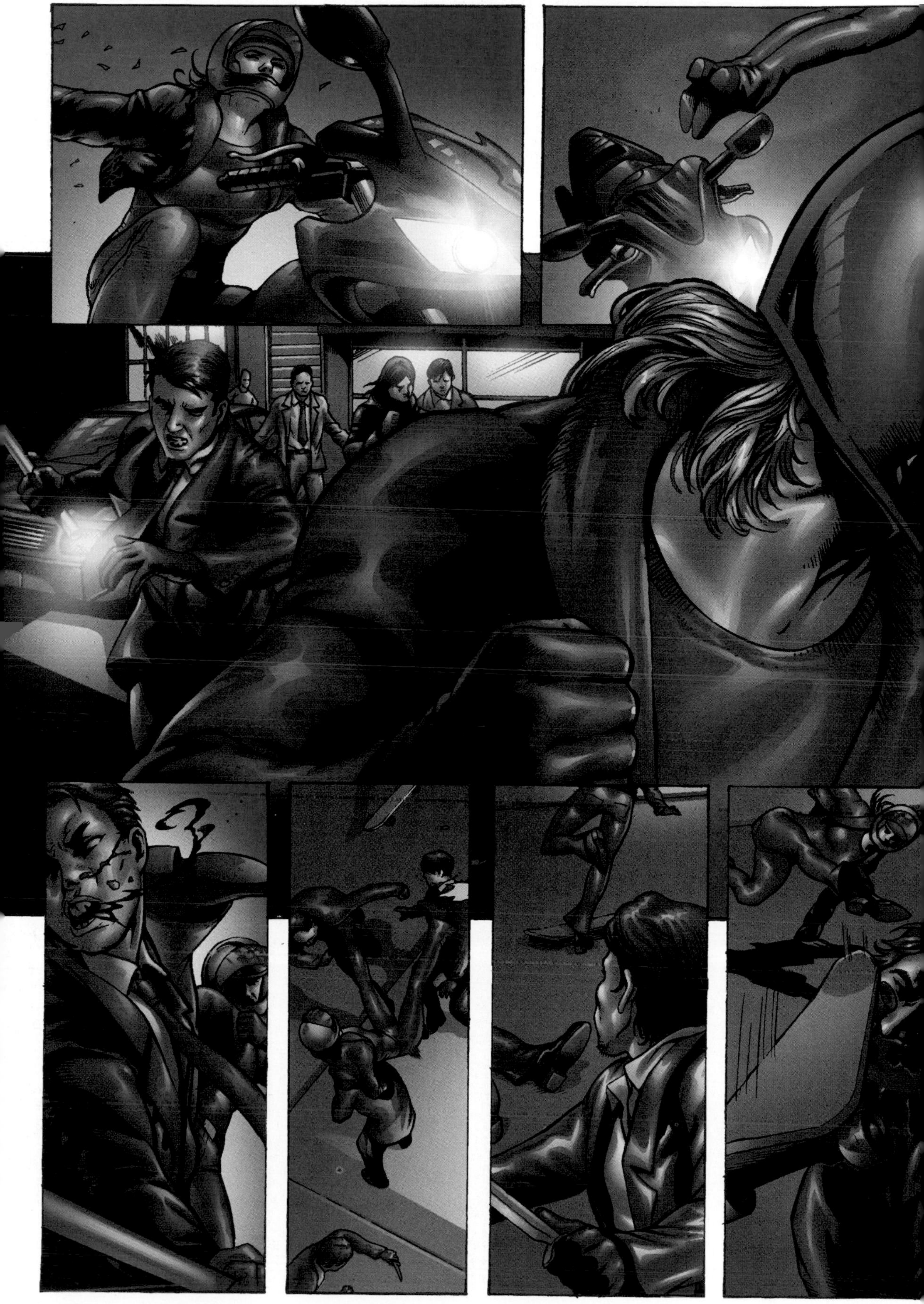

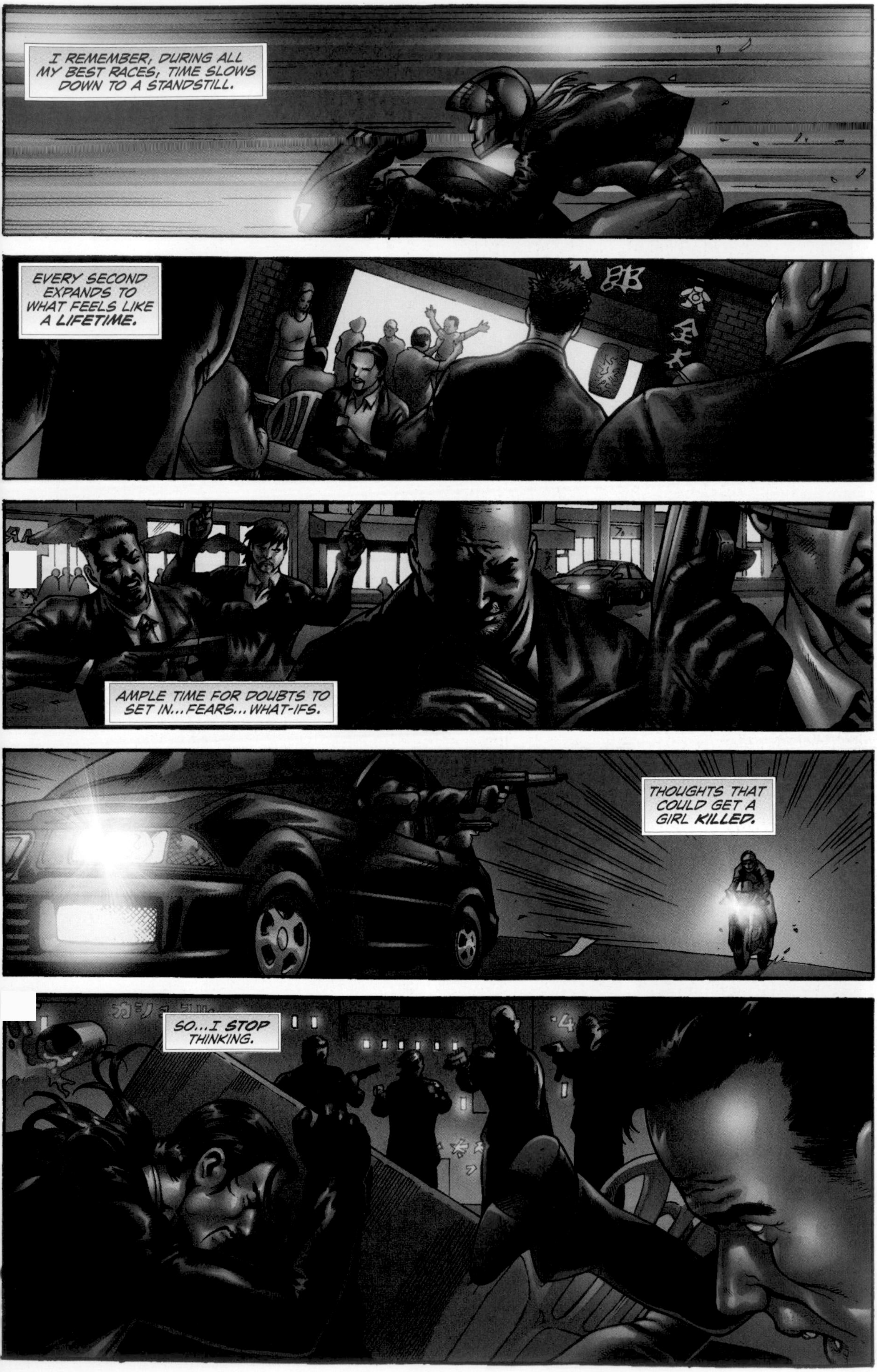
I REMEMBER, DURING ALL MY BEST RACES, TIME SLOWS DOWN TO A STANDSTILL.
EVERY SECOND EXPANDS TO WHAT FEELS LIKE A LIFETIME.
AMPLE TIME FOR DOUBTS TO SET IN... FEARS... WHAT-IFS.
THOUGHTS THAT COULD GET A GIRL KILLED.
SO... I STOP THINKING.

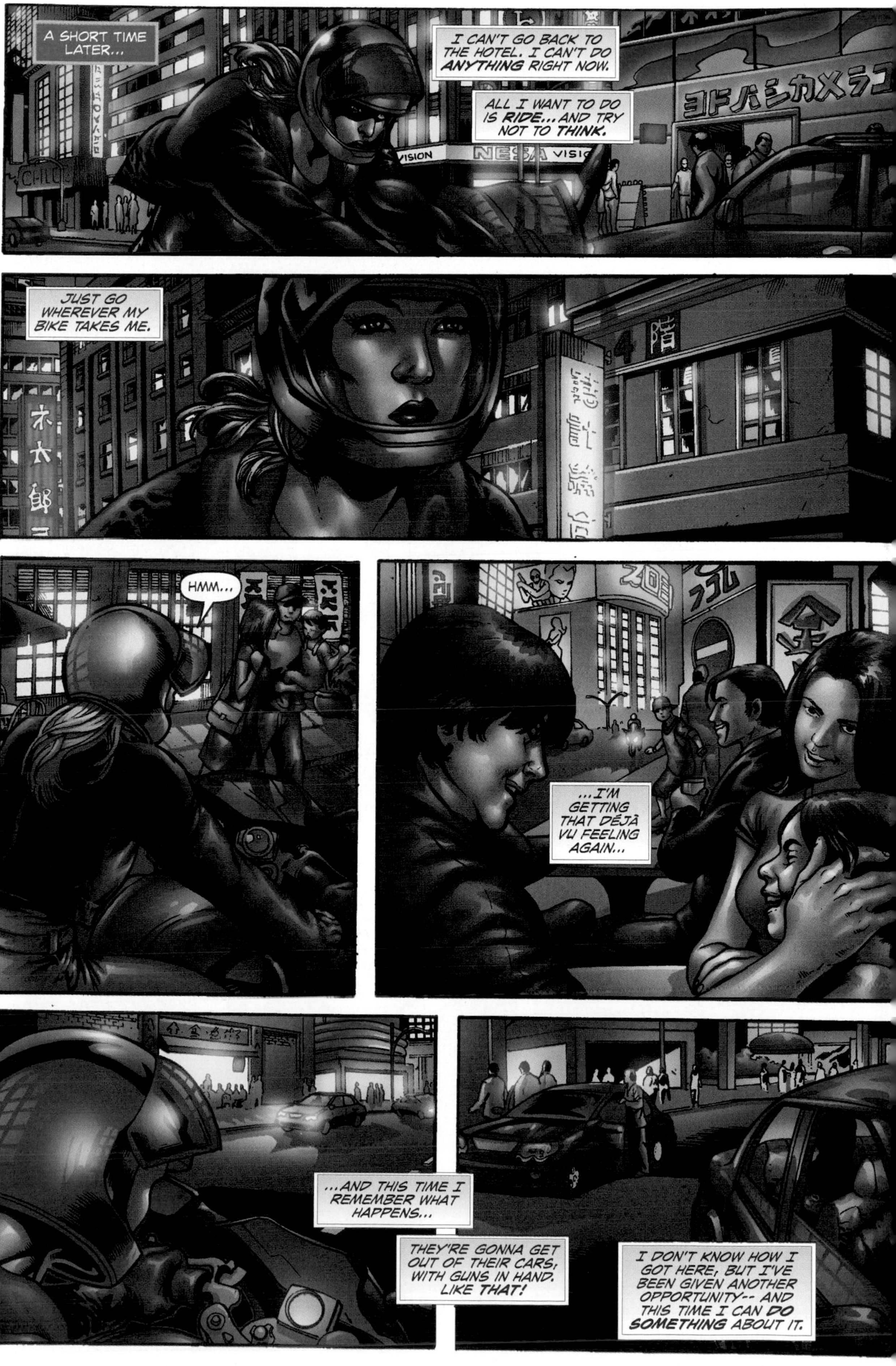
A SHORT TIME LATER...
I CAN'T GO BACK TO THE HOTEL. I CAN'T DO ANYTHING RIGHT NOW.
ALL I WANT TO DO IS RIDE... AND TRY NOT TO THINK.
ヨドバシカメラ
VISION
NESA VISION
JUST GO WHEREVER MY BIKE TAKES ME.
4階
HMM...
...I'M GETTING THAT DÉJÀ VU FEELING AGAIN...
...AND THIS TIME I REMEMBER WHAT HAPPENS...
THEY'RE GONNA GET OUT OF THEIR CARS, WITH GUNS IN HAND. LIKE THAT!
I DON'T KNOW HOW I GOT HERE, BUT I'VE BEEN GIVEN ANOTHER OPPORTUNITY-- AND THIS TIME I CAN DO SOMETHING ABOUT IT.

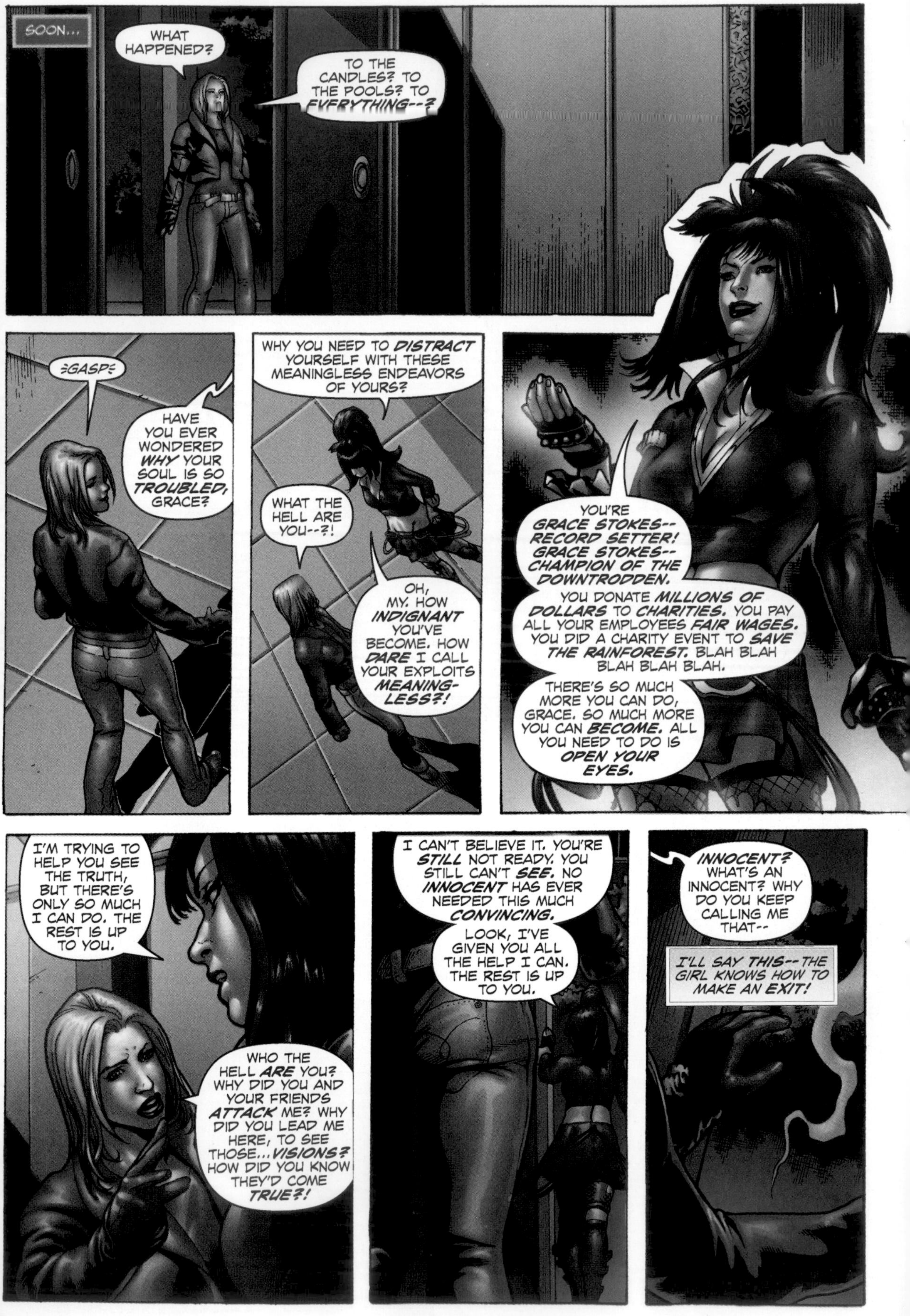
SOON...
WHAT HAPPENED?
TO THE CANDLES? TO THE POOLS? TO EVERYTHING--?
=GASP=
HAVE YOU EVER WONDERED WHY YOUR SOUL IS SO TROUBLED, GRACE?
WHY YOU NEED TO DISTRACT YOURSELF WITH THESE MEANINGLESS ENDEAVORS OF YOURS?
WHAT THE HELL ARE YOU--?!
OH, MY. HOW INDIGNANT YOU'VE BECOME. HOW DARE I CALL YOUR EXPLOITS MEANING-LESS?!
YOU'RE GRACE STOKES-- RECORD SETTER! GRACE STOKES-- CHAMPION OF THE DOWNTRODDEN.
YOU DONATE MILLIONS OF DOLLARS TO CHARITIES. YOU PAY ALL YOUR EMPLOYEES FAIR WAGES. YOU DID A CHARITY EVENT TO SAVE THE RAINFOREST. BLAH BLAH BLAH BLAH BLAH.
THERE'S SO MUCH MORE YOU CAN DO, GRACE. SO MUCH MORE YOU CAN BECOME. ALL YOU NEED TO DO IS OPEN YOUR EYES.
I'M TRYING TO HELP YOU SEE THE TRUTH, BUT THERE'S ONLY SO MUCH I CAN DO. THE REST IS UP TO YOU.
WHO THE HELL ARE YOU? WHY DID YOU AND YOUR FRIENDS ATTACK ME? WHY DID YOU LEAD ME HERE, TO SEE THOSE...VISIONS? HOW DID YOU KNOW THEY'D COME TRUE?!
I CAN'T BELIEVE IT. YOU'RE STILL NOT READY. YOU STILL CAN'T SEE. NO INNOCENT HAS EVER NEEDED THIS MUCH CONVINCING.
LOOK, I'VE GIVEN YOU ALL THE HELP I CAN. THE REST IS UP TO YOU.
INNOCENT? WHAT'S AN INNOCENT? WHY DO YOU KEEP CALLING ME THAT--
I'LL SAY THIS--THE GIRL KNOWS HOW TO MAKE AN EXIT!

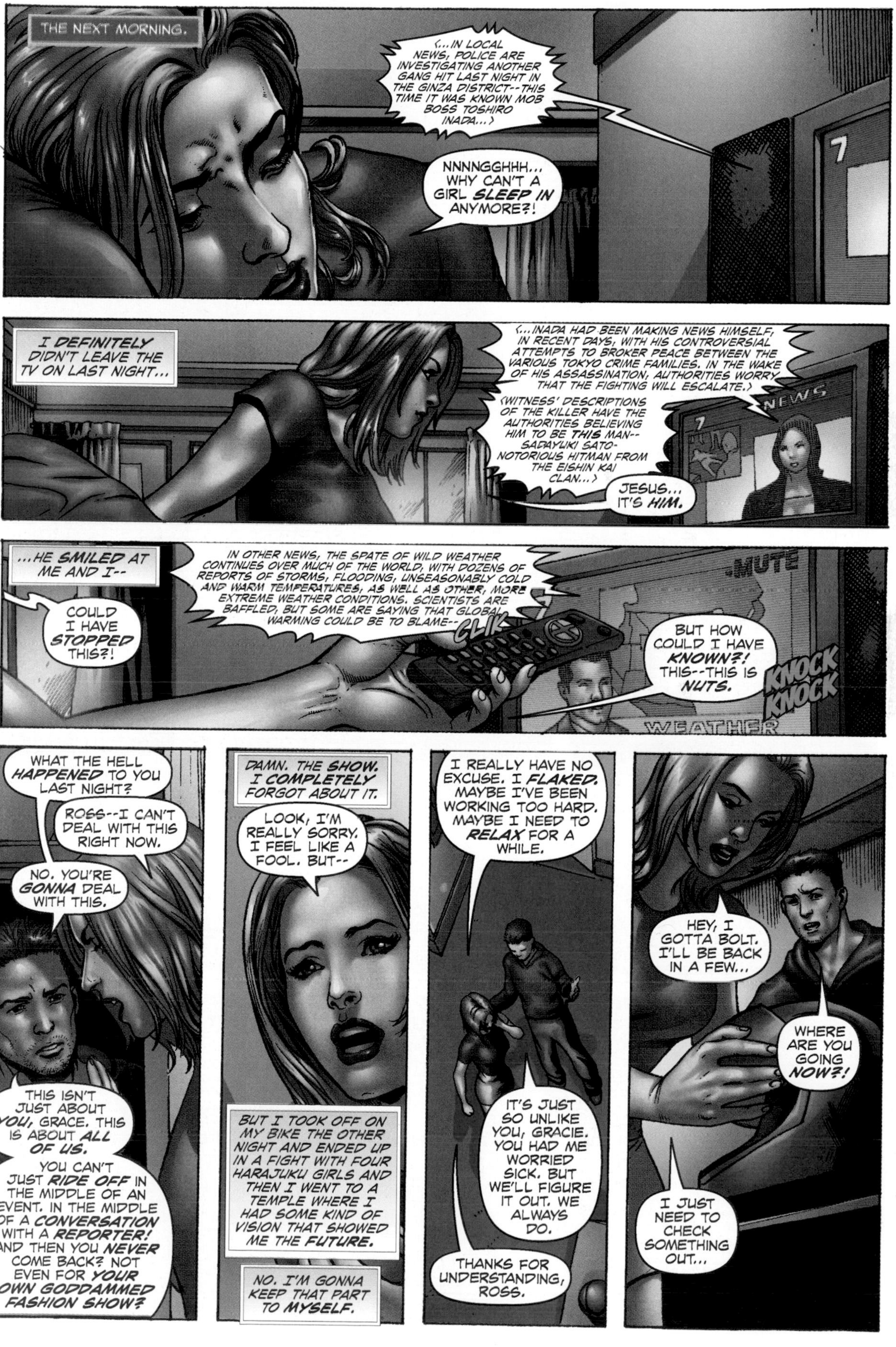
THE NEXT MORNING.
‹...IN LOCAL NEWS, POLICE ARE INVESTIGATING ANOTHER GANG HIT LAST NIGHT IN THE GINZA DISTRICT--THIS TIME IT WAS KNOWN MOB BOSS TOSHIRO INADA...›
NNNNGGHHH... WHY CAN'T A GIRL SLEEP IN ANYMORE?!
7
I DEFINITELY DIDN'T LEAVE THE TV ON LAST NIGHT...
‹...INADA HAD BEEN MAKING NEWS HIMSELF, IN RECENT DAYS, WITH HIS CONTROVERSIAL ATTEMPTS TO BROKER PEACE BETWEEN THE VARIOUS TOKYO CRIME FAMILIES. IN THE WAKE OF HIS ASSASSINATION, AUTHORITIES WORRY THAT THE FIGHTING WILL ESCALATE.›
‹WITNESS' DESCRIPTIONS OF THE KILLER HAVE THE AUTHORITIES BELIEVING HIM TO BE THIS MAN--SADAYUKI SATO-NOTORIOUS HITMAN FROM THE EISHIN KAI CLAN...›
NEWS
7
JESUS... IT'S HIM.
...HE SMILED AT ME AND I--
COULD I HAVE STOPPED THIS?!
IN OTHER NEWS, THE SPATE OF WILD WEATHER CONTINUES OVER MUCH OF THE WORLD, WITH DOZENS OF REPORTS OF STORMS, FLOODING, UNSEASONABLY COLD AND WARM TEMPERATURES, AS WELL AS OTHER, MORE EXTREME WEATHER CONDITIONS. SCIENTISTS ARE BAFFLED, BUT SOME ARE SAYING THAT GLOBAL WARMING COULD BE TO BLAME--
CLIK
MUTE
BUT HOW COULD I HAVE KNOWN?! THIS--THIS IS NUTS.
KNOCK KNOCK
WEATHER
WHAT THE HELL HAPPENED TO YOU LAST NIGHT?
ROSS--I CAN'T DEAL WITH THIS RIGHT NOW.
NO. YOU'RE GONNA DEAL WITH THIS.
THIS ISN'T JUST ABOUT YOU, GRACE. THIS IS ABOUT ALL OF US.
YOU CAN'T JUST RIDE OFF IN THE MIDDLE OF AN EVENT. IN THE MIDDLE OF A CONVERSATION WITH A REPORTER! AND THEN YOU NEVER COME BACK? NOT EVEN FOR YOUR OWN GODDAMED FASHION SHOW?
DAMN. THE SHOW. I COMPLETELY FORGOT ABOUT IT.
LOOK, I'M REALLY SORRY. I FEEL LIKE A FOOL. BUT--
BUT I TOOK OFF ON MY BIKE THE OTHER NIGHT AND ENDED UP IN A FIGHT WITH FOUR HARAJUKU GIRLS AND THEN I WENT TO A TEMPLE WHERE I HAD SOME KIND OF VISION THAT SHOWED ME THE FUTURE.
NO. I'M GONNA KEEP THAT PART TO MYSELF.
I REALLY HAVE NO EXCUSE. I FLAKED. MAYBE I'VE BEEN WORKING TOO HARD. MAYBE I NEED TO RELAX FOR A WHILE.
IT'S JUST SO UNLIKE YOU, GRACIE. YOU HAD ME WORRIED SICK. BUT WE'LL FIGURE IT OUT. WE ALWAYS DO.
THANKS FOR UNDERSTANDING, ROSS.
HEY, I GOTTA BOLT. I'LL BE BACK IN A FEW...
WHERE ARE YOU GOING NOW?!
I JUST NEED TO CHECK SOMETHING OUT...

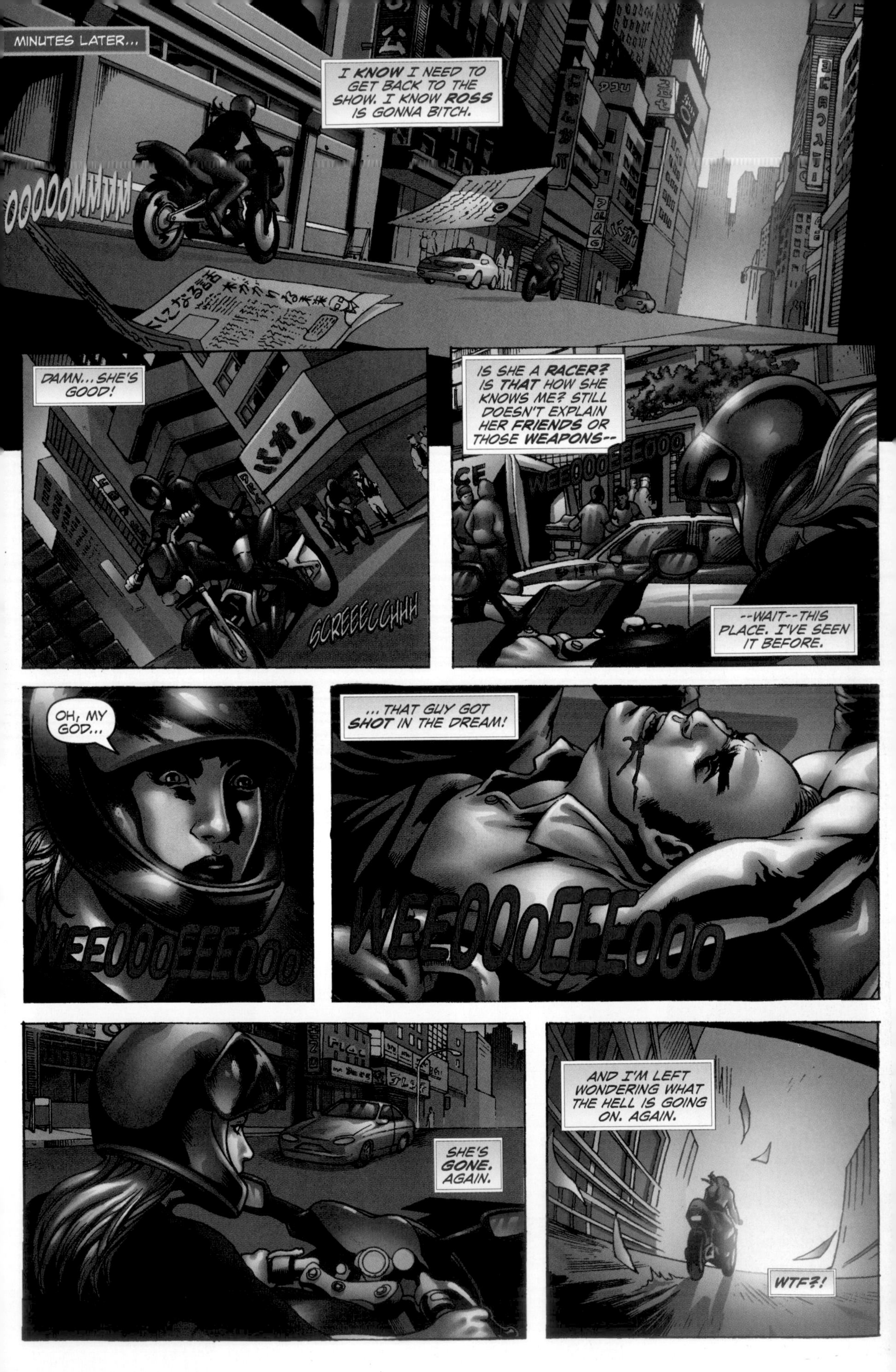
MINUTES LATER...
I KNOW I NEED TO GET BACK TO THE SHOW. I KNOW ROSS IS GONNA BITCH.
OOOOOMMMM
DAMN...SHE'S GOOD!
SCREEECCHHH
IS SHE A RACER? IS THAT HOW SHE KNOWS ME? STILL DOESN'T EXPLAIN HER FRIENDS OR THOSE WEAPONS--
WEEOOOEEEOOO
--WAIT--THIS PLACE. I'VE SEEN IT BEFORE.
OH, MY GOD...
WEEOOOEEEOOO
...THAT GUY GOT SHOT IN THE DREAM!
WEEOOOEEEOOO
SHE'S GONE. AGAIN.
AND I'M LEFT WONDERING WHAT THE HELL IS GOING ON. AGAIN.
WTF?!

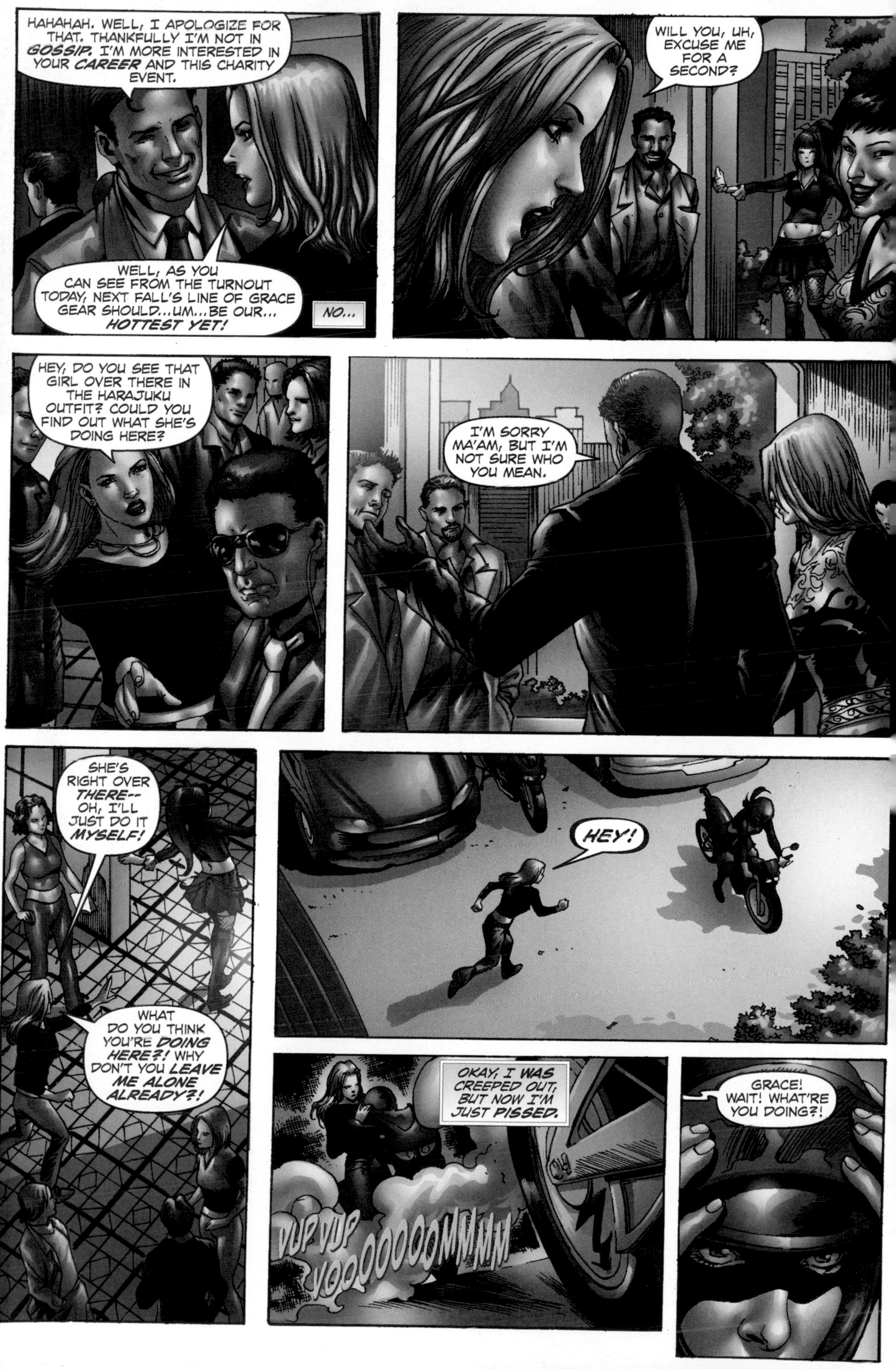
HAHAHAH. WELL, I APOLOGIZE FOR THAT. THANKFULLY I'M NOT IN GOSSIP. I'M MORE INTERESTED IN YOUR CAREER AND THIS CHARITY EVENT.
WELL, AS YOU CAN SEE FROM THE TURNOUT TODAY, NEXT FALL'S LINE OF GRACE GEAR SHOULD...UM...BE OUR... HOTTEST YET!
NO...
WILL YOU, UH, EXCUSE ME FOR A SECOND?
HEY, DO YOU SEE THAT GIRL OVER THERE IN THE HARAJUKU OUTFIT? COULD YOU FIND OUT WHAT SHE'S DOING HERE?
I'M SORRY MA'AM, BUT I'M NOT SURE WHO YOU MEAN.
SHE'S RIGHT OVER THERE-- OH, I'LL JUST DO IT MYSELF!
WHAT DO YOU THINK YOU'RE DOING HERE?! WHY DON'T YOU LEAVE ME ALONE ALREADY?!
HEY!
OKAY, I WAS CREEPED OUT, BUT NOW I'M JUST PISSED.
VUP VUP
VOOOOOOOMMMM
GRACE! WAIT! WHAT'RE YOU DOING?!

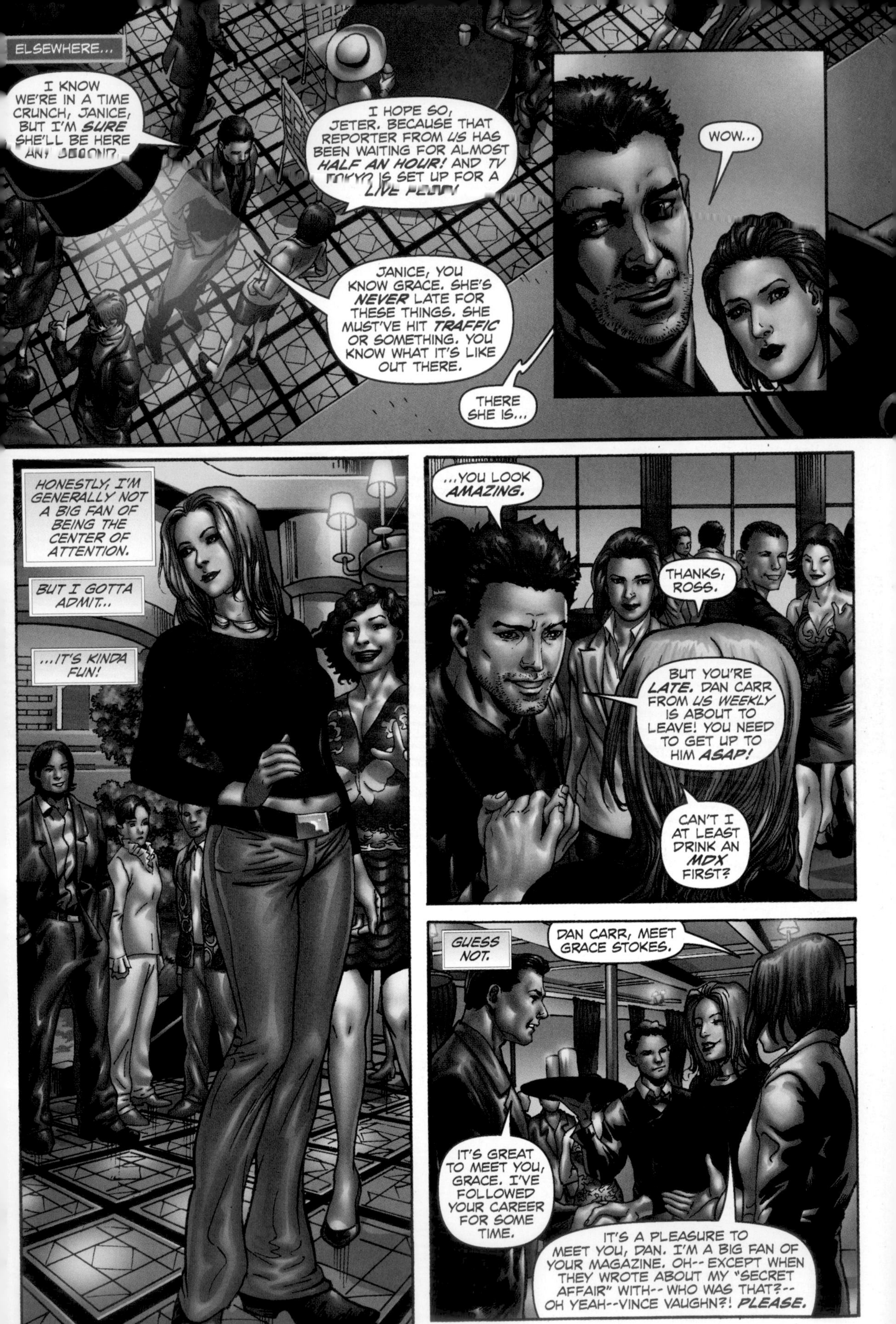
ELSEWHERE...
I KNOW WE'RE IN A TIME CRUNCH, JANICE, BUT I'M *SURE* SHE'LL BE HERE
I HOPE SO, JETER. BECAUSE THAT REPORTER FROM *US* HAS BEEN WAITING FOR ALMOST *HALF AN HOUR!* AND TV TOKYO IS SET UP FOR A *LIVE*
WOW...
JANICE, YOU KNOW GRACE. SHE'S *NEVER* LATE FOR THESE THINGS. SHE MUST'VE HIT *TRAFFIC* OR SOMETHING. YOU KNOW WHAT IT'S LIKE OUT THERE.
THERE SHE IS...
HONESTLY, I'M GENERALLY NOT A BIG FAN OF BEING THE CENTER OF ATTENTION.
BUT I GOTTA ADMIT...
...IT'S KINDA FUN!
...YOU LOOK *AMAZING.*
THANKS, ROSS.
BUT YOU'RE *LATE.* DAN CARR FROM *US WEEKLY* IS ABOUT TO LEAVE! YOU NEED TO GET UP TO HIM *ASAP!*
CAN'T I AT LEAST DRINK AN *MDX* FIRST?
GUESS NOT.
DAN CARR, MEET GRACE STOKES.
IT'S GREAT TO MEET YOU, GRACE. I'VE FOLLOWED YOUR CAREER FOR SOME TIME.
IT'S A PLEASURE TO MEET YOU, DAN. I'M A BIG FAN OF YOUR MAGAZINE. OH-- EXCEPT WHEN THEY WROTE ABOUT MY "SECRET AFFAIR" WITH-- WHO WAS THAT?-- OH YEAH--VINCE VAUGHN?! *PLEASE.*

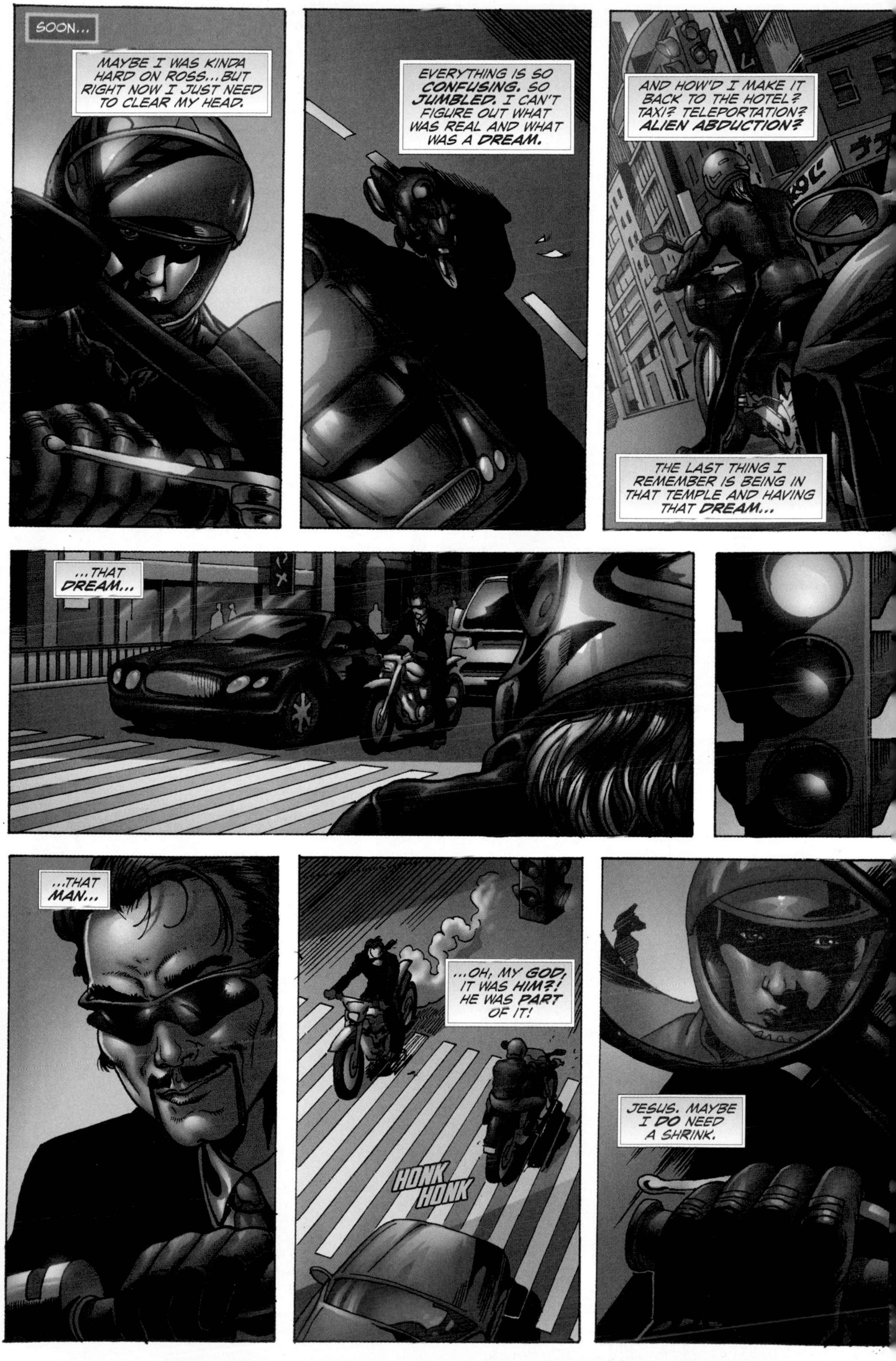
SOON...
MAYBE I WAS KINDA HARD ON ROSS... BUT RIGHT NOW I JUST NEED TO CLEAR MY HEAD.
EVERYTHING IS SO CONFUSING. SO JUMBLED. I CAN'T FIGURE OUT WHAT WAS REAL AND WHAT WAS A DREAM.
AND HOW'D I MAKE IT BACK TO THE HOTEL? TAXI? TELEPORTATION? ALIEN ABDUCTION?
THE LAST THING I REMEMBER IS BEING IN THAT TEMPLE AND HAVING THAT DREAM...
...THAT DREAM...
...THAT MAN...
...OH, MY GOD, IT WAS HIM?! HE WAS PART OF IT!
HONK HONK
JESUS. MAYBE I DO NEED A SHRINK.

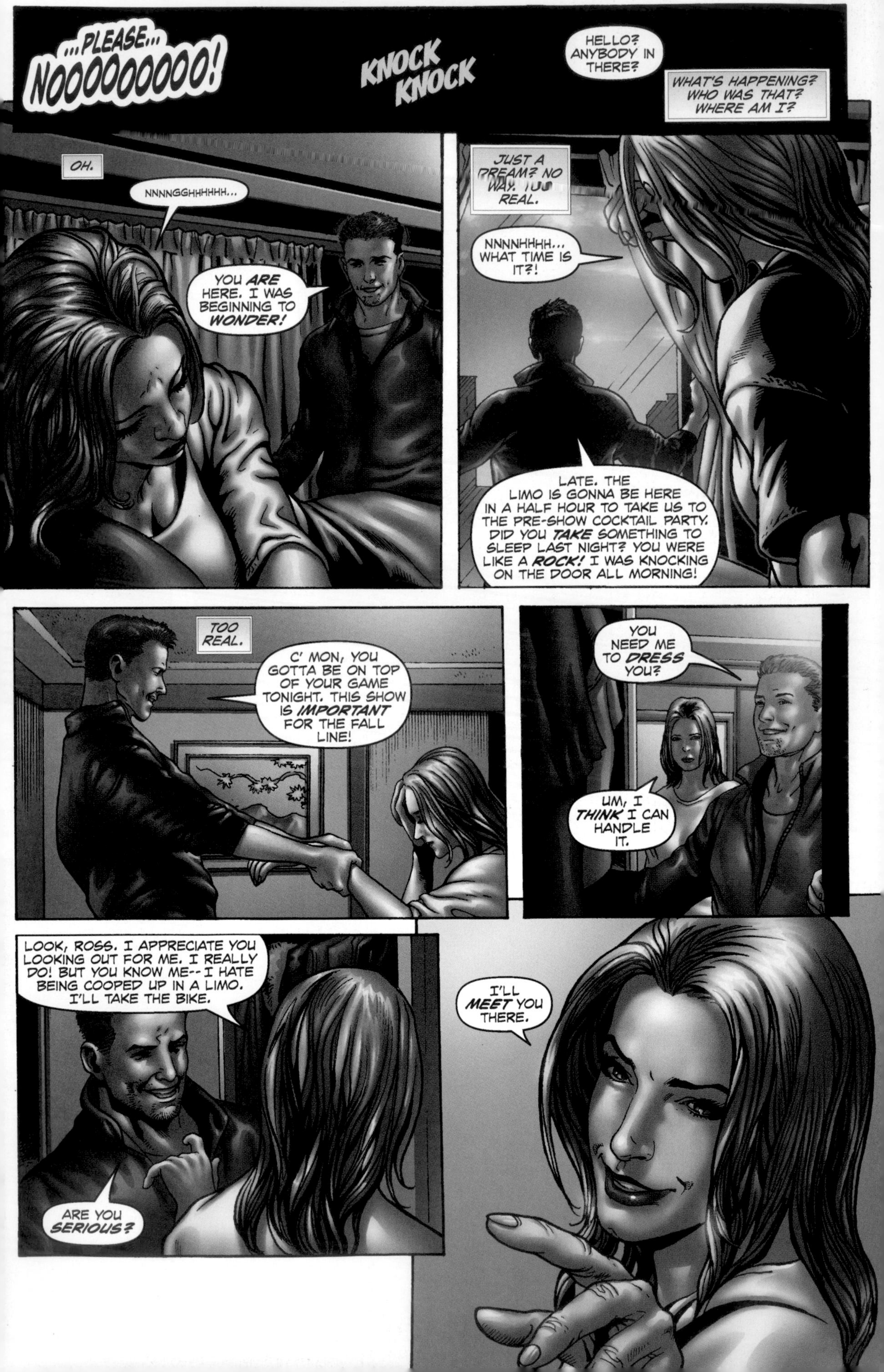
...PLEASE... NOOOOOOOOO!
KNOCK KNOCK
HELLO? ANYBODY IN THERE?
WHAT'S HAPPENING? WHO WAS THAT? WHERE AM I?
OH.
NNNNGGHHHHHH...
YOU ARE HERE. I WAS BEGINNING TO WONDER!
JUST A DREAM? NO WAY. TOO REAL.
NNNNHHHH... WHAT TIME IS IT?!
LATE. THE LIMO IS GONNA BE HERE IN A HALF HOUR TO TAKE US TO THE PRE-SHOW COCKTAIL PARTY. DID YOU TAKE SOMETHING TO SLEEP LAST NIGHT? YOU WERE LIKE A ROCK! I WAS KNOCKING ON THE DOOR ALL MORNING!
TOO REAL.
C' MON, YOU GOTTA BE ON TOP OF YOUR GAME TONIGHT. THIS SHOW IS IMPORTANT FOR THE FALL LINE!
YOU NEED ME TO DRESS YOU?
UM, I THINK I CAN HANDLE IT.
LOOK, ROSS. I APPRECIATE YOU LOOKING OUT FOR ME. I REALLY DO! BUT YOU KNOW ME-- I HATE BEING COOPED UP IN A LIMO. I'LL TAKE THE BIKE.
ARE YOU SERIOUS?
I'LL MEET YOU THERE.

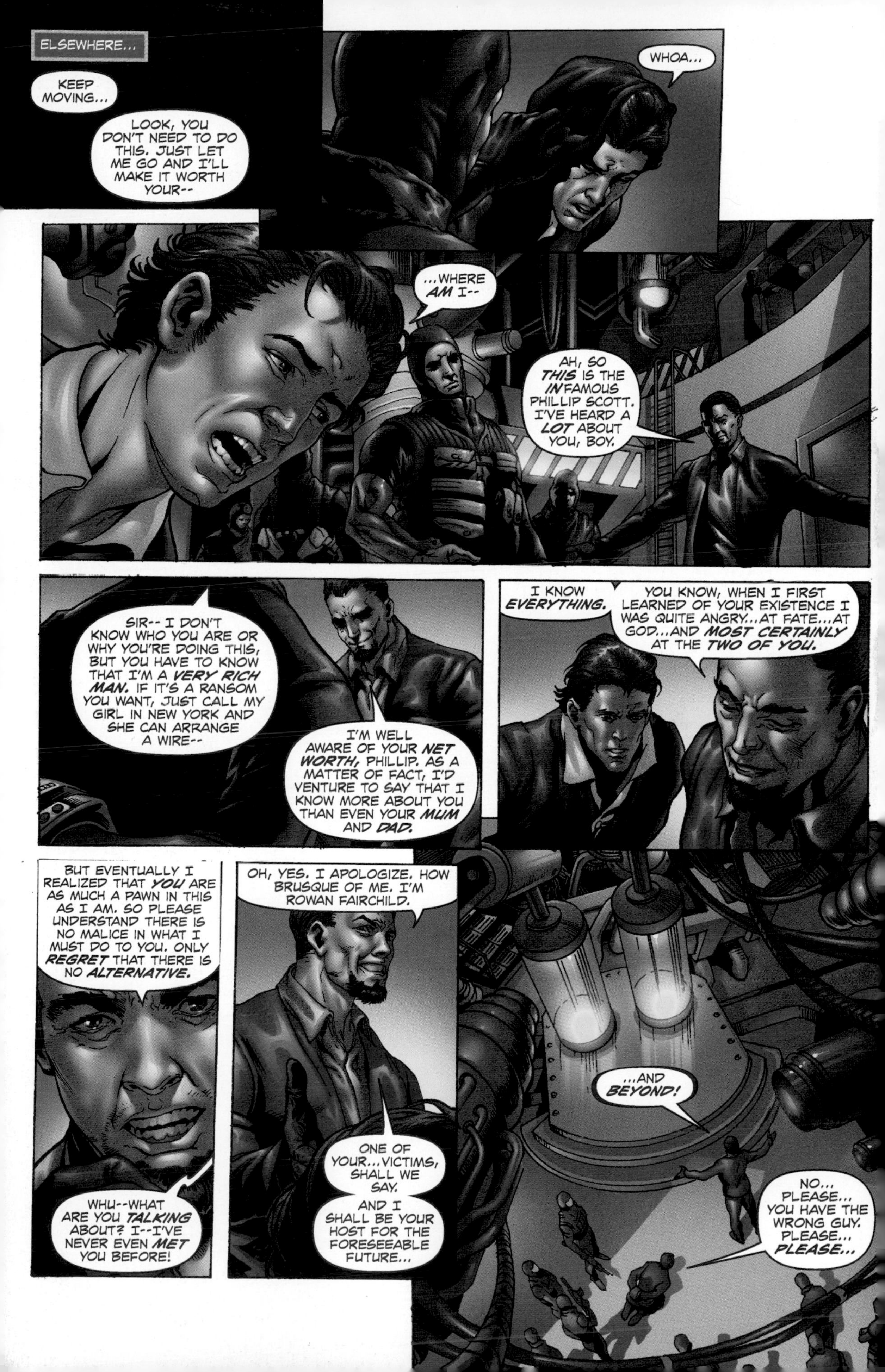
ELSEWHERE...
KEEP MOVING...
LOOK, YOU DON'T NEED TO DO THIS. JUST LET ME GO AND I'LL MAKE IT WORTH YOUR--
WHOA...
...WHERE AM I--
AH, SO THIS IS THE INFAMOUS PHILLIP SCOTT. I'VE HEARD A LOT ABOUT YOU, BOY.
SIR-- I DON'T KNOW WHO YOU ARE OR WHY YOU'RE DOING THIS, BUT YOU HAVE TO KNOW THAT I'M A VERY RICH MAN. IF IT'S A RANSOM YOU WANT, JUST CALL MY GIRL IN NEW YORK AND SHE CAN ARRANGE A WIRE--
I'M WELL AWARE OF YOUR NET WORTH, PHILLIP. AS A MATTER OF FACT, I'D VENTURE TO SAY THAT I KNOW MORE ABOUT YOU THAN EVEN YOUR MUM AND DAD.
I KNOW EVERYTHING.
YOU KNOW, WHEN I FIRST LEARNED OF YOUR EXISTENCE I WAS QUITE ANGRY...AT FATE...AT GOD...AND MOST CERTAINLY AT THE TWO OF YOU.
BUT EVENTUALLY I REALIZED THAT YOU ARE AS MUCH A PAWN IN THIS AS I AM. SO PLEASE UNDERSTAND THERE IS NO MALICE IN WHAT I MUST DO TO YOU. ONLY REGRET THAT THERE IS NO ALTERNATIVE.
WHU--WHAT ARE YOU TALKING ABOUT? I--I'VE NEVER EVEN MET YOU BEFORE!
OH, YES. I APOLOGIZE. HOW BRUSQUE OF ME. I'M ROWAN FAIRCHILD.
ONE OF YOUR...VICTIMS, SHALL WE SAY.
AND I SHALL BE YOUR HOST FOR THE FORESEEABLE FUTURE...
...AND BEYOND!
NO... PLEASE... YOU HAVE THE WRONG GUY. PLEASE... PLEASE...

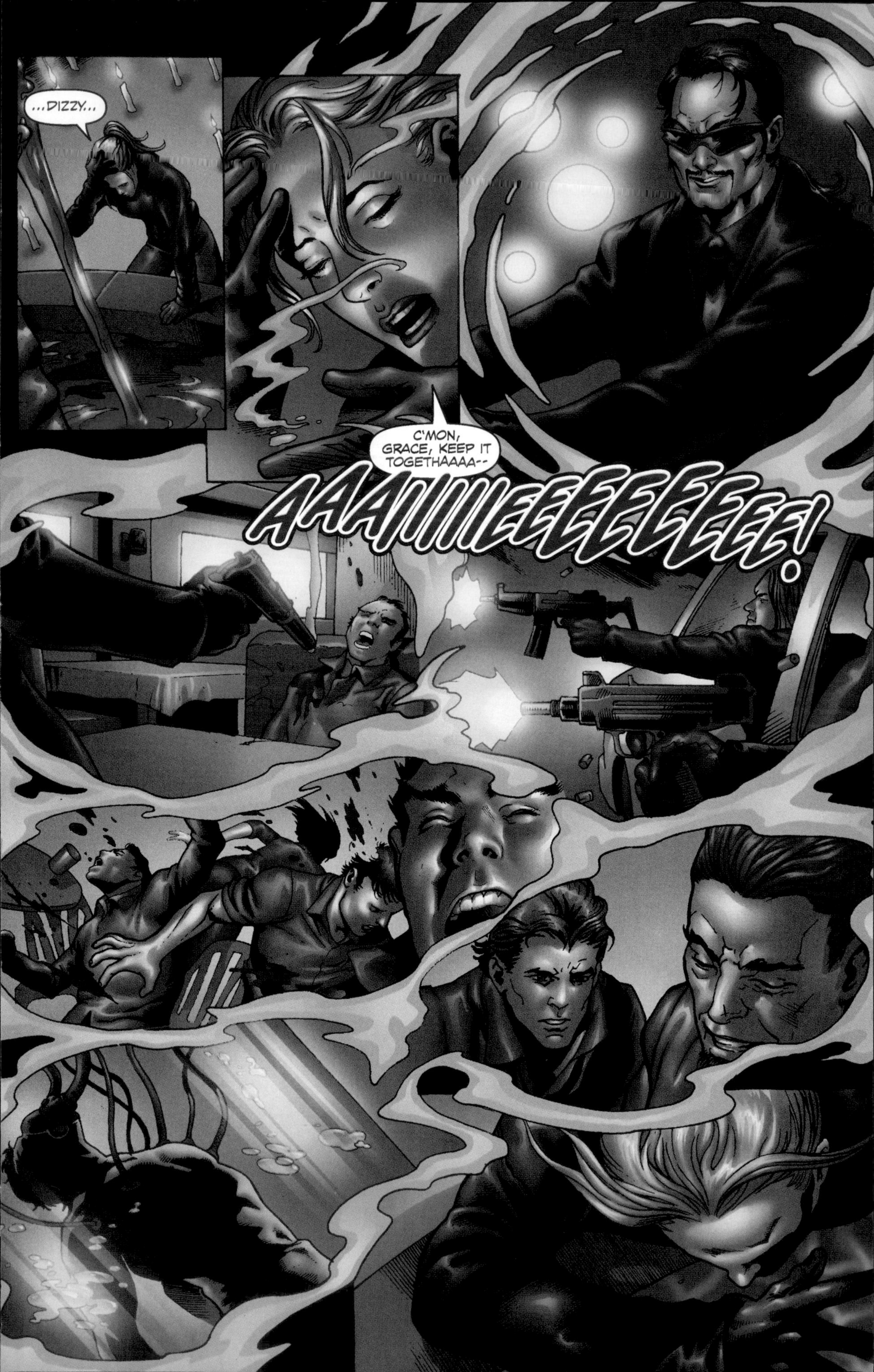
...DIZZY...
C'MON, GRACE, KEEP IT TOGETHAAAA--
AAAIIIIIEEEEEEEEE!

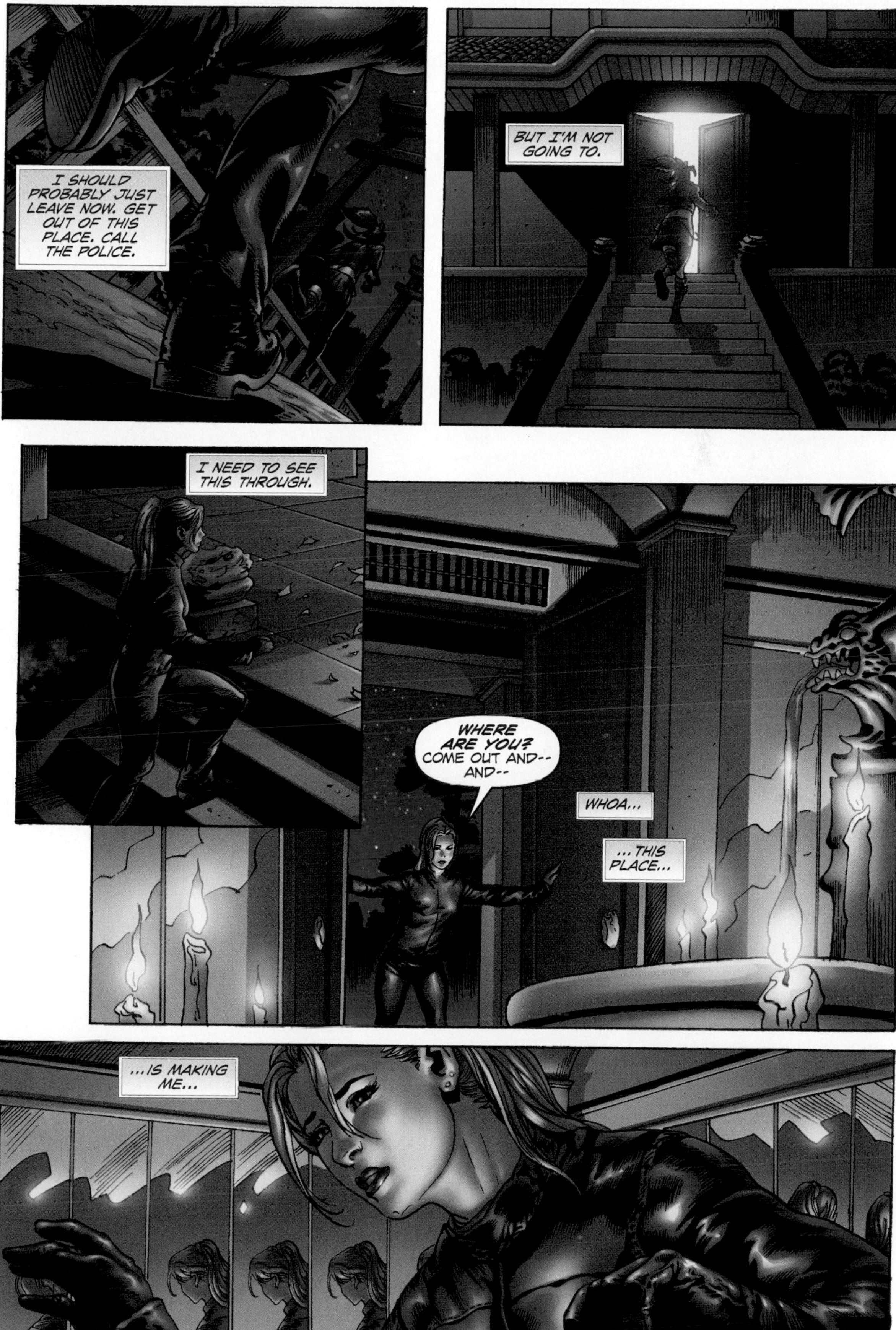
I SHOULD PROBABLY JUST LEAVE NOW. GET OUT OF THIS PLACE. CALL THE POLICE.
BUT I'M NOT GOING TO.
I NEED TO SEE THIS THROUGH.
WHERE ARE YOU? COME OUT AND-- AND--
WHOA...
...THIS PLACE...
...IS MAKING ME...

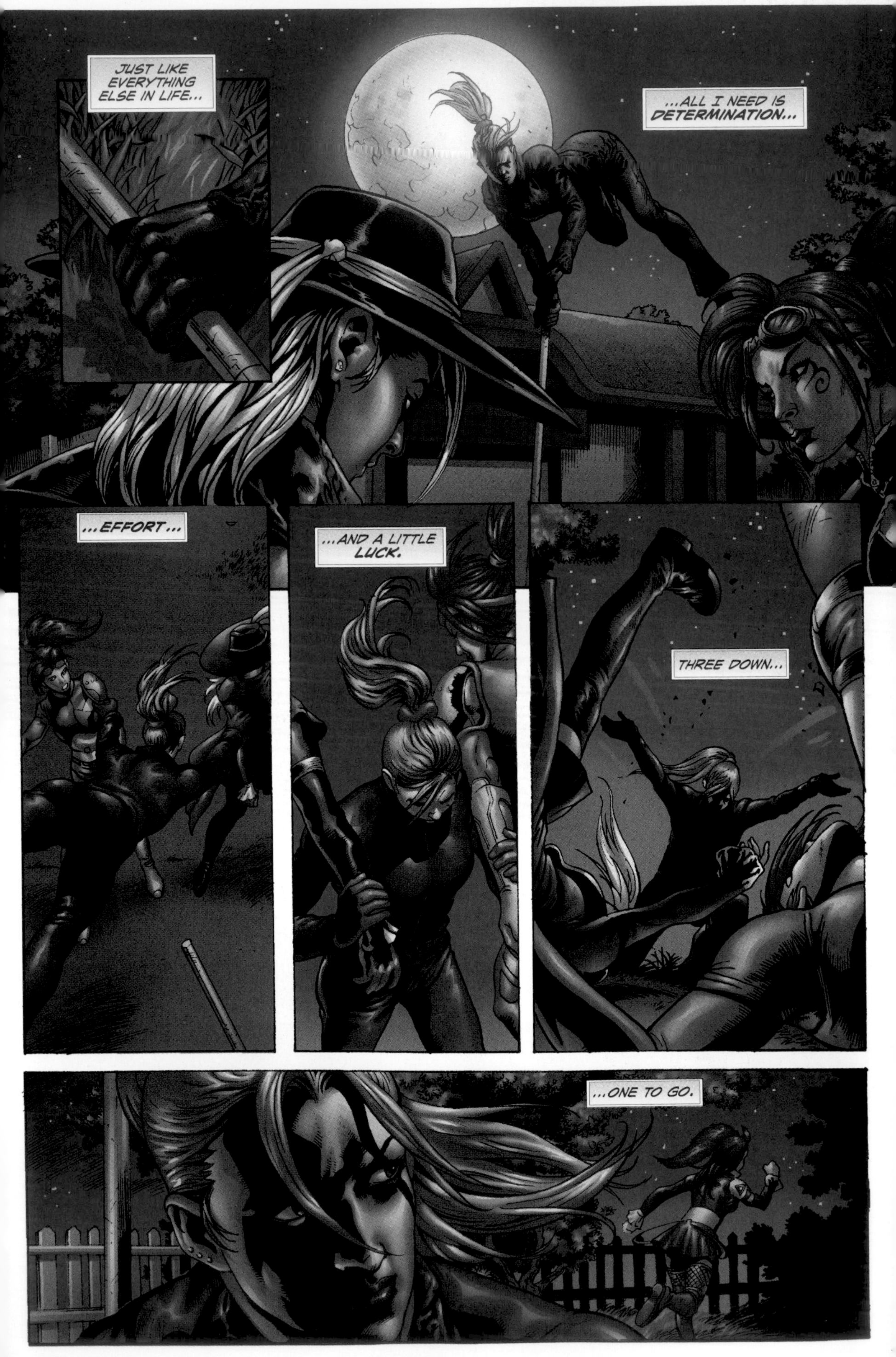
JUST LIKE EVERYTHING ELSE IN LIFE...
...ALL I NEED IS DETERMINATION...
...EFFORT...
...AND A LITTLE LUCK.
THREE DOWN...
...ONE TO GO.

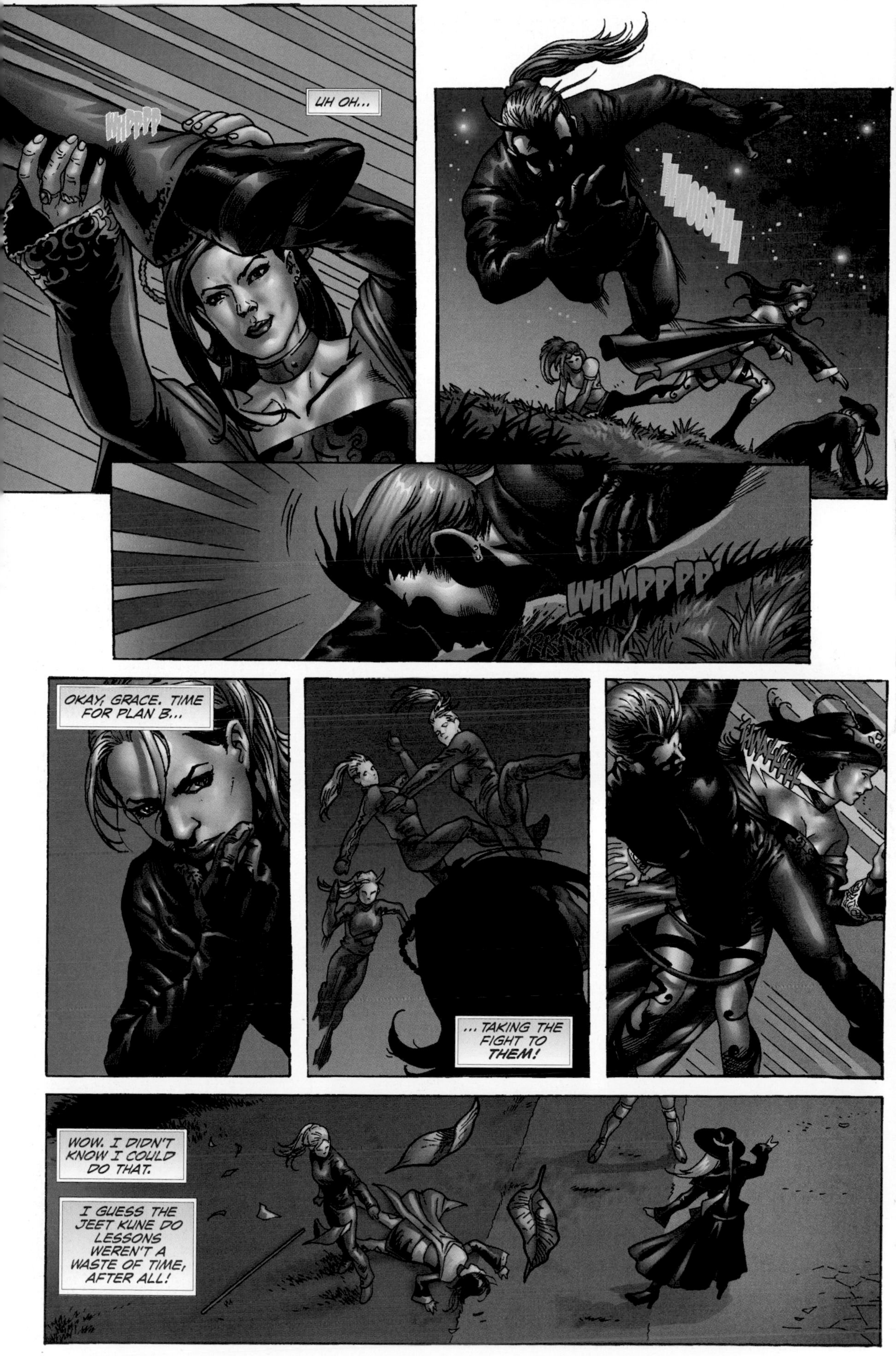
WHPPPP
UH OH...
THWOOSHHH
WHMPPPP
OKAY, GRACE. TIME FOR PLAN B...
...TAKING THE FIGHT TO THEM!
WOW. I DIDN'T KNOW I COULD DO THAT.
I GUESS THE JEET KUNE DO LESSONS WEREN'T A WASTE OF TIME, AFTER ALL!

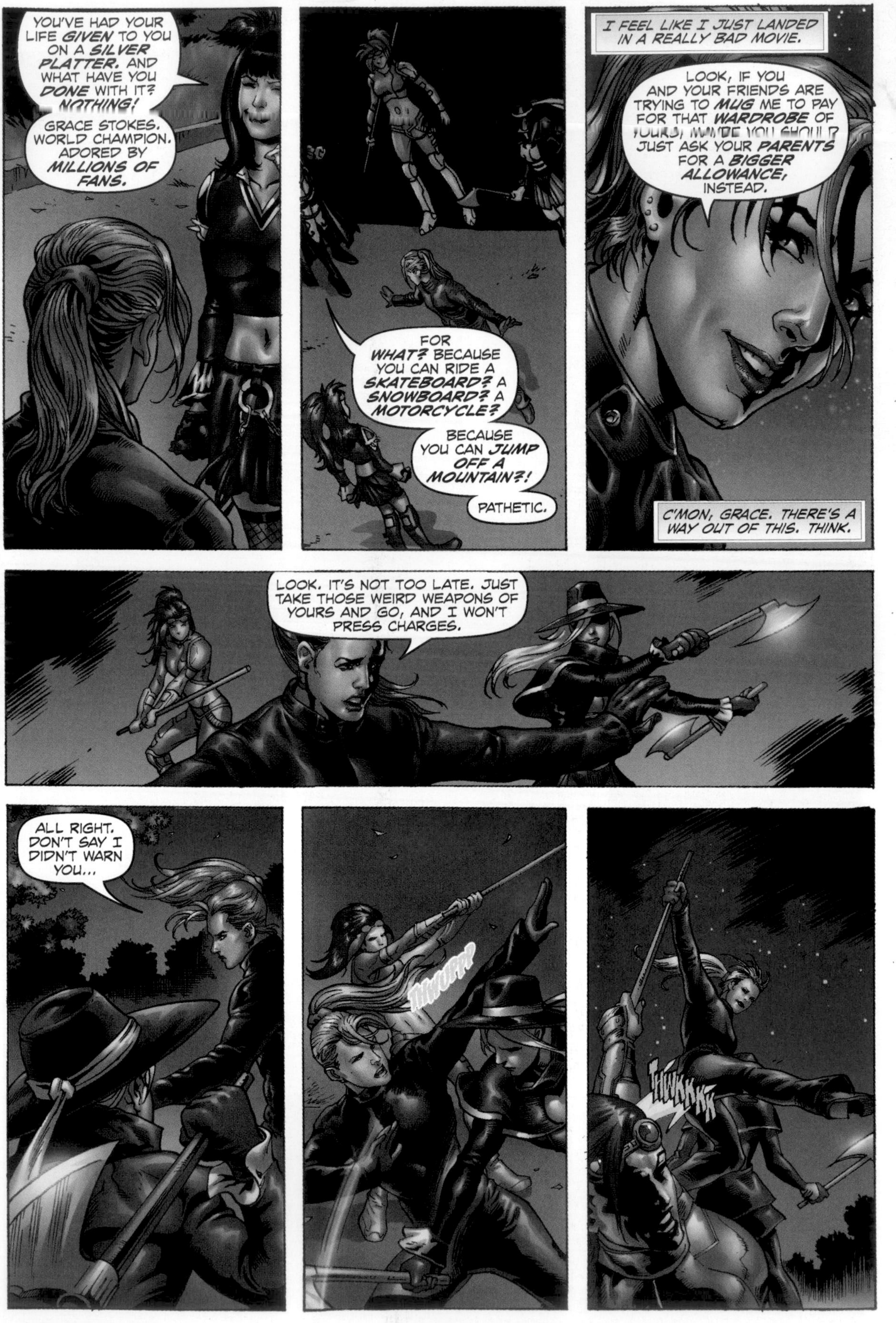
YOU'VE HAD YOUR LIFE GIVEN TO YOU ON A SILVER PLATTER. AND WHAT HAVE YOU DONE WITH IT? NOTHING!
GRACE STOKES. WORLD CHAMPION. ADORED BY MILLIONS OF FANS.
FOR WHAT? BECAUSE YOU CAN RIDE A SKATEBOARD? A SNOWBOARD? A MOTORCYCLE?
BECAUSE YOU CAN JUMP OFF A MOUNTAIN?!
PATHETIC.
I FEEL LIKE I JUST LANDED IN A REALLY BAD MOVIE.
LOOK, IF YOU AND YOUR FRIENDS ARE TRYING TO MUG ME TO PAY FOR THAT WARDROBE OF YOURS, MAYBE YOU SHOULD JUST ASK YOUR PARENTS FOR A BIGGER ALLOWANCE, INSTEAD.
C'MON, GRACE. THERE'S A WAY OUT OF THIS. THINK.
LOOK. IT'S NOT TOO LATE. JUST TAKE THOSE WEIRD WEAPONS OF YOURS AND GO, AND I WON'T PRESS CHARGES.
ALL RIGHT. DON'T SAY I DIDN'T WARN YOU...
THWUPP!
THWAKKK

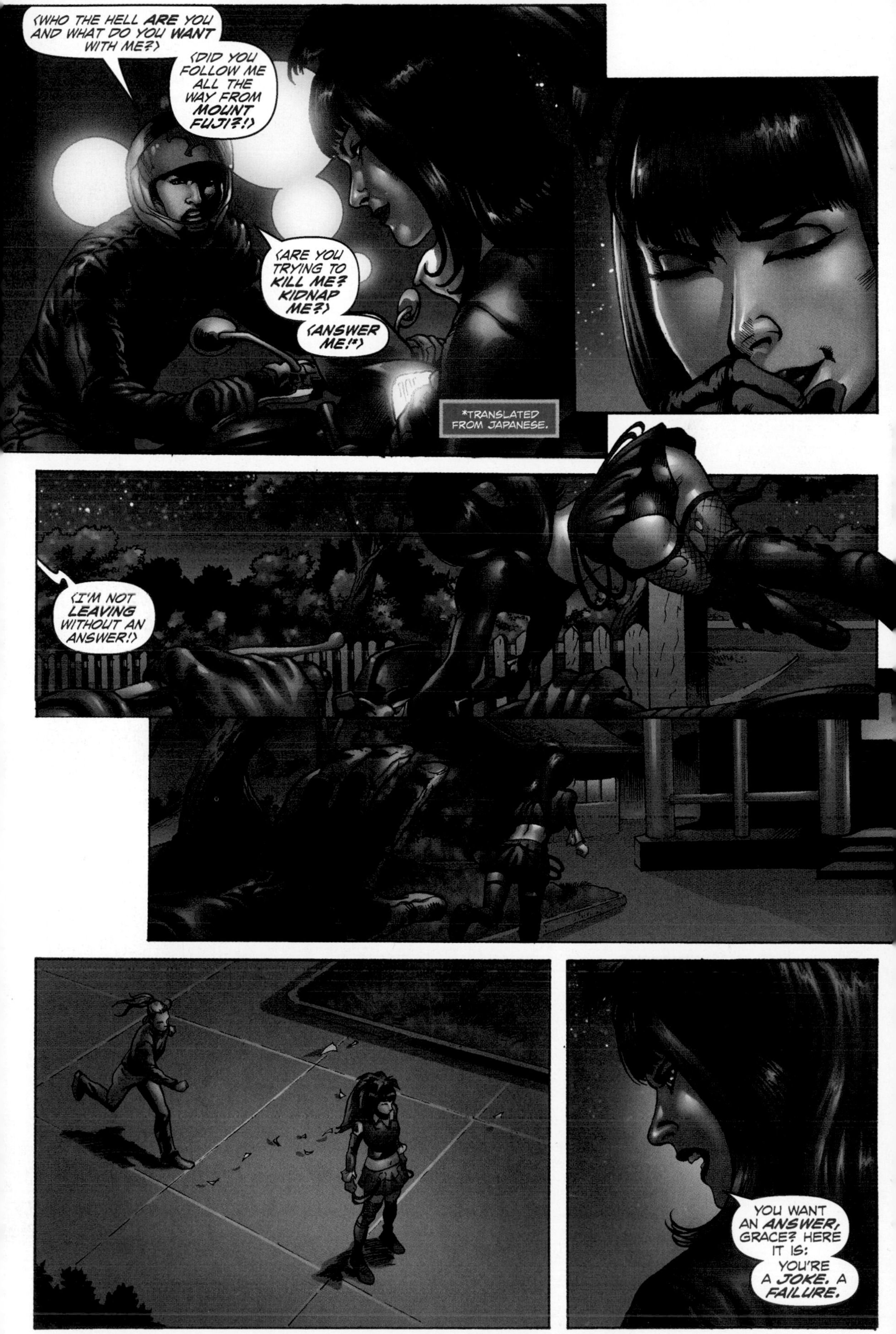

‹WHO THE HELL ARE YOU AND WHAT DO YOU WANT WITH ME?›
‹DID YOU FOLLOW ME ALL THE WAY FROM MOUNT FUJI?!›
‹ARE YOU TRYING TO KILL ME? KIDNAP ME?›
‹ANSWER ME!*›
*TRANSLATED FROM JAPANESE.
‹I'M NOT LEAVING WITHOUT AN ANSWER!›
YOU WANT AN ANSWER, GRACE? HERE IT IS:
YOU'RE A JOKE. A FAILURE.

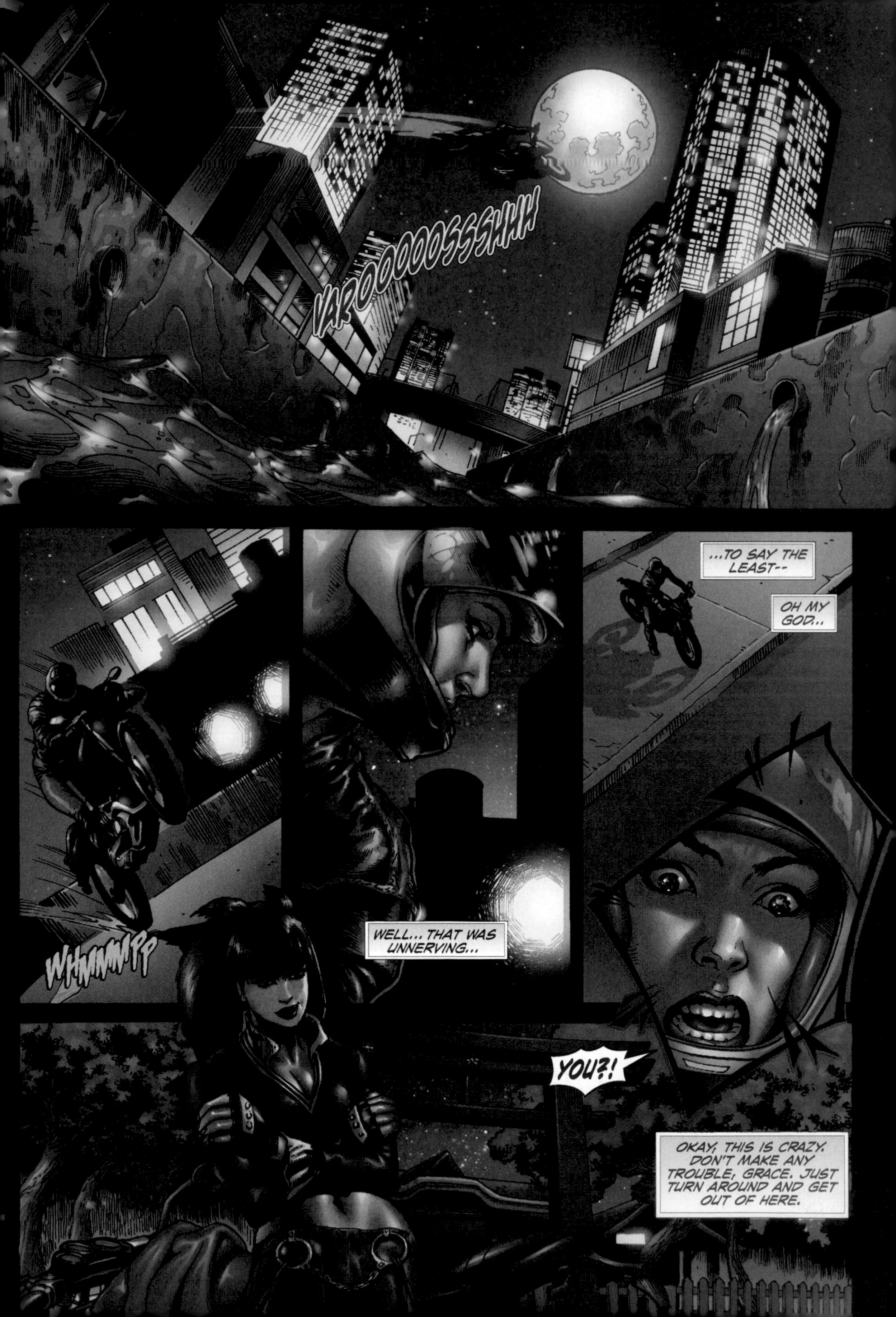
VAROOOOOSSSHHH
WHMMMPP
WELL... THAT WAS UNNERVING...
...TO SAY THE LEAST--
OH MY GOD...
YOU?!
OKAY, THIS IS CRAZY. DON'T MAKE ANY TROUBLE, GRACE. JUST TURN AROUND AND GET OUT OF HERE.

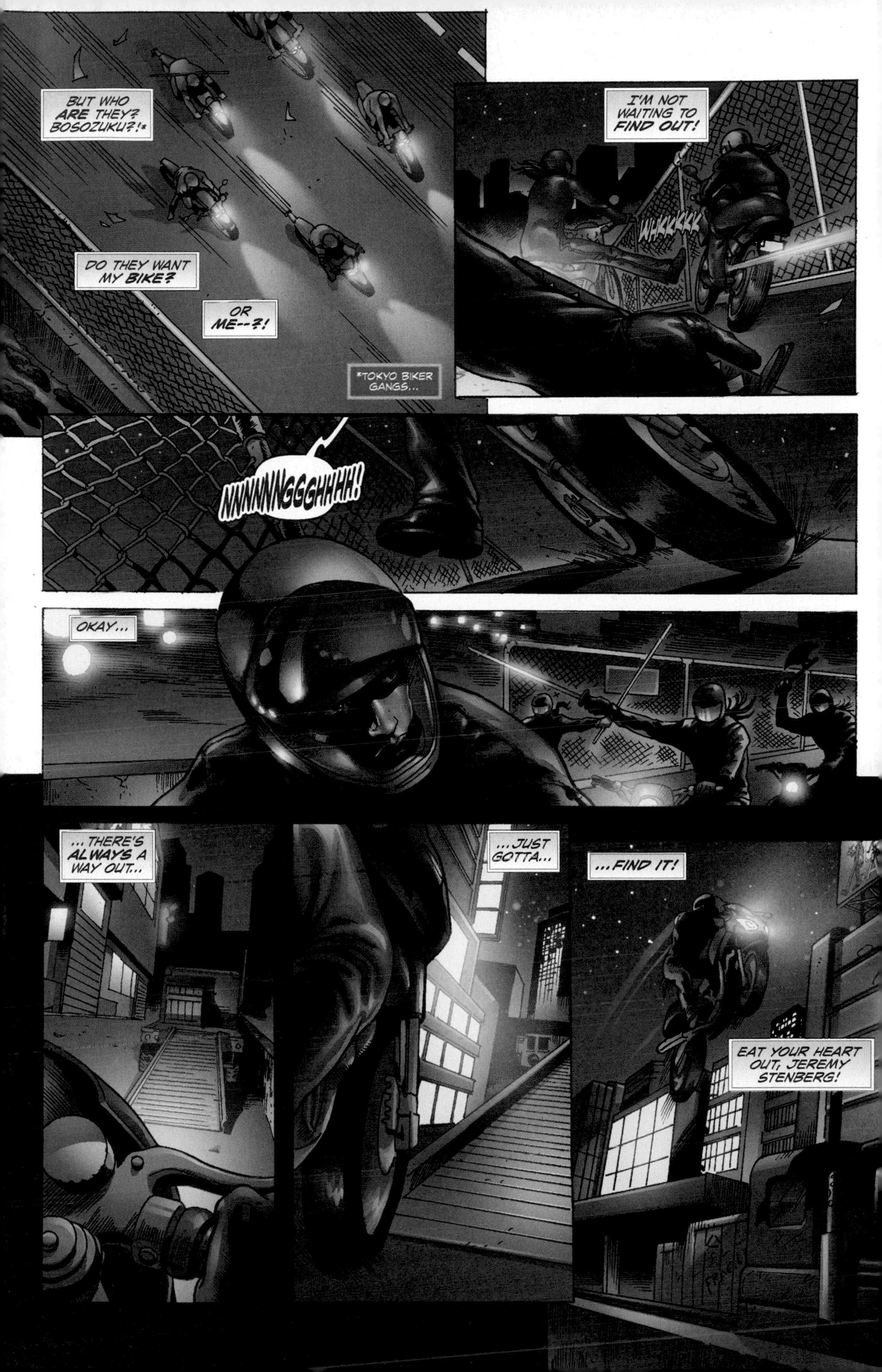
BUT WHO ARE THEY? BOSOZUKU?!*
DO THEY WANT MY BIKE?
OR ME--?!
*TOKYO BIKER GANGS...
I'M NOT WAITING TO FIND OUT!
WHKKKKK
NNNNNNGGGHHHH!
OKAY...
...THERE'S ALWAYS A WAY OUT...
...JUST GOTTA...
...FIND IT!
EAT YOUR HEART OUT, JEREMY STENBERG!

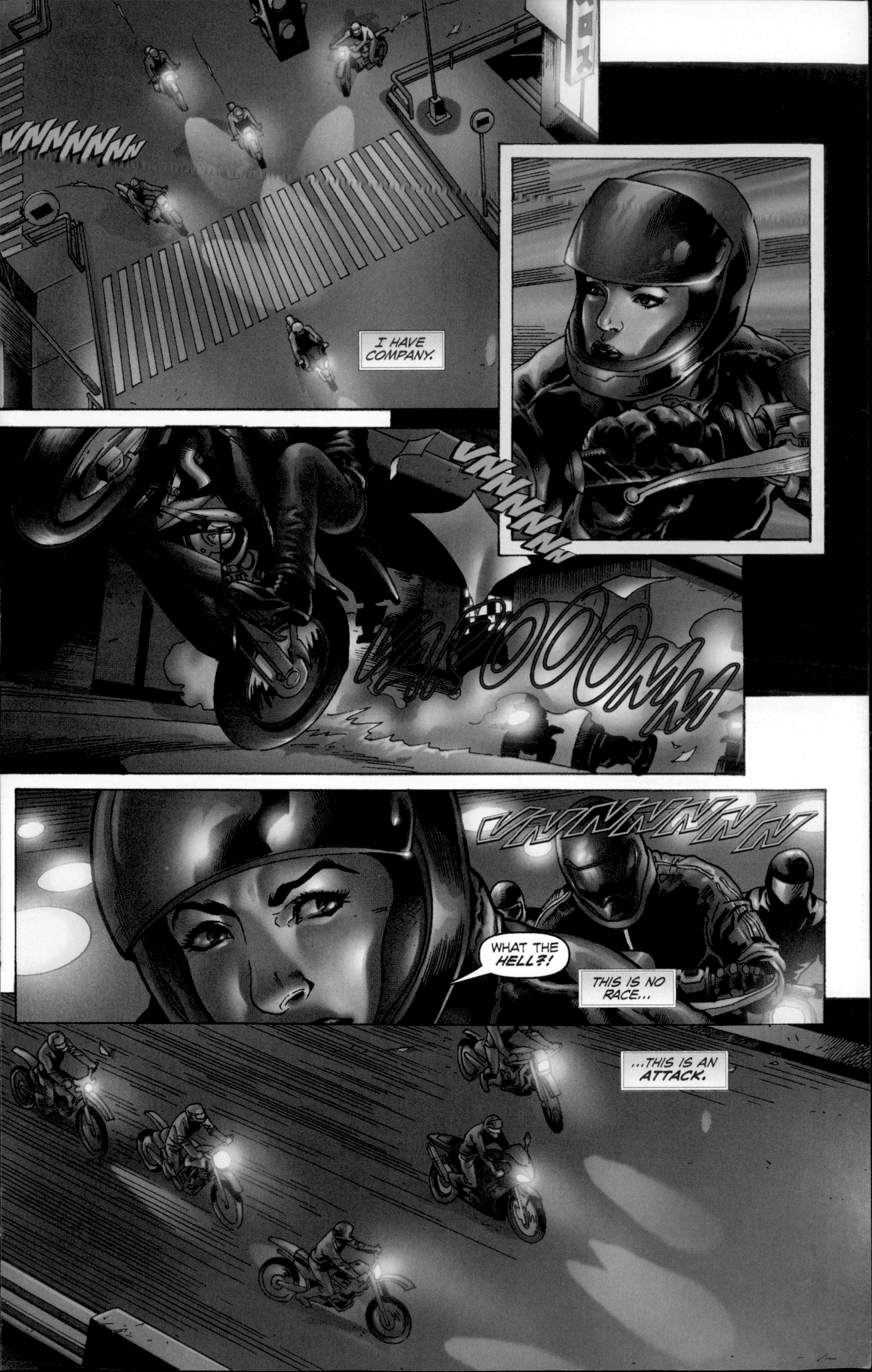
VNNNNNNN
I HAVE COMPANY.
VNNNNNNN
VRROOOOOMM
VNNNNNNNN
WHAT THE HELL?!
THIS IS NO RACE...
...THIS IS AN ATTACK.

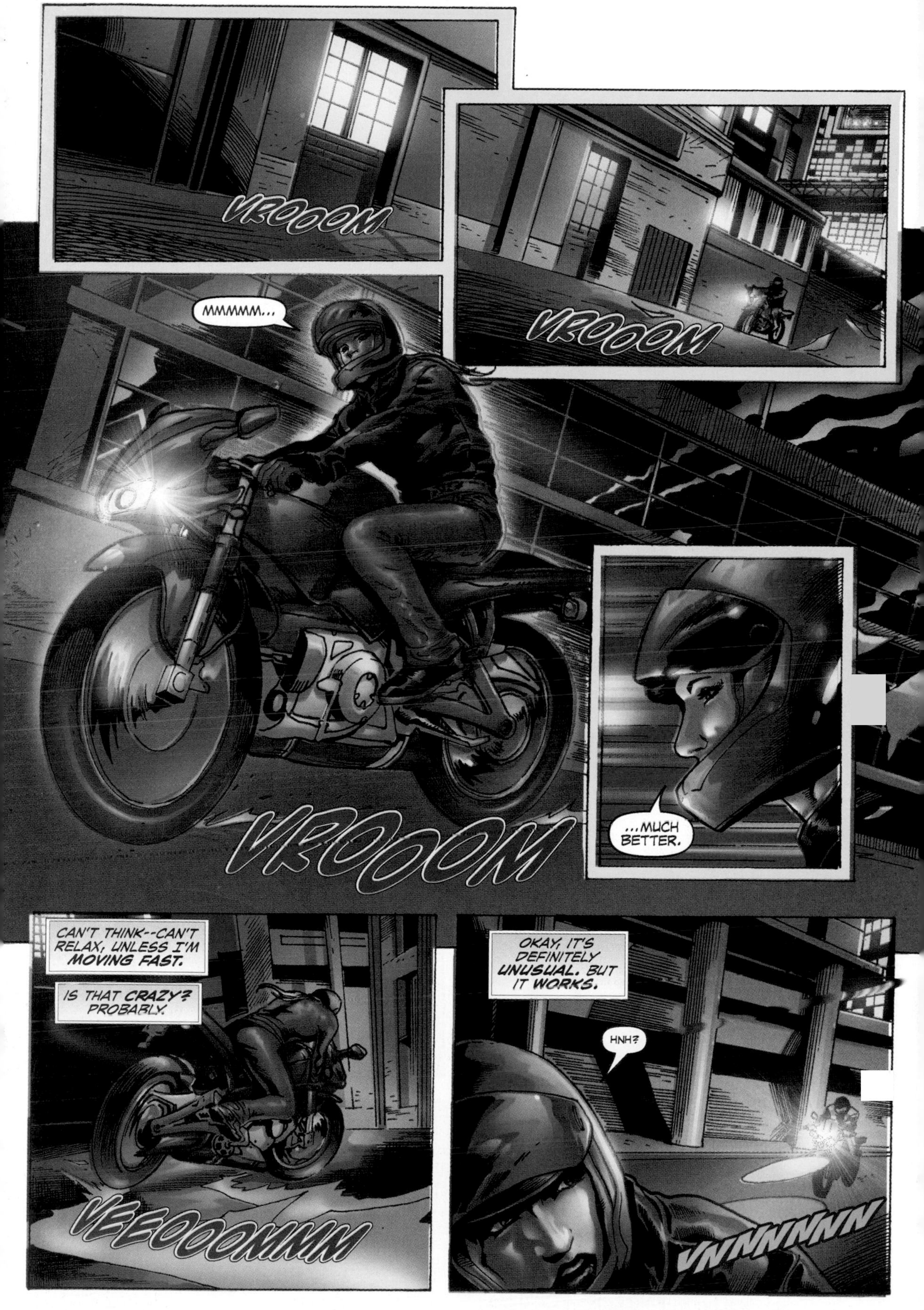
VROOOM
VROOOM
MMMMM...
VROOOM
...MUCH BETTER.
CAN'T THINK--CAN'T RELAX, UNLESS I'M MOVING FAST.
IS THAT CRAZY? PROBABLY.
VEEOOOMMM
OKAY, IT'S DEFINITELY UNUSUAL. BUT IT WORKS.
HNH?
VNNNNNN

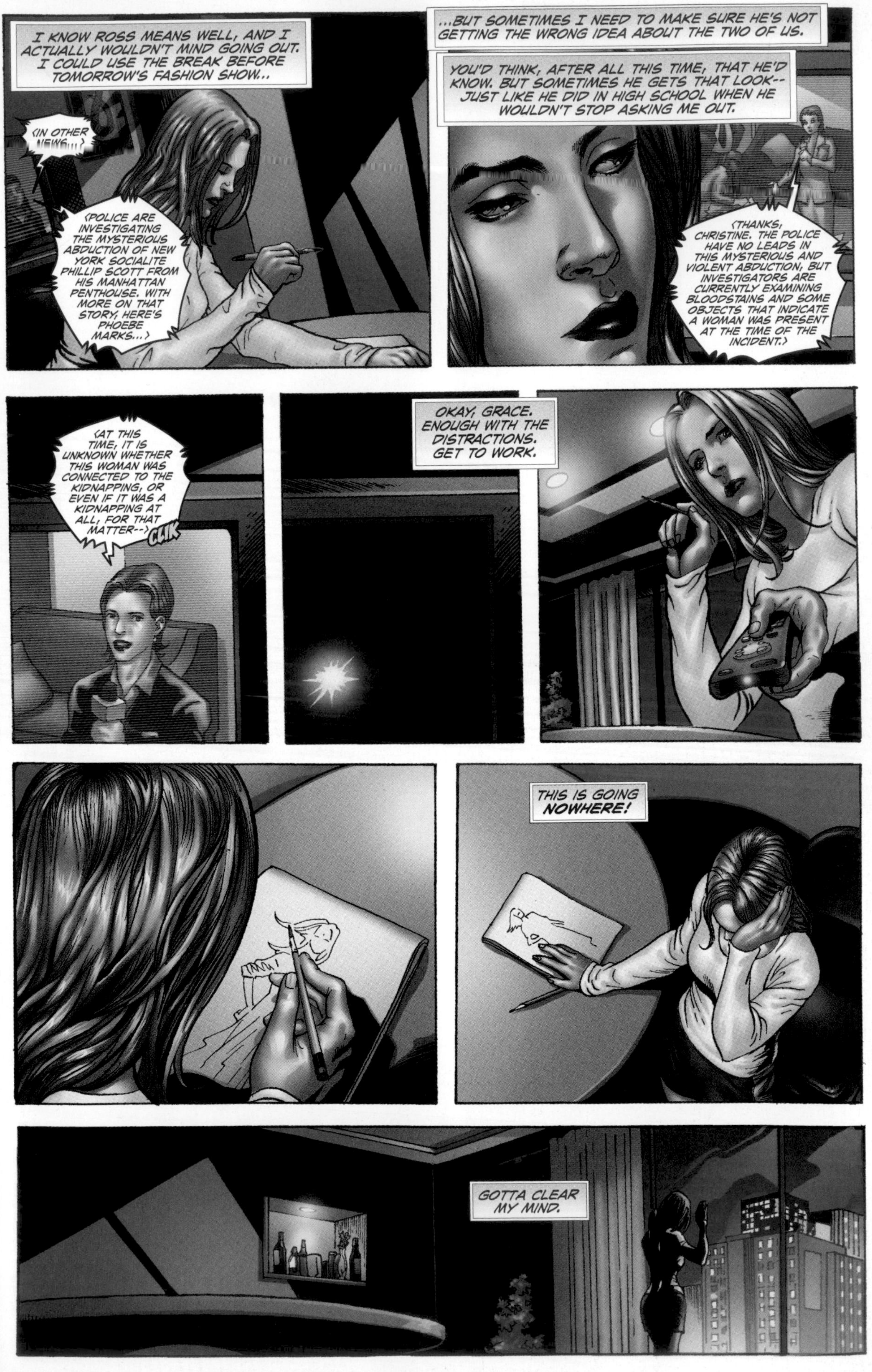
I KNOW ROSS MEANS WELL, AND I ACTUALLY WOULDN'T MIND GOING OUT. I COULD USE THE BREAK BEFORE TOMORROW'S FASHION SHOW...
<IN OTHER NEWS...>
<POLICE ARE INVESTIGATING THE MYSTERIOUS ABDUCTION OF NEW YORK SOCIALITE PHILLIP SCOTT FROM HIS MANHATTAN PENTHOUSE. WITH MORE ON THAT STORY, HERE'S PHOEBE MARKS...>
...BUT SOMETIMES I NEED TO MAKE SURE HE'S NOT GETTING THE WRONG IDEA ABOUT THE TWO OF US.
YOU'D THINK, AFTER ALL THIS TIME, THAT HE'D KNOW. BUT SOMETIMES HE GETS THAT LOOK-- JUST LIKE HE DID IN HIGH SCHOOL WHEN HE WOULDN'T STOP ASKING ME OUT.
<THANKS, CHRISTINE. THE POLICE HAVE NO LEADS IN THIS MYSTERIOUS AND VIOLENT ABDUCTION, BUT INVESTIGATORS ARE CURRENTLY EXAMINING BLOODSTAINS AND SOME OBJECTS THAT INDICATE A WOMAN WAS PRESENT AT THE TIME OF THE INCIDENT.>
<AT THIS TIME, IT IS UNKNOWN WHETHER THIS WOMAN WAS CONNECTED TO THE KIDNAPPING, OR EVEN IF IT WAS A KIDNAPPING AT ALL, FOR THAT MATTER-->
CLIK
OKAY, GRACE. ENOUGH WITH THE DISTRACTIONS. GET TO WORK.
THIS IS GOING NOWHERE!
GOTTA CLEAR MY MIND.

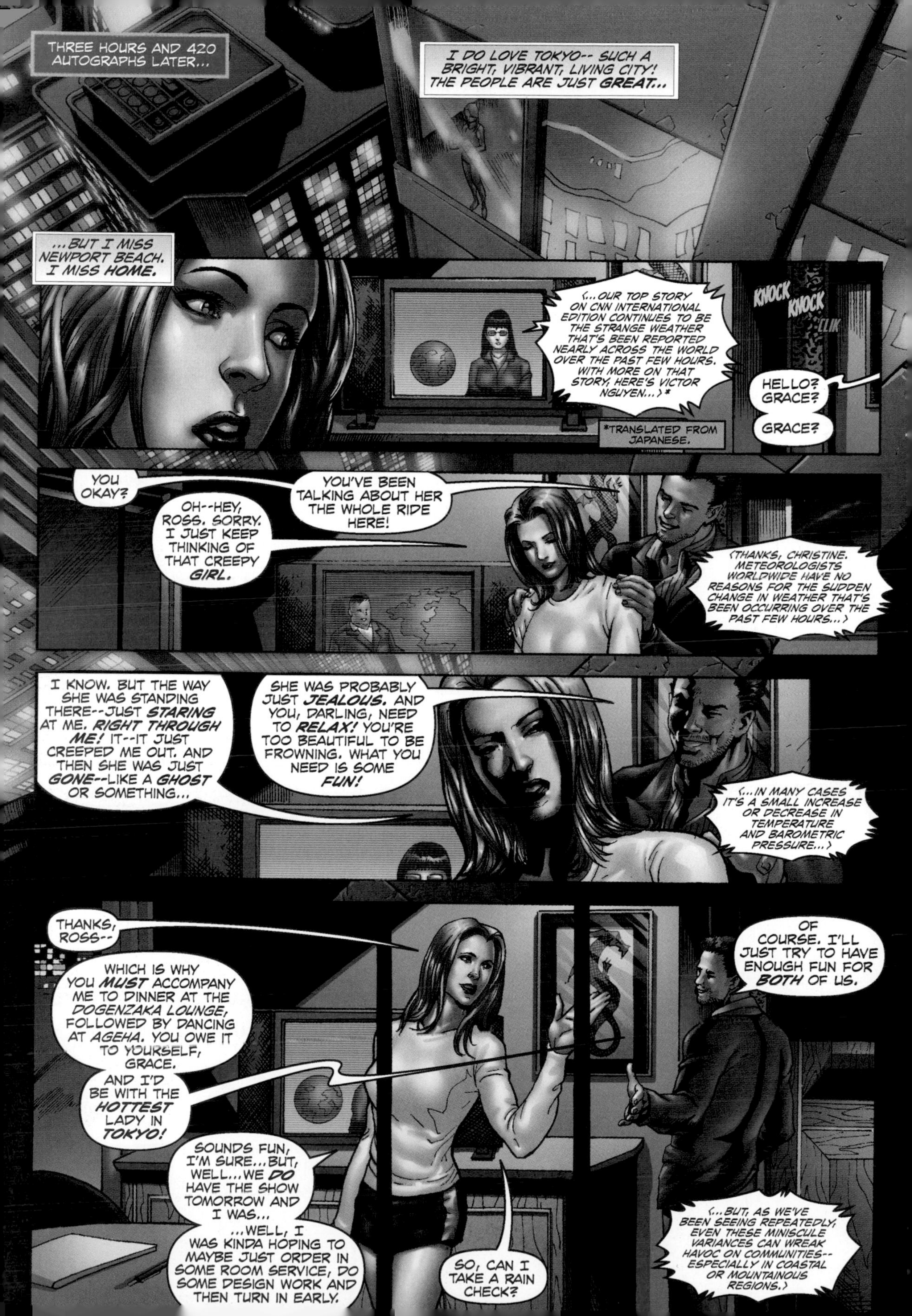
THREE HOURS AND 420 AUTOGRAPHS LATER...
I DO LOVE TOKYO-- SUCH A BRIGHT, VIBRANT, LIVING CITY! THE PEOPLE ARE JUST GREAT...
...BUT I MISS NEWPORT BEACH. I MISS HOME.
‹...OUR TOP STORY ON CNN INTERNATIONAL EDITION CONTINUES TO BE THE STRANGE WEATHER THAT'S BEEN REPORTED NEARLY ACROSS THE WORLD OVER THE PAST FEW HOURS. WITH MORE ON THAT STORY, HERE'S VICTOR NGUYEN...›*
*TRANSLATED FROM JAPANESE.
KNOCK KNOCK CLIK
HELLO? GRACE?
GRACE?
YOU OKAY?
YOU'VE BEEN TALKING ABOUT HER THE WHOLE RIDE HERE!
OH--HEY, ROSS. SORRY. I JUST KEEP THINKING OF THAT CREEPY GIRL.
‹THANKS, CHRISTINE. METEOROLOGISTS WORLDWIDE HAVE NO REASONS FOR THE SUDDEN CHANGE IN WEATHER THAT'S BEEN OCCURRING OVER THE PAST FEW HOURS...›
I KNOW. BUT THE WAY SHE WAS STANDING THERE--JUST STARING AT ME. RIGHT THROUGH ME! IT--IT JUST CREEPED ME OUT. AND THEN SHE WAS JUST GONE--LIKE A GHOST OR SOMETHING...
SHE WAS PROBABLY JUST JEALOUS. AND YOU, DARLING, NEED TO RELAX! YOU'RE TOO BEAUTIFUL TO BE FROWNING. WHAT YOU NEED IS SOME FUN!
‹...IN MANY CASES IT'S A SMALL INCREASE OR DECREASE IN TEMPERATURE AND BAROMETRIC PRESSURE...›
THANKS, ROSS--
WHICH IS WHY YOU MUST ACCOMPANY ME TO DINNER AT THE DOGENZAKA LOUNGE, FOLLOWED BY DANCING AT AGEHA. YOU OWE IT TO YOURSELF, GRACE.
AND I'D BE WITH THE HOTTEST LADY IN TOKYO!
OF COURSE. I'LL JUST TRY TO HAVE ENOUGH FUN FOR BOTH OF US.
SOUNDS FUN, I'M SURE...BUT, WELL...WE DO HAVE THE SHOW TOMORROW AND I WAS...
...WELL, I WAS KINDA HOPING TO MAYBE JUST ORDER IN SOME ROOM SERVICE, DO SOME DESIGN WORK AND THEN TURN IN EARLY.
SO, CAN I TAKE A RAIN CHECK?
‹...BUT, AS WE'VE BEEN SEEING REPEATEDLY, EVEN THESE MINISCULE VARIANCES CAN WREAK HAVOC ON COMMUNITIES-- ESPECIALLY IN COASTAL OR MOUNTAINOUS REGIONS.›

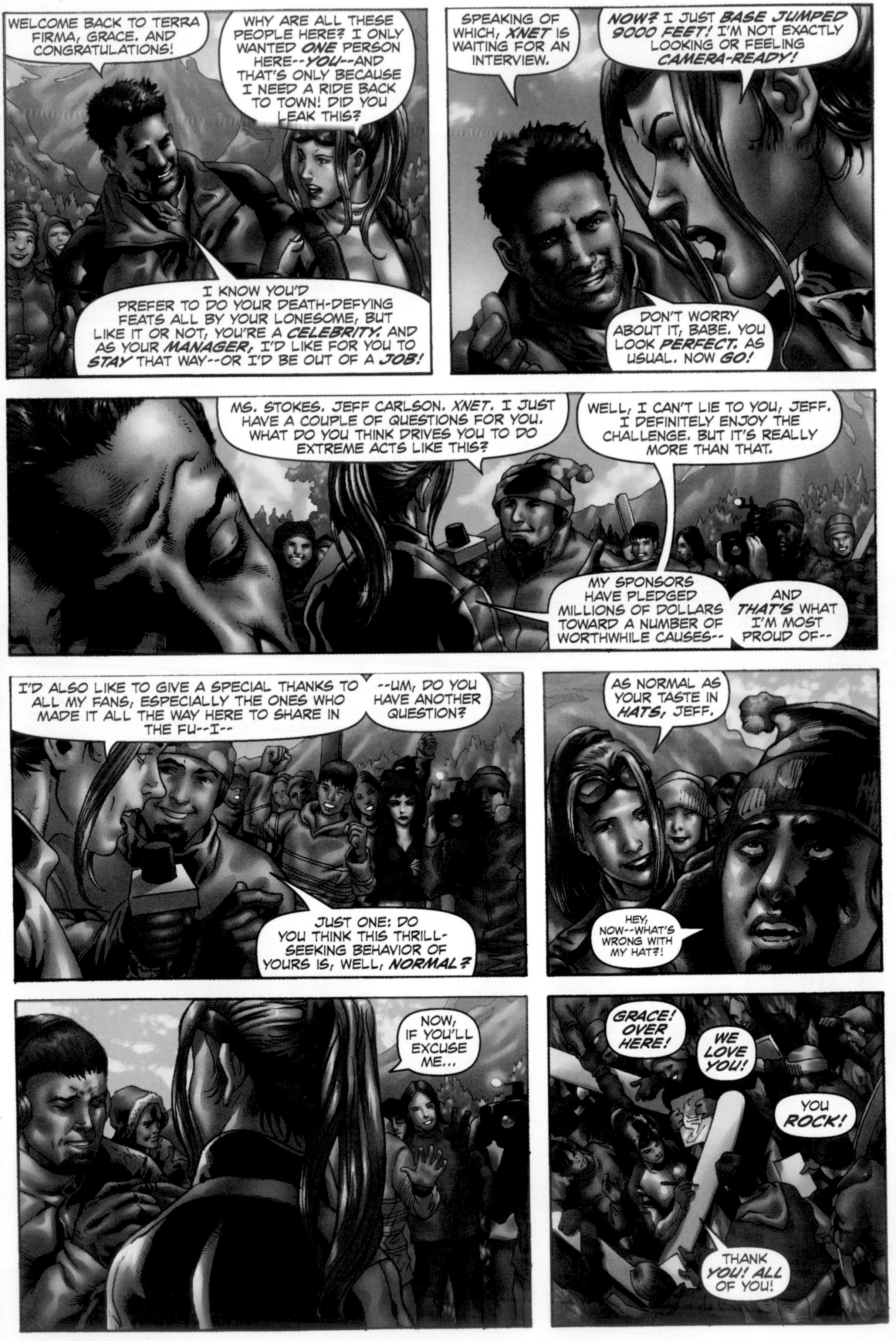
WELCOME BACK TO TERRA FIRMA, GRACE. AND CONGRATULATIONS!
WHY ARE ALL THESE PEOPLE HERE? I ONLY WANTED ONE PERSON HERE--YOU--AND THAT'S ONLY BECAUSE I NEED A RIDE BACK TO TOWN! DID YOU LEAK THIS?
I KNOW YOU'D PREFER TO DO YOUR DEATH-DEFYING FEATS ALL BY YOUR LONESOME, BUT LIKE IT OR NOT, YOU'RE A CELEBRITY. AND AS YOUR MANAGER, I'D LIKE FOR YOU TO STAY THAT WAY--OR I'D BE OUT OF A JOB!
SPEAKING OF WHICH, XNET IS WAITING FOR AN INTERVIEW.
NOW? I JUST BASE JUMPED 9000 FEET! I'M NOT EXACTLY LOOKING OR FEELING CAMERA-READY!
DON'T WORRY ABOUT IT, BABE. YOU LOOK PERFECT. AS USUAL. NOW GO!
MS. STOKES. JEFF CARLSON. XNET. I JUST HAVE A COUPLE OF QUESTIONS FOR YOU. WHAT DO YOU THINK DRIVES YOU TO DO EXTREME ACTS LIKE THIS?
WELL, I CAN'T LIE TO YOU, JEFF. I DEFINITELY ENJOY THE CHALLENGE. BUT IT'S REALLY MORE THAN THAT.
MY SPONSORS HAVE PLEDGED MILLIONS OF DOLLARS TOWARD A NUMBER OF WORTHWHILE CAUSES--
AND THAT'S WHAT I'M MOST PROUD OF--
I'D ALSO LIKE TO GIVE A SPECIAL THANKS TO ALL MY FANS, ESPECIALLY THE ONES WHO MADE IT ALL THE WAY HERE TO SHARE IN THE FU--I--
--UM, DO YOU HAVE ANOTHER QUESTION?
JUST ONE: DO YOU THINK THIS THRILL-SEEKING BEHAVIOR OF YOURS IS, WELL, NORMAL?
AS NORMAL AS YOUR TASTE IN HATS, JEFF.
HEY, NOW--WHAT'S WRONG WITH MY HAT?!
NOW, IF YOU'LL EXCUSE ME...
GRACE! OVER HERE!
WE LOVE YOU!
YOU ROCK!
THANK YOU! ALL OF YOU!

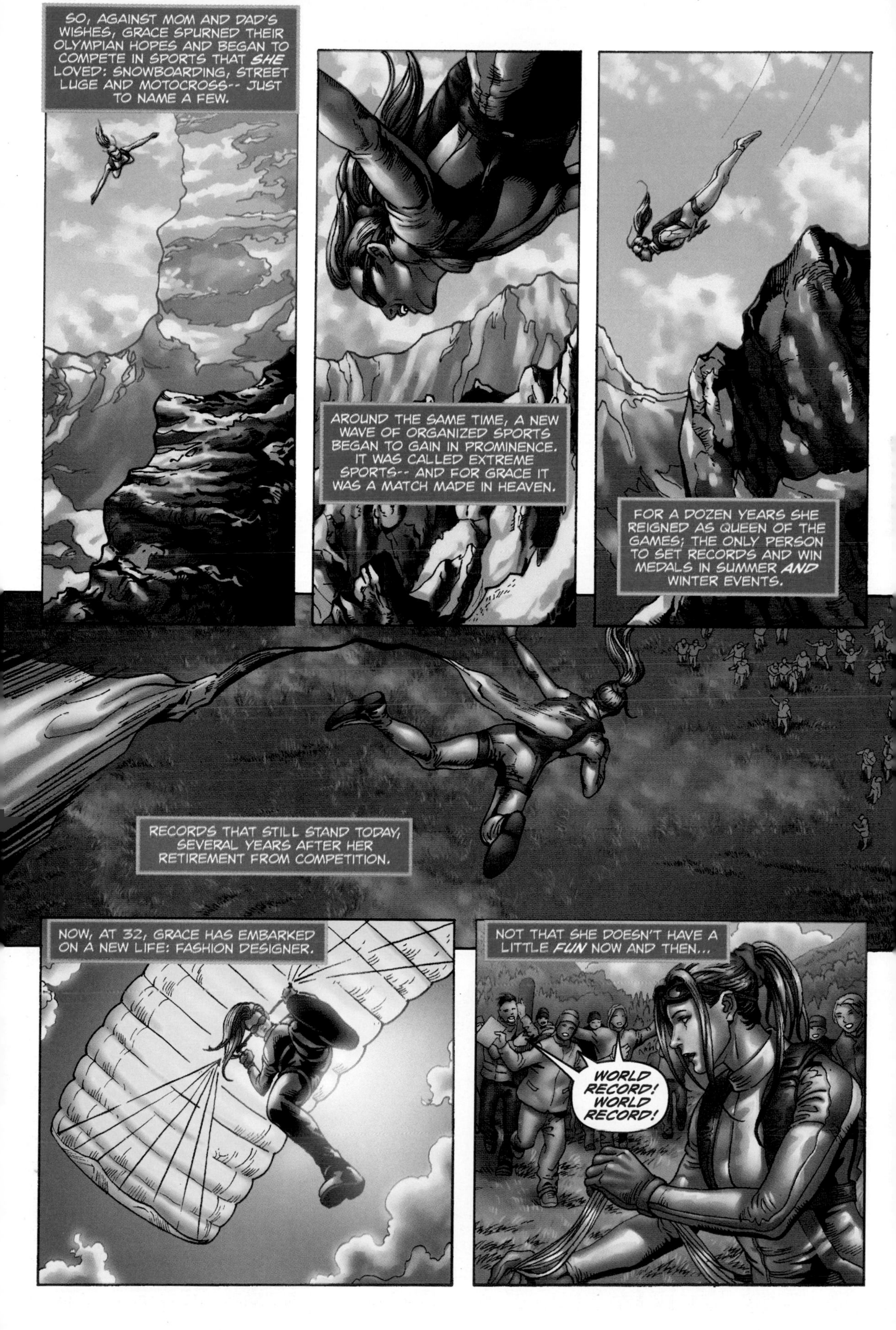
SO, AGAINST MOM AND DAD'S WISHES, GRACE SPURNED THEIR OLYMPIAN HOPES AND BEGAN TO COMPETE IN SPORTS THAT SHE LOVED: SNOWBOARDING, STREET LUGE AND MOTOCROSS-- JUST TO NAME A FEW.
AROUND THE SAME TIME, A NEW WAVE OF ORGANIZED SPORTS BEGAN TO GAIN IN PROMINENCE. IT WAS CALLED EXTREME SPORTS-- AND FOR GRACE IT WAS A MATCH MADE IN HEAVEN.
FOR A DOZEN YEARS SHE REIGNED AS QUEEN OF THE GAMES; THE ONLY PERSON TO SET RECORDS AND WIN MEDALS IN SUMMER AND WINTER EVENTS.
RECORDS THAT STILL STAND TODAY, SEVERAL YEARS AFTER HER RETIREMENT FROM COMPETITION.
NOW, AT 32, GRACE HAS EMBARKED ON A NEW LIFE: FASHION DESIGNER.
NOT THAT SHE DOESN'T HAVE A LITTLE FUN NOW AND THEN...
WORLD RECORD! WORLD RECORD!

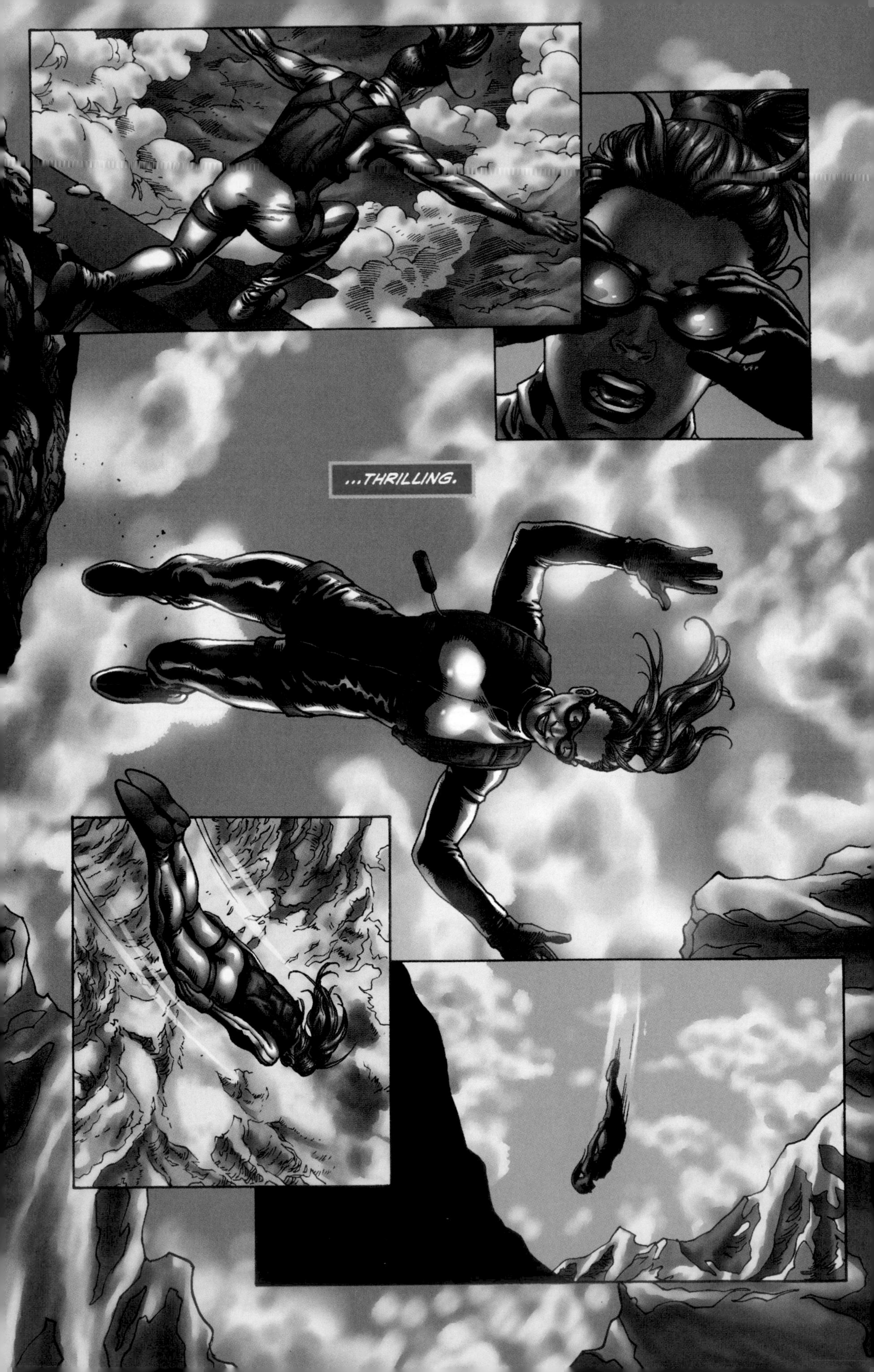
...THRILLING.

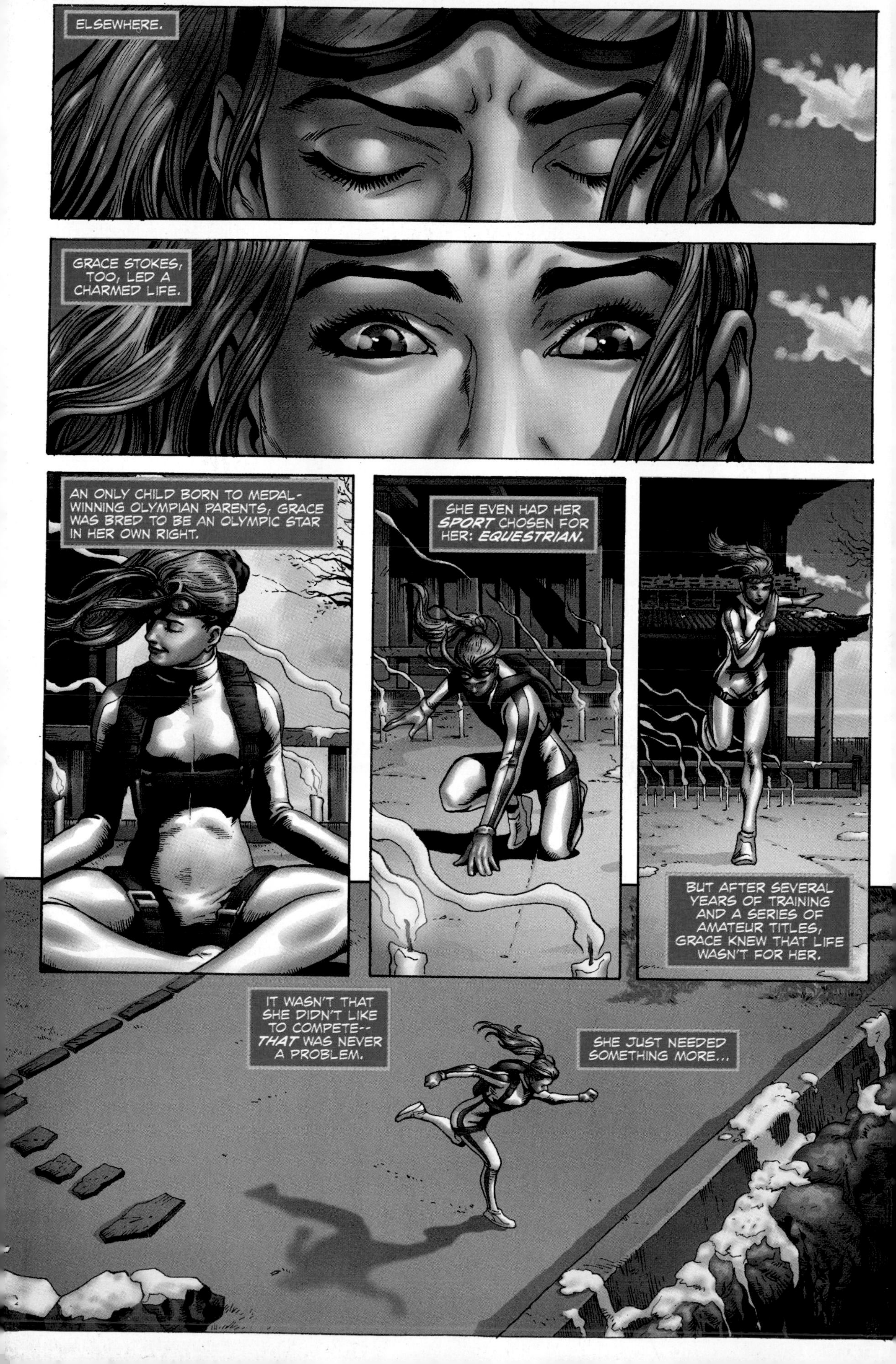
ELSEWHERE.
GRACE STOKES, TOO, LED A CHARMED LIFE.
AN ONLY CHILD BORN TO MEDAL-WINNING OLYMPIAN PARENTS, GRACE WAS BRED TO BE AN OLYMPIC STAR IN HER OWN RIGHT.
SHE EVEN HAD HER SPORT CHOSEN FOR HER: EQUESTRIAN.
BUT AFTER SEVERAL YEARS OF TRAINING AND A SERIES OF AMATEUR TITLES, GRACE KNEW THAT LIFE WASN'T FOR HER.
IT WASN'T THAT SHE DIDN'T LIKE TO COMPETE-- THAT WAS NEVER A PROBLEM.
SHE JUST NEEDED SOMETHING MORE...

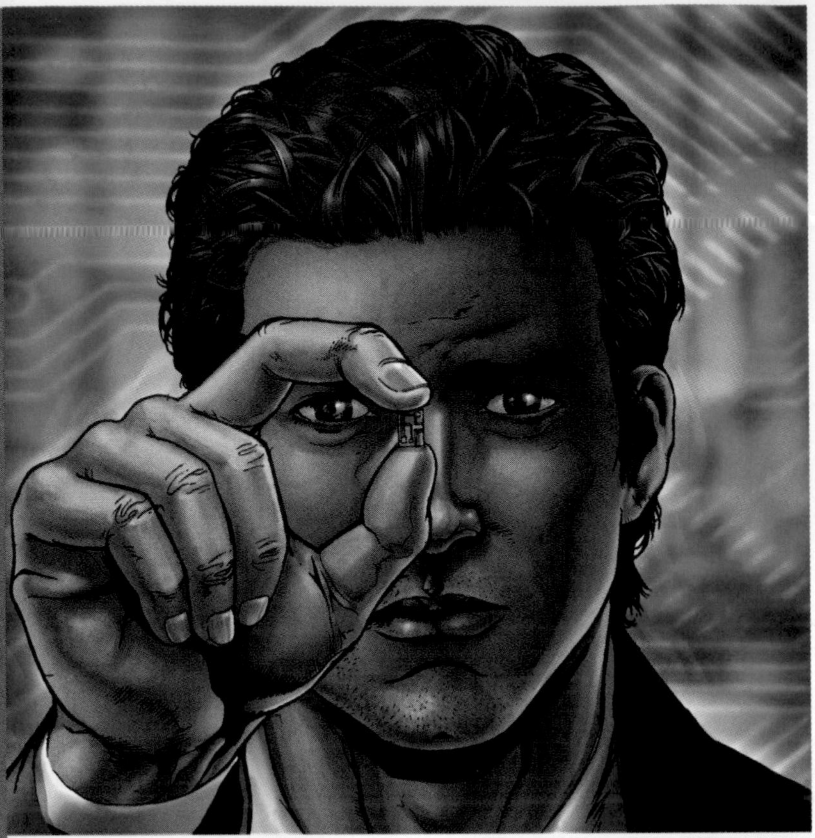

PHILLIP SCOTT

The Midas Touch

[BY MARK PHILLIPS]

Forget the notion that all high tech gurus look like Dilbert, obsess over *Star Trek* and are clueless about all things hip… that's so last century. Increasingly, the new leaders in Silicon Valley are the hip young entrepreneurs reared in the age of the Internet. Freed up from having to invent an industry from scratch, the leaders of tomorrow are deconstructing the status quo of high tech piece by piece and revolutionizing the industry one bit at a time. The poster child for this new wave is Phillip Scott, as likely to be seen in the pages of *GQ* among the most eligible bachelors the world over as in a stuffy boardroom. We caught up with Scott at his posh Tribeca penthouse. Dripping with charisma and charm, we picked Scott's brain over a thirty-year-old Bordeaux and the finest cigars Havana has to offer. (As I told my editor, he insisted…)

Scott's story of success is truly an affirmation of the American dream. From humble beginnings in unwired middle America, rural Nebraska to be precise, Scott established himself as a stellar student, but also connected with the world at large though the earliest versions of the Internet. In fact, Scott coyly admits to "borrowing" computer games directly from the companies' mainframes. Self admittedly coasting through high school, Scott still managed to be named valedictorian. After notching an SAT score only a few points from perfect, though he humbly refuses to give an exact number, he received a full academic scholarship to Brown. In college, Scott began making waves by creating a network for his friends to share music. We all know how that ended…

After graduating near the top of his class from Brown and playing CEO in his free time, Scott went on to MIT where he led the school's artificial intelligence department, spearheading advancements in CPU speed and capacity. Phillip's contributions to the early days of the World Wide Web are widely documented, not only in the computer development community, but the "hacker" net as well. His cutting edge, out-of-the-box solutions struck a chord with both seasoned programmers and the cyberpunks of the day, who are now Scott's peers as the leaders in the Valley.

From Massachusetts, Scott moved on to a number of notable IT companies in Silicon Valley and eventually New York. Within a matter of months Phillip had become controlling partner in computer giant CompRise. By selling off his CompRise stock just ahead of the Internet bubble bursting, Scott was left with the resources to personally acquire several other smaller IT firms as their stock prices plummeted. Each company Scott acquired doubled its annual profit within three years; thus earning Scott the nickname Midas, which sticks even to this day.

Every bit as noteworthy as his achievements in the world of business have been Scott's well publicized flings with several A list celebrities. This includes his most recent tete-a-tete with Lauren Perry, the leading lady in this summer's blockbuster film *The Gold Standard,* coming soon to a multiplex near you. Even in the wake of several public break-ups, Scott still remains very popular in the public eye with his charisma and self-deprecating humor.

As his star continues to rise, some leading minds in the Valley have privately questioned Scott's actual contributions to his companies' successes, stating that he merely seems to have a knack for always being in the right place at the right time. Scott laughs this off, quipping, "Sometimes it's better to be good and sometimes it's better to be lucky." And perhaps it's the very lack of proof of his genius that makes Phillip Scott so alluring to the world audience. And as we polished off that bottle of Bordeaux, Scott charmed one more skeptic into believing his vision for the future of the tech industry probably will be coming to a computer near you one day very soon.. •

Illustration by Bing Cansino and Annette Kwok